ACCOMPLISHING THE ACCOMPLISHED

The Society for Asian and Comparative Philosophy Monograph Series was started in 1974. Works are published in the series that deal with any area of Asian philosophy, or in any other field of philosophy examined from a comparative perspective. The aim of the series is to make available scholarly works that exceed article length, but may be too specialized for the general reading public, and to make these works available in inexpensive editions without sacrificing the orthography of non-Western languages.

ACCOMPLISHING THE ACCOMPLISHED

THE *VEDAS* AS A SOURCE OF VALID KNOWLEDGE IN ŚAṄKARA

Anantanand Rambachan

MONOGRAPH NO. 10
SOCIETY FOR ASIAN AND COMPARATIVE PHILOSOPHY

University of Hawaii Press
Honolulu

Printed in the United States of America

Library of Congress Cataloging-in-Publication Data

Rambachan, Anantanand, 1951-
Accomplishing the accomplished : the Vedas as a source of valid knowledge in Śaṅkara / Anantanand Rambachan.
p. cm. — (Monograph / Society for Asian and Comparative Philosophy ; no. 10)
Includes bibliographical references and index.
ISBN 0-8248-1358-8
1. Vedas—Criticism, interpretation, etc.—History.
2. Śaṅkarācārya. 3. Knowledge, Theory of (Hinduism)—History.
I. Title. II. Series: Monograph . . . of the Society for Asian and Comparative Philosophy ; no. 10.
BL1112.46.R35 1991
181'.482—dc20 91-10279
CIP

Camera-ready copy was prepared by the author.

University of Hawaii Press books are printed on acid-free paper and meet the guidelines for permanence and durability of the Council on Library Resources *for Geeta, Ishanaa, and Aksharananda*

Contents

Abbreviations

AI.U	*Aitareya Upaniṣad*
B.G.	*Bhagavadgītā*
Bhāmatī	*Bhāmatī of Vācaspati Miśra*
B.S.	*Brahma-sūtra*
BR.U.	*Bṛhadāraṇyaka Upaniṣad*
CH.U.	*Chāndogya Upaniṣad*
IS.U.	*Īśa Upaniṣad*
KA.U.	*Kaṭha Upaniṣad*
KE.U.	*Kena Upaniṣad*
MA.U.	*Māṇḍūkya Upaniṣad*
MA.U.K.	*Māṇḍūkya Upaniṣad Kārikā of Gauḍapada*
M.S.J.	*Pūrva-Mīmāṁsā Sūtras of Jaimini*
MU.U.	*Muṇḍaka Upaniṣad*
N.S.	*Naiṣkarmyasiddhi of Sureśvara*
N.Y.S.G.	*Nyāya Sūtras of Gotama*
PR.U.	*Praśna Upaniṣad*
SV.U.	*Śvetāśvatāra Upaniṣad*
TA.U.	*Taittirīya Upaniṣad*
T.B.	*Tattvabodha of Śaṅkara*
V.P.	*Vedānta Paribhāṣā of Dharmarājā*
V.S.	*Vedāntasāra of Sadānanda*

The letter *B* added to the abbreviation of any text (as BR.U.B.) indicates the commentary (*bhāṣya*) of Śaṅkara on the said text. Thus, B.G.B. means Śaṅkara's *bhāṣya* on the *Bhagavadgītā*.

Preface

All major schools of Indian philosophical and religious thought originated and developed with the aim of providing a viable means for the attainment of *mokṣa.* This is not to affirm that this end was uniformly conceived in all systems. The point is that Indian philosophy always had a practical or pragmatic end in view, if these terms can be admitted in respect to the quest for *mokṣa.* This subservience to the accomplishment of *mokṣa* is what makes it difficult to distinguish Indian philosophy from Indian religion. Philosophy aimed at transcending or overcoming human suffering, however conceived, and part of the criteria for evaluating any system was its adequacy as a means to *mokṣa. Jijñāsā* or the desire to know, from which is derived *jijñāsu* (the one who desires to know), was in relation to *mumukṣutvam* or the intense desire for *mokṣa.* The *mumukṣu* was one who intensely desired *mokṣa.* In other words, the *jijñāsu* was a *mumukṣu.* Philosophical texts and treatises were written with the *mumukṣu* in view, and often commenced by identifying the aspirant aimed at and the qualifications necessary for a successful undertaking of the inquiry.

The centrality of the *mokṣa* concern is one of the keys to understanding the motivation which prompts Indian philosophy and the nature of argument both within and among the various schools. It is also the interest which influences and lies at the center of this study. This study is undertaken in the general spirit of philosophical inquiry as *sādhana.* In the specific context of the *Advaita Vedānta* system with which it is concerned, this study is an exercise in the discipline of *manana* or rational reflection upon some of its fundamental propositions. This discipline, which is explained more fully in the body of this text, aimed essentially at clarification, evaluation, the removal of doubts, and the assessment of rival views. Various methods were used in achieving these aims, including scriptural exegesis and philosophical argument. It offered the scope for both criticism and creativity, and it is in the tradition of this kind of analysis that my work belongs.

Advaita Vedānta, as systematized and expressed by Śaṅkara, is widely represented in contemporary studies as positing a special experience (*anubhava*) to be the ultimately valid source of the knowledge of *brahman* (*brahmajñāna*). According to these studies, Śaṅkara only accorded a provisional validity to the knowledge gained by inquiry into the words of the *śruti* (*Vedas*) and did not see the latter as the unique source (*pramāṇa*) of *brahmajñāna.* The affirmations of the *śruti,* it is argued, need to be verified and confirmed by the knowledge gained through direct experience (*anubhava*) and the authority of the *śruti,* therefore, is only secondary.

My own study of the commentaries of Śaṅkara suggests, however, that these interpretations grossly misrepresent his epistemology in failing to apprehend the meaning and significance which he ascribes to the *śruti* as the definitive source of the knowledge of *brahman*. It is clear that in relation to the gain of *brahmajñāna*, Śaṅkara saw all other sources of knowledge as being subordinate to the *śruti* and supported his view by detailed and well-reasoned arguments. This study, therefore, is concerned primarily with investigating Śaṅkara's understanding of the *śruti* as the source of *brahmajñāna* and the processes through which this knowledge is gained. It is undertaken with the aim of refuting certain widely held interpretations.

The Introduction offers a survey of prevalent interpretations of the significance of *śruti* and *anubhava* in Śaṅkara, most of which are questioned in my analysis. In Chapter 1, I consider the nature of the six valid sources of knowledge accepted by *Advaita Vedānta* and outline certain central epistemological theories held by its proponents. This discussion provides the basis and background for Chapter 2, in which I treat Śaṅkara's justification of the *śruti* as a valid source of knowledge (*pramāṇa*). Through words, whose references are finite objects known to us, *śruti* attempts to inform us of *brahman*, which is unknown to us and which possesses none of the characteristics of anything known to us. In Chapter 3, I examine the methods of instruction and exegesis suggested in Śaṅkara's commentaries for dealing with this problem of communicating *brahmajñāna*. Chapter 4 seeks to clarify further the relationship between *śruti, brahmajñāna*, and *mokṣa* by discussing Śaṅkara's conception of the nature of knowledge, the mode and conditions of its attainment, and its distinction from action (*karman*). Chapter 5 studies the roles of *śravaṇa* (listening), *manana* (reflection), and *nididhyāsana* (contemplation) in relation to the gain of *brahmajñāna*. I seek here to refute the sharp distinctions made among them and the claim that they are intended for different ends. Many of the conclusions about Śaṅkara's epistemology are derived from different perceptions of the character and aims of these processes.

Śaṅkara selected the medium of commentaries (*bhāṣya*) to express his views. For this study, I have relied primarily on those commentaries of his which are widely accepted as being authentic. Śaṅkara's commentaries on the following works have been cited: *Aitareya Upaniṣad, Bhagavadgītā, Bṛhadāraṇyaka Upaniṣad, Brahma-sūtra, Chāndogya Upaniṣad, Īśa Upaniṣad, Kaṭha Upaniṣad, Kena Upaniṣad, Māṇḍūkya Upaniṣad, Māṇḍūkya Upaniṣad Kārikā of Guadapada, Muṇḍaka Upaniṣad, Praśna Upaniṣad*, and *Taittirīya Upaniṣad.*

Of these thirteen commentaries, only the authenticity of the commentaries on the *Māṇḍūkya Upaniṣad* and the *Māṇḍūkya Upaniṣad Kārikā of Gaudapada* has been seriously questioned. The other works have all been listed by K. H. Potter among the authentic works of Śaṅkara (*The Encyclopedia of Indian Philosophies*, Vol. 1: Bibliography [Delhi: Motilal Banarsidass, 1970]). My references to these two works, however, are very few indeed, and none of the principal arguments depends on them.

Similarly, I have avoided using and establishing any conclusions on the evidence of the many expository treatises attributed to Śaṅkara. The authenticity of all of these, except perhaps for the *Upadeśasahasrī*, remains very doubtful. I have made only a single reference to *Tattvabodha*, in Chapter 1.

I have sought objectivity in the presentation of Śaṅkara by citing principally and frequently from his commentaries. For this reason, I have made very limited use of secondary writings from the *Advaita* tradition. In the major chapters on Śaṅkara, the writings of Sureśvara, Vācaspati, and Sadānanda have been alluded to on a few occasions to amplify certain arguments.

Acknowledgments

I am indebted to Swami Dayananda Saraswati, with whom I had the privilege of studying the *Advaita Vedānta* tradition through Śaṅkara's commentaries on the principal *Upaniṣads*, the *Brahma-sūtra*, and the *Bhagavadgītā*. He taught me to see that the *Upaniṣads*, properly approached and unfolded as a *pramāṇa*, afford a knowledge which is an immediate and sufficient solution to the perennial human quest for fullness. I have been encouraged by his approval of this study and the continued interest he has shown in it.

This work originally commenced as a doctoral dissertation in the Department of Theology and Religious Studies at the University of Leeds, United Kingdom. The research was made possible by a three-year scholarship from the University of Leeds and a grant which enabled me to undertake further study in India. For these, and for the many facilities provided, I wish to express my appreciation.

I am most grateful to Dr. Ursula King for her unfailing kindness and assistance throughout my stay at the University of Leeds and for her close supervision and guidance of this research in all of its stages. Her criticisms and suggestions have always been of great benefit.

The Faculty Development Committee of Saint Olaf College provided a grant which made it possible for me to be free from my teaching responsibilities during the spring semester (1987/88). This enabled me to devote my attention to the preparation of this study for publication. I am thankful to the Committee for its interest and support.

My wife, Geeta, has been a tremendous source of encouragement and assistance. In spite of the pressing demands of her own profession, she has always happily found the time to diligently proofread drafts of this work and has patiently listened to and considered its various arguments. For all of this, and much more, I am grateful.

Dr. Jon Moline, Dean of Saint Olaf College, generously supported the preparation of this manuscript, and Jody Greenslade, Mark Christianson, and Craig Rice undertook the typing and formatting. I am much obliged to all of them.

Finally, I wish to thank Professor Henry Rosemont, Jr., editor of the SACP Monograph Series, and Sharon F. Yamamoto of the University of Hawaii Press for their interest and guidance.

ACCOMPLISHING THE ACCOMPLISHED

Introduction

A Review of Current Interpretations of the Significance of *Śruti* and *Anubhava* in Śaṅkara

In his well-known and widely used study, *The Spiritual Heritage of India,* Swami Prabhavananda writes:

> Indian philosophy is not merely metaphysical speculation, but has its foundation in immediate perception. God and the soul are regarded by the Hindu mind, not as concepts, speculative and problematical, as is the case in Western Philosophy, but as things directly known. They can be experienced not by a chosen few, but, under right conditions, by all humanity.[1]

Immediate perception, according to Prabhavananda, is the source from which springs all Indian thought. Another writer who, perhaps more than anyone else, has popularized this view in the West is Radhakrishnan. The Hindu philosophy of religion, in his view, starts from and returns to an experimental basis. In a popular work of his, *The Hindu View of Life,* Radhakrishnan writes:

> While fixed beliefs mark off one religion from another, Hinduism sets itself no such limits. Intellect is subordinate to intuition, dogma to experience, outer expression to inward realization. Religion is not the acceptance of academic abstractions or the celebration of ceremonies, but a kind of life or experience.... Religious experience is of a self-certifying character. It is *svatassiddha.*[2]

Proponents of this interpretation of Hinduism resist the use of the term, *philosophy,* as a description of any system of Indian thought. They seem to find its connotations of speculation and intellectualism quite inapt. The term preferred is *darśana,* often rendered as "direct vision" or "seeing." Chandradhar Sharma sums up this predilection in a representative manner.

> Western Philosophy has remained more or less true to the etymological meaning of "philosophy," in being essentially an intellectual quest for truth. Indian philosophy has been, however, intensely spiritual and has emphasized the need of practical realization of truth. The word *darshana* means "vision" and also "the in-

> strument of vision." It stands for the direct, immediate and intuitive vision of Reality, the actual perception of Truth, and also includes the means which lead to this realization.[3]

In this review, it is useful to focus on Radhakrishnan because of his wide influence and the high esteem with which his views are generally regarded.[4] Early in his discussion, Radhakrishnan seeks to present the *Advaita Vedānta* attitude to the *Vedas*.[5] His views at this point can be summarized as follows:

1. Scriptural authority is accepted by *Advaita* as an independent means of knowledge.
2. The *Vedas* are eternal in terms of their significance but not as texts, for these are reuttered by *īśvara* in each world age. The *Vedas* embody the ideal form of the universe, and since this is constant, the *Vedas* are described as eternal.
3. The *Vedas* are of superhuman origin (*apauruṣeya*) and express the mind of God. They reveal God's character and embody God's ideas.
4. Their validity is self-evident and direct, even as the light of the sun is the direct means for our knowledge of forms.

What is of significance here is that Radhakrishnan's brief discussion is the only place in which he attempts to formulate and present the traditional *Advaita* attitude to the *Vedas*. Even here, however, his summary, as will be evident later, misrepresents the *Advaita* position and makes it appear, in some parts, contradictory. There is a conflict, for example, between the position that the authority of the *Vedas* is direct and self-evident and the argument that their authority derives from God. In fact, his entire treatment of the *pramāṇas*, in relation to *Advaita*, is scant and inadequate. Although he does give some recognition at this point to the authoritativeness of the *Vedas*, as his argument develops he presents a view of the *Vedas* which sharply contrasts with this earlier one. There is no hint of any awareness of the tension between both views, and it remains unresolved throughout his entire discussion. This unresolved tension between two different sets of assertions about the *Vedas* can be discerned in many other writers.

The *Vedas*, as far as Radhakrishnan is concerned, are the records of transcendental experiences, not texts of theological affirmations.

> The chief sacred scriptures of the Hindus, the *Vedas*, register the intuitions of the perfected souls. They are not so much dogmatic dicta as transcripts from life. They record the spiritual experiences of souls strongly endowed with the sense of reality. They are held to be authoritative on the ground that they express the experiences of the experts in the field of religion. If the

> utterances of the *Vedas* were uninformed by spiritual insight, they would have no claim to our belief.[6]

This understanding of the nature and derivation of these texts is a very common one. The conclusions of the *Vedas* are quite often presented as the fruits of laborious spiritual experiments conducted over a long period of time by the ancients. There is a deliberate and intentional attempt to draw a scientific analogy and image.

> The *Upaniṣads* which are the end of the *Veda* (*vedānta*) or the crown of the *śruti* (*śruti-śiras*) contain the discoveries made by the ancient seers in the realm of the spirit; they are a record of the declarations made by the sages and are designed to initiate the votary into the secrets of the intuitive or mystic experience. Even as in the sphere of physical science an investigator cannot afford to neglect the researches already made by others in the field, in the realm of the super-physical also a seeker of the truth must take into account the realizations of the sages. The appeal to the authority of *śruti* means no more and no less.[7]

In a very similar view, another writer sees the *Vedas* as the culmination of the experiences of various saints "working independently in different places and times, on subjects of such unique type as God and soul, reality or unreality of Existence and so on."[8] They record what occurred during moments of exalted imagination in the minds of these saints.[9]

Closely linked to the idea of the *Vedas* as records of mystic experiences, and even more important, is the perception of their authority as being derived from the so-called self-certifying and intrinsically valid nature of these experiences. To cite Radhakrishnan again:

> The highest evidence is perception, whether it is spiritual or sensuous and is capable of being experienced by us on compliance with certain conditions. The authoritativeness of the *śruti* is derived from the fact that it is but the expression of experience, and since experience is of a self-certifying character, the *Vedas* are said to be their own proof, requiring no support from elsewhere.[10]

The appeal to *śruti*, therefore, is ultimately based on the validity of a particular experience. Only the latter is seen as capable of conveying a knowledge which is immediate and at the same time indubitable.[11] According to some writers, the basis of the traditional acceptance of the authority of this experience is the fact that it has always been of a uniform nature. The spiritual experiments, in other words, have yielded an unvarying result.

> In the traditional view in which Śaṅkara was brought up, the Hindu scriptures have an absolute authority — not because a personal God wrote them or inspired individuals to write them; but because they embody the fruits of the spiritual insight of many sages who had searched for ultimate truth with single-minded devotion. They are, so to say, the fruits of many spiritual experiments, all of which have yielded the same result.[12]

This experience, when recorded in language and transmitted through a succession of teachers and students, comes to be known as *śruti* (that which is heard). *Śruti* therefore, is the "visible garment of the experiences of the awakened soul."[13] Radhakrishnan seeks to justify this recording of experience (*anubhava*) in a linguistic medium by arguing that while the former carries the greatest degree of certitude, it has a low degree of conceptual clarity.[14]

> This is why interpretation is necessary, and those interpretations are fallible and so require endless revision. *Śruti* attempts to say things which are not fully to be said.[15]

Besides the problem of reconciling the "highest degree of certitude" with "a low degree of conceptual clarity," this view starkly contrasts with earlier pronouncements about *śruti* as "eternal wisdom," and "the timeless rules of all created existence," possessing a direct and self-evident authority.

From the nature of *śruti* as the record of mystic or transcendental experiences and the derivation of its authority from the self-certifying nature of the same comes another important proposition of current opinion. This is the conclusion that for one who is in search of self-knowledge, the declarations of the *śruti* have only a provisional validity. *Śruti* is not itself a definitive or conclusive source of knowledge. Mahadevan again draws his scientific analogy.

> The students of *Vedānta* are required to place faith in *śruti*, even as learners of science must begin with a sense of confidence in the scientific theories formulated by the masterminds in the field. The final test in *Vedānta*, however, is experience, just as in science the arbiters of theory are said to be facts... .*Śruti*, to start with, is others' experience; and the knowledge one derives therefore is but mediate (*parokṣa*). Unless this

> becomes immediate (*aparokṣa*), the goal of *Vedānta*, which is self-realization, will not be reached.[16]

According to Menon and Allen, the recorded experiences are there only to guide us, but the "experiments" must be repeated in order that the conclusions can be tested and verified by us.[17] The truths of the *śruti*, therefore, are not the monopoly of any exclusive group but could be ascertained and verified by anyone.[18]

> The *Vedas*, therefore, contain truths which man could by the exercise of his own faculties discover, though it is to our advantage that they are revealed, seeing that not all men have the courage, time and equipment to face such an enterprise.[19]

A different view is expressed elsewhere by Radhakrishnan, and *śruti* becomes a secondary and poor substitute for those incapable of the first-hand experience and confirmation of *anubhava*.

> Those who have had no direct insight into reality are obliged to take on trust the Vedic views which record the highest experiences of some of the greatest minds who have wrestled with this problem of apprehending reality. For the ordinary man the central truth of the ultimate consciousness is revealed, and not ascertained by any human evidence like that of perception or inference.[20]

This view of the function of the *śruti* is shared by Belvalkar, according to whom the *Advaitin* found it necessary to appeal to the authority of the *śruti* only because the experience upon which it was founded was beyond the reach of all. Whenever, Belvalkar claims, the scriptures are cited, it is merely for the purpose of supporting a conclusion "which has been reached independently of the scriptures."[21] Śaṅkara's reliance on the *śruti* is sometimes seen only as an attempt to show his agreement with orthodox authority.[22] *Śruti*, then, does not incontrovertibly establish anything but awaits the confirmation of *anubhava* for the conversion of its hypothetical assertions into fact.

Radhakrishnan reveals his focus on experience by rejecting the traditional term *jñāna* because of its empirical associations, preferring the word *anubhava*, which he renders as "integral experience."[23] *Anubhava* is elevated by him to the status of an independent *pramāṇa* and becomes the equal of direct perception (*pratyakṣa*). It is the basis of whatever we know and believe of the supersensual world. In his view, then, *śruti* occupies a decidedly secondary position to direct mystical insight in the religious outlook of Śaṅkara. Radhakrishnan claims that it is difficult to find support in the writings of Śaṅkara for the view that inquiry into the *Vedas* is the only means to knowledge of *brahman.*[24] He is unambiguous in his final conclusion about the relationship between *śruti* and *anubhava* in Śaṅkara.

> For him, integral experience or *anubhava* is the basal fact. It is the highest religious insight. It supplies the proof — if proof be the name for it — of man's awareness of a spiritual reality.[25]

Radhakrishnan's final conclusions about the roles of *śruti* and *anubhava* in Śaṅkara are shared by many other Indian writers. Prabhavananda also sees direct personal experience as the ultimate satisfactory proof in Śaṅkara. The *śruti* is a mere provisional pointer along the way.[26] Sharma also upholds the view that immediate spiritual realization, which he terms "supra-relational intuition," is the ultimate criterion of truth in Śaṅkara. Like Radhakrishnan, he links up the authority of the *Vedas* in Śaṅkara with the self-certifying nature of experience.[27] According to R. P. Singh, Śaṅkara's conclusion that *anubhava* is the only *pramāṇa* of *brahman* is the result of the nature of the *brahman* experience. In other words, epistemology is determined by experience. The nature of the object determines the *pramāṇa* through which it can be known.[28] Whereas in some cases sensuous perception may be appropriate, in others the nature of the object demands reliance only on spiritual perception (*anubhava*).[29] Singh emphasizes that all reasoning and reflection are only preparatory for what he terms the "scientia visionis," the final and highest court of appeal. Belvalkar argues for the superiority of experience over *śruti* from what he sees to be the dominant role of the former in ordinary life.

> Reason — and by this term should be understood to include Analogy and the other *Pramanas* admitted by traditional *Vedānta* — gets its eventual sanction from Experience, and so likewise does the authority of the Scriptures. Scriptures are therefore subordinate to Reason where we are concerned with matters of actual sensuous *anubhava*, such as the heat of the fire. On the other hand, Reason has to yield the palm to the Scriptures where it is a question of matters where Scriptures can appeal to a distinct supra-sensuous experience of their own. Eventually the *Vedānta* acknowledges only one criterion of truth, viz., *anubhava.* Such being the case, it will certainly not do to style *Vedānta* as mere exegetics, or dogmatism, or theology, or whatever other appellation it may be fashionable to us to characterize the system.[30]

N. K. Devaraja is largely in agreement with the general view of the relationship between *śruti* and *anubhava* in Śaṅkara.[31] The interesting point about Devaraja's analysis, however, is that he, unlike other writers, broadens the concept of experience. He acknowledges the central role of the *pramāṇas* in Śaṅkara but sees Śaṅkara's insistence that *brahman* is to be known only through the *śruti* merely as an expression of his "ultra-orthodox mood."[32] His reason for not seeing this as an inveterate tenet of Śaṅkara seems to be due to the latter's emphasis that *brahman* is not an object of scriptural knowledge.[33] *Śruti* is by no means unique in bringing about the final intuition of *brahman.* It is merely a more direct and effective means.

> All the *pramāṇas* play their part in bringing about that final intuition, and if Śaṅkara is at moments inclined to assign a higher place to *śruti*, it is probably because he feels that the utterances of the *Upaniṣads*, being vital poetic records of spiritual experience, can induce that intuition earlier than the mere negative operations of the logical understanding. Or, if we are unkind critics, we may say that, occasionally, the orthodox in Śaṅkara overwhelms the empiricist and rationalist in him.[34]

Devaraja, as mentioned, broadens the concept of experience with reference to Śaṅkara. Experience is superior to *śruti* not only in the sense of intuitive or mystical experience but also in the wider sense of perceptual or everyday (*loka*) experience. This very interesting contention of Devaraja will be evaluated later, but here it is just necessary to state his evidence for this conclusion. It is based on two references from Śaṅkara's commentary on the *Bṛhadāraṇyaka Upaniṣad* and the *Brahma-sūtra.* In the first quotation, that *śruti* must communicate in familiar concepts is seen as evidence for the superior authority of *loka.*

> It is not the purpose of the scripture to distort the nature of things; on the contrary, its aim is to make the unknown known as it is. . . .Not a hundred illustrations can establish that fire is cold or that the sun gives out no heat. For other *pramāṇas* represent the objects to be different in nature. Nor is one *pramāṇa* contradicted by another. Every *pramāṇa* makes known only what is not an object of another *pramāṇa.* Nor can scripture make the unknown intelligible without depending upon the relationship of words and their meaning as recognized by the *loka.*[35]

The second quotation is actually one of Śaṅkara's hypothetical opponents (*pūrvapakṣin*) whose voice Devaraja perplexingly thinks Śaṅkara employs to assert the superiority of everyday experience.

> *Yukti* or reasoning which affirms the unseen on the analogy of the seen, is nearer to experience than *śruti*, for the latter's authority is traditional merely.[36]

Taken by themselves, both references are very tenuous grounds for asserting his conclusions. The first merely avers the authority of each *pramāṇa* in its respective sphere and suggests the absence of any conflict among them. The implication that Śaṅkara resorts to an opponent to voice his views makes the second reference very insubstantial evidence.

Hiriyanna's conclusions about the respective roles of *śruti* and *anubhava* in Śaṅkara are somewhat surprising in the light of the fact that he is one of the few writers who discuss in fair detail the *pramāṇa* concept.[37] He sees no essential difference between the *Pūrva-Mīmāṁsā* concept of the *Vedas* and the *Advaita* concept, except the role of *īśvara* in the latter's scheme.[38] With this background, it is indeed strange that he also, like the other writers considered, credits the intuitive experience with a separate, superior, and final epistemological status.

> The ultimate philosophic fact is no doubt to be known through the testimony of the *Upaniṣads*; but if the knowledge conveyed by it is to bring real freedom, one should verify it by one's own living experience in the form "I am Brahman" or *Aham Brahma Asmi*. It is this immediate experience or direct intuition of the Absolute which is described as *vidvadanubhava* to distinguish it from lay experience, that accordingly becomes the final criterion of Truth here.[39]

Hiriyanna is also united with others in concluding that the *Upaniṣads*, should in the last resort, be regarded as recording the intuitional knowledge of the ancient sages. While the *Upaniṣads* are necessary, they have only an instrumental value in conveying merely mediate knowledge. In resorting to direct experience, one has to go beyond the texts.[40]

In view of the consensus among Eastern scholars about the primacy of *anubhava* over *śruti*, it is perhaps not surprising to find their Western counterparts generally agreeing with these conclusions. Smart endorses the opinion of the essentially mystical nature of knowledge in Śaṅkara.

> The full understanding of his system and its conclusive "verification" comes through the nondualistic realization of identity between Self and Holy Power. Thus knowledge, at the higher level of metaphysical truth, is not theoretical; but it is essentially contemplative or mystical.[41]

As a direct consequence of his stress on an experience, Smart argues for a basic similarity between *Mahāyāna* and *Advaita*. He ventures so far as to dismiss the dependence of the latter on the *Vedas* as being of no consequence, since revelation, in his view, culminates in nondual experience.[42] The pivotal role of the mystical experience considerably modifies, according to Smart, the intrinsic-validity concept of the scripture. This brings Śaṅkara, in Smart's view, very close to the *Yoga* standpoint.

> In other words, the scriptures are valid at the higher level in so far as they point towards a certain supreme experience. In the last resort, therefore, their truth is pragmatic and provisional. What confirms them is direct experience, and by then they are useless. This clearly modifies considerably the concept of their being self-authenticated. Here Śaṅkara's view is not far from that of *Yoga*, namely that the scriptures originate from the supreme perception or intuition of yogis. Hence the issue about the validity of revelation is shifted to that of the trustworthiness of mystical — in particular yogic — experience.[43]

Smart reiterates this position in his later work, *The Yogi and the Devotee*, emphasizing the place of *dhyāna* and the *Yoga* parallel.[44]

R.V. de Smet is one of the few writers treating substantially Śaṅkara's method, and emphasizing the primacy of *śruti*.[45] He describes Śaṅkara as a *śrutivādin* (one for whom the *śruti* is the primary authority) and discusses the superiority of *śruti* in relation to all other *pramāṇas*.

> As to testimony, it is of two kinds: *pauruṣeya* and *apauruṣeya*, i.e., it either originates from an individual witness (*puruṣa*) or it does not. *Smṛti*, for instance, is mere human tradition and its authority is therefore defective, for men are fallible. But *śruti* (i.e., the Vedic and Brahmanic scriptures, especially the *Upaniṣads*) is entirely free from dependence upon individual authors; it is absolutely infallible and its authority is supreme.[46]

With such a clear comprehension of the unrivalled status of the *Vedas* in Śaṅkara and a detailed discussion of his procedure in interpreting the same, one expected de Smet to diverge in his conclusion from the general view. It comes as an anticlimax to find in him the selfsame unacknowledged and unresolved contradiction between an initial emphasis on the unmitigated authority of *śruti* and their reliance for verification on an experience. This tension was also highlighted in the case of Radhakrishnan.

> Thus Vedic faith, which at first was a mere reliance on the intuition of the *ṛṣis*, becomes fully validated when it turns into that final transcendental experience.[47]

Writers who argue for *anubhava* as the true *pramāṇa* of *brahmajñāna* generally treat the process of knowledge in Śaṅkara as progressing through three different phases. The original reference to this threefold process comes from the *Bṛhadāraṇyaka Upaniṣad* where Yājñavalkya, instructing his wife Maitreyī, says,

> The Self, my dear Maitreyī, should be realized — should be heard of, reflected on, and mediated upon. By the realization of the Self, my dear, through hearing, reflection, and meditation, all this is known.[48]

Śravaṇa (listening) is the initial exposure to the context of the *Upaniṣads* as unfolded by the qualified teacher. *Manana* (reflection) is the employment of reason to refute and eliminate doubts arising within one's own mind, as well as objections tendered by rival schools of thought. These two processes are generally characterized as entirely intellectual and merely preliminary. They culminate in the final phase of *nididhyāsana* (contemplation or meditation), in which the truth of the self is directly apprehended, all doubts finally fall away, and freedom (*mokṣa*) is attained. In the general presentation of this threefold process, it is the final procedure that is considered salient and all-important. The contention is that only here does the gain of knowledge in the true sense occur.

> Deep reflection (*manana*) leads the aspirant to the next stage, namely, *nididhyāsana*. This third stage, called *nididhyāsana*, is constant and uninterrupted meditation or intense contemplation on the convinced doctrines of *tat tvam asi* and other *mahāvākyas* propounding the Advaitic mystic doctrine. This *nididhyāsana* is the immediate preparation for the *Brahmajñāna* or the transcendental experience, i.e., the supra-mental consciousness. After *nididhyāsana*, the aspirant attains to the experience that transcends all world-consciousness and ego-consciousness. In that experience he realizes the truth of the *Upaniṣadic* utterance: "There is no diversity here."[49]

Mere *Śravaṇa*, it is contended, will not take the student very far.[50] Only the direct and immediate knowledge which uninterrupted meditation (*nididhyāsana*) affords, enables the mediate instruction of the teacher to dispel false notions.[51] The experience which supposedly confers true knowledge is sometimes presented as one over which the student has no control but upon which one simply waits after completing *śravaṇa* and *manana*.

> He has listened with faith to the *guru's* teaching and explanation of the *śruti*; with the help of all the resources of secular reasoning, he has successfully

> contradicted all the objections that could be raised against the doctrine he has heard; now, all the obstacles to *advaita* — Knowledge being destroyed, his mind is peaceful and there is nothing more to drive him away from the contemplation of the Truth; calm and happy, he concentrates all his thoughts on the revealed truth and awaits silently the flash-like illumination which is to change his high but still complex knowledge into the simplest and most immediate consciousness of the Absolute.[52]

Writers who affirm the primacy of *anubhava* are generally vague on the actual nature of the experience which gives us immediate knowledge of *brahman*. *Anubhava* is generally equated by them with "intuition" and presented as a form of "direct insight," "direct access," or "direct acquaintance." It is described as a form of internal perception comparable to external perception, on the basis that perception (internal or external) alone can give us direct knowledge of any existent entity.[53] *Anubhava* is not a movement around the object of knowledge but a vision from the inside.[54] In its immediacy, it is more like feeling than thinking, transcending the discursive-reasoning fuctions of the mind. Unlike our knowledge of the physical world, which progresses in stages, enlightenment, like all intuitions, descends in a sudden flash when we least expect it.[55] As noted earlier, it is supposed to leave no room for doubt.

> The intuition of the Absolute resembles perception rather than conception. It is as inevitable, as direct, as absolute as perception. It forces itself irresistibly on our consciousness. There can be no scope for doubt, hesitation, option "this or that" in this act of realization. Reality as soon as it rises into view carries its conviction about itself; it lays hold upon our nature with absolute violence. It is objective certainty we attain and not subjective assurance, or rather it is absolute certitude, and neither subjective nor objective assurance, which we get.[56]

Most of the writers we have considered equate *anubhava* with the *Yoga* experience of *nirvikalpa samādhi*, the state in which the mind transcends its usual divisions of knower, knowledge, and process of knowing and becomes free from all mental content.

In view of the general tendency to assign epistemological supremacy to *anubhava* in relation to *śruti*, the common designation of *Advaita* as "mysticism" is not surprising, and any consideration of the role of these two factors in Śaṅkara must take note of and evaluate this proclivity. One of the earliest writers to so treat *Advaita* was S. N. Dasgupta.[57] In his work, *brahman* is considered as identical with the experience, and the latter is referred to as "reality." Intuitive experience is the immediate means of self-knowledge and is his key concept.

> Only persons who have realized this truth can point this out to us as an experience which is at once self-illuminating and blissful and which is entirely different from all else that is known to us. Once it is thus exhibited, those who have the highest moral elevation and disinclination to worldly enjoyments can grasp it by an inner intuitive contact with the reality itself (*adhyātmayoga*). This truth is indeed the culmination of all the teaching of the *Vedas.*[58]

Dasgupta's definition of mysticism as "the belief that God is realized through ecstatic communion with Him," is obviously inadequate to deal with the diversity of the material he subsumes under the category.[59] But then, Dasgupta shows little sensitivity to variation. The method of *Yoga* is seen by him as supplying the definite technique lacking in the *Upaniṣads* for the perception of the truths discussed there. There is little regard for divergent theological presuppositions, and Dasgupta's unhesitant recourse to *Yoga* is significant.

> In the most advanced state of this *yoga* intuition, all the truths regarding the nature of the true Self, of the mind, and of the material world and its connection with the mind, become clear, and as a result of this and also as a result of the gradual weakening of the constitution of the mind, the latter ceases to live and work and is disassociated forever from the spirit or the Self.[60]

R. C. Zaehner, in his works on mysticism, also treats Śaṅkara's *Advaita* primarily as an experience.[61] More recently Geoffrey Parrinder has done the same.[62] Parrinder does not proffer any definition of his own, but for him the crucial terms are *experiment* and *experience.* Two definitions he does quote are "reliance on spiritual intuition or exalted feeling as a means of acquiring knowledge of mysteries inaccessible to intellectual apprehension," and "belief in the possibility of union with the Divine nature by means of ecstatic contemplation."[63] It is interesting that Parrinder confesses the difficulty of finding an Indian term to correspond to the European word, mysticism, in the sense of union, and more interesting that he selects the term *yoga.*

Although Parrinder expresses no misgivings about his label of mysticism on *Advaita*, two significant passages in his work suggest the difficulties of this assumption. These, however, do not direct him to any re-evaluation. In the first of these, he writes about the *Upaniṣads*,

> A few other examples of world-renunciation are given but it is remarkable that the *Upaniṣads*, which are often regarded as mystical treatises, have very few autobiographical details, and the experiences upon which they seem to be founded have to be deduced from their teachings. There is a search for mystical unity, but it is expressed in a dogmatic statement rather than in described experience.[64]

After describing Śaṅkara's mysticism as cool and unimpassioned, characterized by argument and assertion than by autobiography, he writes in the second passage,

> The proof of the existence of the divine being is in the human self, and this is established by asserting the identity of divine and self. This dogmatic declaration results from reflection and intuition, but it is strongly supported by appeals to the authority of scripture, the *Vedas* and *Upaniṣads.* In this Śaṅkara reveals himself as a theologian rather than a logical philosopher.[65]

These two passages, suggesting perhaps Parrinder's own unconfessed doubts, reveal also the difficulty of many of the other writers on mysticism. *Advaita Vedānta* is treated as mystical without any satisfactory definition of the latter. Mysticism seems to be an alternative heading, attractive, perhaps, for the discussion of doctrinal matters.[66]

It seems, therefore, that there is a certain consensus in current opinion about the respective roles of *śruti* and *anubhava* in Śaṅkara.[67] The primacy of experience and intuition over *śruti* is, in fact, considered to be a unique characteristic of Indian philosophy in general, which places it in a distinctively superior category from Western philosophy. Many of the conclusions I have isolated have achieved an a priori status over the years and greatly influenced the study of and approach to Śaṅkara and to Indian religious thought. It is my contention, however, that these views gravely misrepresent Śaṅkara's position, and I aim to argue for radically different conclusions about the status and functions of *śruti* and *anubhava.* I can now summarize the chief features of the relationship between *śruti* and *anubhava*, as formulated in the studies examined:

1. The *Vedas* are the records of the transcendental experiences of the ancient mystics, through which they conclusively apprehended the exact nature of reality. *Śruti* is the linguistic record of *anubhava.*

2. The *Vedas* derive their authority from the self-certifying nature of religious experience. Religious experiences, being intrinsically valid and authoritative, lends this character to the texts recording them.
3. For the aspirant, the declarations of the *Vedas* are only provisional. They are subject to the confirmation of direct experience, which is in the last resort the final criterion of truth and the ultimate satisfactory proof. As records of mystical experiences, the *Vedas* merely indicate what can be known. They are primarily useful to the lesser-qualified aspirant who is incapable of *anubhava*.
4. The *Vedas* contain truth which human beings could, by the exercise of their faculties, rediscover and verify.
5. The *Vedas* are by no means unique as a source of knowledge about *brahman*.
6. Knowledge of *brahman* (*brahmajñāna*) is gained through the three-fold process of *śravaṇa*, *manana*, and *nididhyāsana*. The first two are viewed as merely preliminary and intellectual. It is only the experience which contemplation (*nididhyāsana*) affords that conclusively informs us about *brahman*.
7. *Anubhava* is accorded the status of an independent means of knowledge (*pramāṇa*). It is the basis on which all knowledge of the supersensuous rests — the equivalent, in the spiritual context, of direct perception in the empirical world.

Chapter 1

The Ascertainment and Sources of Valid Knowledge

Orthodox and heterodox systems of Indian philosophy demonstrate a great concern about the nature, validity, and sources of knowledge. It was considered important for each school of thought to elucidate the authoritative basis of its postulates, and the character of debate was shaped by a clear comprehension of each other's standpoint. The code of disputation did not allow attempts to refute opposing arguments by reference to an authoritative source of knowledge which was not mutually acceptable. This principle is clearly evident throughout Śaṅkara's commentaries, in which the kind of argument employed and the authority specified depend on the epistemology of the opponent. The authority of the *Vedas*, for example, is not generally resorted to in contention with Buddhist schools of thought. The growth and refinement of sophisticated theories of knowledge were undoubtedly quickened by the birth of heterodox systems like Jainism and Buddhism, which rejected the authority of the *Vedas* and claimed to found their propositions exclusively on reason and human experience.

Śaṅkara, in his commentaries, does not undertake any independent systematic analysis of the sources of knowledge. He treats them throughout as being well known.[1] Nevertheless, it is a great error to assume that he was indifferent to problems of epistemology. His commentaries clearly belie any such conclusion. There may be a number of reasons for the absence of any independent systematic treatment of this subject in his works. First, he saw his role primarily as a commentator on the *Upaniṣads*, and the kind of discussion he developed was largely dictated by the content of any particular verse before him. Second, the absence could be accounted for by his agreement with the exponents of rival systems. One gets the impression that Śaṅkara's concern was not with the elaboration of a theory about the sources of knowledge but with the evaluation of their respective worth. It is a concern which arises directly out of his desire to uphold the authoritative source for our knowledge of *brahman*.

1.1 The Nature and Criterion of Valid Knowledge

The Sanskrit word *jñāna*, in a broad sense, refers to all kinds of cognition, without regard to the question of truth or error. To "know," in this sense of the term, is simply to have a notion, doubt, desire, feeling, dream or incorrect idea. In this strict sense, therefore, its opposite, *ajñāna*, indicates the complete absence of any cognition. *Jñāna*, therefore, may refer to both valid and invalid cognitions, and I have used the word *knowledge* in this study as equivalent to *jñāna*. *Ajñāna* has been used by Śaṅkara to include the absence of knowledge, but also error and doubt (BRU.B. 3.3.1.). The word *pramā*, however, denotes only valid cognitions.

The special source of a particular *pramā* or knowledge is termed, *pramāṇa*. It is defined as the cause (*karaṇa*) of valid knowledge (*pramā karaṇam pramāṇam*).[2] A *karaṇa* is conceived as "the unique or special cause through the *action* of which a particular effect is produced."[3] In the case of external perceptual knowledge, for instance, the causes are many. There is the particular sense organ as well as the mind. The mind, however, is common to all kinds of perception and so cannot be regarded as the unique cause. In external perception, it is the particular sense organ which is considered as the *karaṇa*. In addition to being unique, a *karaṇa* should also possess an active function. The contact between the sense organ and the sense object is unique because it is a feature of perception alone. It is not, however, considered as the *karaṇa* of perception because it is itself a function of the sense organ. A *pramāṇa*, then, can be defined as "an active and unique cause (*karaṇa*) of the *pramā* or knowledge."[4] Its special feature is its capacity to produce valid knowledge. On this characteristic, Śaṅkara is clear.

> A means of knowledge is or is not such according as it leads or does not lead to valid knowledge. Otherwise even a post, for instance, would be considered a means of knowledge in perceiving sound, etc.[5]

The reverse of this proposition is also true for Śaṅkara. Knowledge is only generated by a valid means of knowledge (*pramāṇa*).[6]

The function of knowledge, according to Śaṅkara, is to reveal the nature of things, and valid knowledge conforms to the nature of the object it seeks to reveal. Any object must be known as it is, and thus knowledge is not governed by human choice but by the character of the object to be known.

> But a thing cannot be judged diversely to be of such a kind and not to be of such a kind, to be existent and nonexistent (simultaneously). Options depend on human notions, whereas valid knowledge of the true nature of a thing is not dependent on human notions. On what does it depend then? It is dependent on the thing itself. For an awareness of the form, "This is a stump, or a man, or something else," with regard to the same stump cannot be valid knowledge. In such a case the awareness of the form, "This is a man or something else" is erroneous, but "This is a stump to be sure" is valid knowledge; for it corresponds to the thing itself. Thus the validity of knowledge of an existing thing is determined by the thing itself.[7]

Dharmarājā, in *Vedānta Paribhāṣā*, defines *pramā* as "that knowledge which has for its object something that is not already known and is uncontradicted."[8] Here, novelty (*anadhigatatvam*) and non-contradictedness (*abādhitatvam*) are considered the crucial characteristics of *pramā*. Non-contradictedness, as far as *Advaita* is concerned, is the crucial test of truth. All other tests are seen as conforming to this. Any invalid proposition or erroneous experience, such as the cognition of a rope as a snake, can be refuted on the ground of being contradicted. In this case, the object of knowledge, the snake, is contradicted by the knowledge of the rope. The principle of non-contradictedness implies that a cognition, the purpose of which is to reveal reality, is held to be valid until it is falsified by a superior *pramāṇa*. The objection may be forwarded that since *Advaita* posits *brahman* as the ultimate reality, it is impossible to speak of a valid knowledge of ordinary objects. This contention is anticipated by Dharmarājā, who qualifies "uncontradicted" in his definition to mean "not contradicted during the transmigratory state."[9] In the absolute sense, of course, *brahman* alone is uncontradicted, and the notion of reality ascribed to the world of diversity is held to be valid until *brahman* is known.[10]

There is no doubt that Śaṅkara sees the operation of the *pramāṇas*, secular and sacred, as being founded on ignorance (*avidyā*). What is not often emphasized is the distinctive manner of the relationship between *avidyā* and the *pramāṇas*. It is not, as it is sometimes understood, that the *pramāṇas* are incapable of producing right knowledge, empirical and absolute. It is the generally implicit and assumed identification between the Self and non-Self in the operation of the *pramāṇas* that reveals their location in *avidyā*. Unless this very specific understanding of *avidyā* is kept in mind, the claim that the *pramāṇas* are founded on ignorance and are also capable of producing valid knowledge may seem inconsistent. The working of the *pramāṇas* proceeds from the natural superimposition (*adhyāsa*) of the nature of the Self on the non-Self and vice versa.

> Since a man without self-identification with the body, mind, senses, etc., cannot become a cognizer, and as such, the means of knowledge cannot function for him; since perception and other activities (of a man) are not possible without accepting the senses, etc. (as his own); since the senses cannot function without (the body as) a basis; since nobody engages in any activity with a body that has not the idea of the Self superimposed on it; since the unrelated Self cannot become a cognizer unless there are all these (mutual superimposition of the Self and the body and their attributes on each other); and since the means of knowledge cannot function unless there is a cognizership; therefore, it follows that the means of knowledge, such as direct

> perception as well as the scriptures, must have a man as their locus who is subject to nescience.[11]

The ultimate refutation of the presupposed superimposition, upon which the function of any *pramāṇa* is generally based, does not diminish its function in the production of valid knowledge.[12] Śaṅkara does not propose any alternative avenue to knowledge, empirical and spiritual, besides the legitimate *pramāṇas*. He does not anywhere express doubts or reservations about the competence of the *pramāṇas* to produce valid knowledge in their respective spheres. He claims, in fact, that practical affairs will become impossible if the *pramāṇas* are regarded as fundamentally perverse. Defending inference, for example, as a means of knowledge, Śaṅkara writes

> If you challenge the validity of an inference of the kind not based on a causal relation, all our activities, including eating and drinking, would be impossible, which you certainly do not desire. We see in life that people who have experienced that hunger and thirst, for instance, are appeased by eating and drinking, proceed to adopt these means, expecting similar results; all this would be impossible. As a matter of fact, however, people who have the experience of eating and drinking infer, on the ground of similarity, that their hunger and thirst would be appeased if they ate and drank again, and proceed to act accordingly.[13]

Another of Śaṅkara's compelling arguments for the indispensability of the *pramāṇas* occurs in one of his many discussions with the various Buddhist schools. Here the controversy is with the *Vijñānavāda* proponent, arguing for the nonexistence of external objects and the validity of ideas alone, which appears as different external objects.

> *Buddhist*: Since no object can possibly exist externally, I come to the conclusion that it appears as though it is outside.
>
> *Vedāntin*: This conclusion is not honest, since the possibility or impossibility of the existence of a thing is determined in accordance with the applicability or non-applicability of the means of knowledge to it, but the applicability or non-applicability of the means of knowledge is not ascertained in accordance with the possibility or impossibility (of the thing). What is known through anyone of the means of knowledge, such as direct perception etc., is possible, and what cannot be known through any one of these means of knowledge is impossible. In the case under discussion,

> the external things are known individually by the respective means of knowledge; so how can they be declared to be impossible by raising such alternatives as different, non-different, etc.?[14]

The second characteristic of valid knowledge, as mentioned above, is novelty (*anadhigatatva*). The question of novelty as a feature of *pramā* revolves around the acceptance of memory as a distinct *pramāṇa*. Vedāntists, however, on the whole, seem uninterested in this controversy. The *Vedānta-Paribhāṣā* offers a definition of *pramā* to exclude and include memory. Generally speaking, it is excluded from valid knowledge because it is not produced by any one of the accepted *pramāṇas* but originates from the impressions of a past cognition. This does not imply that memory is invalid. It is true if it arises out of the impressions of a valid cognition and false if it does not. In other words, it is the original or archetypal cognition that is paramount.

1.2 The Self-Validity of Knowledge (*Svataḥ-Prāmāṇya-Vāda*)

The self-validity of knowledge is a very important but little discussed area of *Advaita* thought. It is one of the many epistemological theories taken from the *Pūrva-Mīmāṁsā* by *Advaita*, and its understanding is vital in apprehending the independent and definitive role of each *pramāṇa* in giving rise to valid knowledge. *Svataḥ-prāmāṇya* may be translated as the self-validity or intrinsic validity of knowledge.[15]

The theory suggests that the causes which give rise to a particular cognition also produce a belief in its validity. This belief does not require verification through another cognition. If all the conditions necessary for the successful operation of any one of the *pramāṇas* are fulfilled, valid knowledge will result as well as a belief in that validity. The important point is that the source of knowledge should be free from deficiencies. The necessary conditions required for the production of any knowledge will, of course, vary with the *pramāṇas*. In the case of the perception of forms, for example, the conditions will include a healthy organ of vision and sufficient light. When a cognition, initially believed to be true, is later found to be invalid, this invalidity cannot be attributed to the causal factors themselves but to some adventitious defects (*doṣa*) in them. A cognition may be questioned when it is later contradicted by another source of knowledge or when a defect is subsequently discovered in its cause. Valid knowledge arises when the necessary conditions which give rise to it are present and, along with it, there is a belief in its validity. Both do not owe their rise to any external conditions and require no verification from anything else.[16] Thus *Pūrva-Mīmāṁsā* and *Advaita* claim that while validity is intrinsic, invalidity is extrinsic.[17]

On the question of the validity of knowledge, the *Advaita* view is best contrasted with the arguments of the *Nyāya* school. The contention between both schools on this matter has become one of the classic controversies in the history of Indian philosophical thought. Both schools are in agreement as far as the invalidity of knowledge is concerned, regarding it as due to extraneous factors. They disagree, however, about the cause of validity. *Nyāya* proposes the theory of the extrinsic in both cases. The *Nyāya* argument is that if invalidity (*apramā*) is due to defects existing along with the common causes of knowledge, then *pramā* must be due to the presence of some favorable factor (*guṇa*) along with the common causes. Hence, knowledge is not self-valid, but its validity and invalidity are derived from extraneous causes. This argument is refuted by *Advaita* on the ground that the favorable factor of *Nyāya* is not independent of the causes themselves.[18] Valid knowledge can be accounted for by the absence of defect and contradiction, and the excellence of the causes of knowledge (*guṇa*) is not an extraneous factor but an intrinsic condition for the rise of *pramā*.

The *parataḥ-prāmāṇya-vāda* of *Nyāya* advocates the extrinsic apprehension of validity. Valid knowledge, in the *Nyāya* view, corresponds with its object, and this correspondence can be put to the test in fruitful activity. One infers from the capacity or incapacity of knowledge to produce successful activity its validity or invalidity. A mirage in a desert, for example, is an optical illusion because of its failure to quench the thirst of a traveller.[19]

Advaitins generally respond in a twofold manner to the *Nyāya* objections. In the first case, it is argued that a false cognition may, and sometimes does, lead to successful activity. The lustre of a distant jewel may be mistaken for the jewel itself but can lead the one who desires it to successfully obtain it.[20]

The stronger argument urged against the *Nyāya* position is that it leads to infinite regression. If the validity of one cognition is to depend on another cognition, then the second will require a third, and so on. This is the import of Śaṅkara's statement that the validity of the *Upaniṣads* does not depend on another means of knowledge like inference.[21] Knowledge produced by a defect-free *pramāṇa* is apprehended as valid unless contradicted by the knowledge of a higher reality.[22] The self-validity of knowledge does not preclude the possibility of doubt about the truth of any particular cognition. Properly speaking, however, if one entertains doubt about the truth of a cognition, there is no cognition. It involves a vacillation between two notions and can sometimes be removed by repeating the same cognition after removing the cause of doubt.

The importance of the self-validity argument for *Advaita* is that any defect-free *pramāṇa* can independently generate knowledge. The knowledge produced by any *pramāṇa* does not have to be authenticated by another. On the evidence of the sense of taste alone, for example, the sweetness of sugar is indubitably accepted. It follows from this that the *Vedas* also, as a means of knowledge in the form of words (*śabda-pramāṇa*) can generate valid knowledge independently of other means. The knowledge is not necessarily of a provisional nature, awaiting confirmation. We can anticipate here a clear difference of view with those who propose the necessity for *anubhava* as a kind of certifying experience for the hypothetical propositions of the *Vedas*.

1.3 The Self-Luminosity of Knowledge (*Svataḥ-Prakāśa-Vāda*)

Like the idea of self-validity discussed above, the concept of self-luminosity is an essential epistemological theory of *Advaita*. They are the premises for understanding the knowledge process in this system. The idea may be summed up by saying that whenever there is knowledge of an object, the fact of this knowledge is immediately known. According to *Advaita*, material things, which are all inert, are not revealed except by cognitions of them. A cognition, however, is revealed as soon as it arises, needing no other cognition for its revelation. Knowledge of a tree, for example, is dependent on its objectification by the cognition "This is a tree." This cognition, however, is immediately apprehended. One is immediately aware of one's knowledge of the tree.

In *Advaita*, self-luminosity belongs to the *ātman* alone. In its light everything is illumined and known. The Self is the knower (*kṣetrajña*) and everything else is known (*kṣetra*).[23] As the unchanging witness of all mental modifications, it is referred to as *sākṣi*.[24] The same awareness, reflected in the mind and identified with it, becomes the *jīva*, who functions as the perceiver (*pramātā*). The cognizer, the object cognized (*prameya*), and the cognition (*pramiti*) are all revealed by the Self as witness (*sākṣi*). In any act of perception, the cognitive mode objectifies and reveals the object because it is illumined by the Self. This cognition, however, does not require another cognitive mode for its manifestation. It is revealed directly by the Self as *sākṣi*, as soon as it originates.

On the question of the self-luminosity of knowledge, *Advaita* is at issue with the *Bhāṭṭa* school of *Pūrva-Mīmāṁsā* who advocate the theory of *parataḥ-prakāśa-vāda*, according to which any knowledge is not self-revealed but dependent for its revelation upon another knowledge.[25] The *Bhāṭṭa Mīmāṁsā* argues that cognitions, being formless, cannot be directly apprehended but can be inferred. When a tree, for example, is known, it acquires the quality of "knownness" which is perceptible. By perceiving this mark of "knownness," one infers one's prior knowledge of the tree. Thus, while an object may be directly apprehended, its knowledge is gained only indirectly by an inferential process of reasoning. This *Bhāṭṭa* argument is unmistakably refuted by Śaṅkara.

> Those who hold that cognition (*jñāna*) is formless and is not known by immediate perception must admit that, since an object of knowledge is apprehended through cognition, cognition is quite as immediately known as pleasure or the like.
>
> Moreover, it cannot be maintained that cognition is a thing which one seeks to know. If cognition were unknown, it would be a thing which has to be sought after just as an *object* of cognition is sought after. Just as, for example, a man seeks to reach by cognition the cognizable object such as a pot, so also would he have to seek to reach cognition by means of another *cognition*. But the fact is otherwise. Wherefore *cognition* is self-revealed, and therefore, also, is the cognizer self-revealed.[26]

His second argument is the same as that used in refuting the *parataḥ-prāmāṇya* theory. If one cognition needs another for its revelation, the second will need a third, and the result will be infinite regression.[27]

The undoubted motivation behind *Advaita's* powerful advocacy of the theories of the self-validity and self-luminosity of knowledge is the necessity for incontrovertibly establishing the possibility of valid knowledge. This possibility is imperative in any outlook, like *Advaita*, where ultimate human freedom (*mokṣa*) lies in the gain of valid knowledge. Alternative theories are seen as leading to infinitive regression, making knowledge and freedom an impossibility. The very definition of a *pramāṇa* implies, as we have seen, the capacity to produce valid knowledge.

Before embarking on an analysis of Śaṅkara's justification of the *Vedas* as a source of valid knowledge, it is necessary to outline the *Advaita* view of the nature and operation of the other five *pramāṇas*. It is only in the light of our understanding of the mechanism of these sources, the kind of knowledge apprehended through each one and their limitations, that we can properly see the centrality and indispensability of the *Vedas* as a *pramāṇa* for Śaṅkara. Each *pramāṇa* has a unique way of transmitting knowledge, and each one presents a distinct type.[28]

There is no unanimity among the schools of Indian philosophy about the nature and number of these sources of knowledge. The *Cārvākas* only admit sense perception as a valid means of knowledge. The schools of Buddhism and *Vaiśeṣika* acknowledge perception and inference. The *Sāṅkhya* and *Yoga* systems go further in recognizing perception, inference, and *śabda*. To these three, the *Naiyāyikas* add comparison as a source. *Nyāya* has contributed immensely to the development of inference as a *pramāṇa*. The *Prabhakara* school of *Pūrva-Mīmāṁsā* goes beyond *Nyāya* and adds postulation as a source of knowledge. The process comes to an end with the *Bhāṭṭa* school of *Mīmāṁsā* and *Advaita*, who include non-apprehension as the sixth *pramāṇa*.

1.4 The Six *Pramāṇas*

I. PERCEPTION (*Pratyakṣa*)

Used as an adjective, *pratyakṣa* indicates that which is direct and immediate. As a noun, it signifies immediate knowledge. *Pratyakṣa* principally designates knowledge produced from the direct contact of the external senses with their objects. *Advaita*, however, accepts the validity of internal perception where mental states such as love, hate, anger, and desire are directly known by the *ātman* without the instrumentality of the sense organs and the mind.[29] In the view of *Advaita*, mental states are apprehended as soon as they arise, and the mind is not conceived of as the organ of internal perception.

> It cannot be urged that if the mind thus be not an organ, the perception of happiness, etc., will not be immediate (*sākṣāt*); because the immediacy of knowledge does not lie in its being due to an organ; for in that case inference, etc., also, being up to the mind, would be immediate, and God's knowledge, which is not due to any organ, would not be immediate.[30]

The five external senses comprise the special cause (*asādhārana kāraṇam*) of perception. The *Advaita* understanding of the nature of the sense organs differs from that of other Indian systems, particularly the Buddhists and the *Mīmāṁsā*. The former conceives the sense organs (*indriyas*) as the *golokas* or sense-orifices, while the latter sees them as the capacities (*śakti*) of the physiological organs. According to *Advaita*, the actual organs of perception are not the outer organs located in the physical body. The real sense organs are their subtle counterparts located in the subtle body (*sukṣma śarīra*) and composed of the five elements before they have undergone the process of grossification (*pañcīkaraṇa*).[31] Prior to this stage, the elements of space, air, fire, water, and earth exist in a pure subtle form, characterized by the qualities of *sattva*, *rajas*, and *tamas*. Out of the subtle *sattva* aspect of space (*ākāśa*) is evolved the organ of hearing, the ear. The organ of touch, the skin, evolves out of the *sattva* aspect of air (*vāyu*); the organs of sight from the *sattva* aspect of fire (*agni*); the organ of taste, the tongue, from the *sattva* aspect of water (*apaḥ*); and from the *sattva* aspect of earth is evolved the organ of smell. From the total *sattva* aspect of these five elements emerges the *antaḥkaraṇa* (internal organ) constituted of the *manas* (mind), *buddhi* (intellect), *ahaṁkāra* (ego), and *citta* (memory).[32] It is the fivefold nature of the elements which necessitates the fivefoldness of the *indriyas*, and it is the special relationship which each sense organ enjoys with a particular element that enables it to perceive its respective object.

> The organs are but modes of the objects in order to perceive them, as a lamp, which is but a mode of color, is an instrument for revealing all colors. Similarly, the organs are but modes of all particular objects in order to perceive them, as is the case with the lamp.[33]

Śaṅkara goes to great lengths to justify the existence of the internal organ (*antaḥkaraṇa*). He argues inductively for its reality.

> For it is a well-known fact that even when there is a connection between the external organ, the object, and the self, a man does not perceive that object which may be just in front, and when asked, "Have you seen this form?" he says, "My mind was elsewhere — *I was absent-minded, I did not see it.*" Similarly when asked, "Have you heard what I have said?" he says, "*I was absent-minded, I did not hear it.*" Therefore it is understood that something else, viz., the internal organ called the mind, which joins itself to the objects of all the organs, exists, in the absence of which the eye and other organs fail to perceive their respective objects such as form and sound, although they have the capacity to do so, and in the presence of which they succeed in it. Hence *it is through the mind that* everybody *sees and hears*, for vision and the like are impossible when the mind is engaged.[34]

The existence of the *antaḥkaraṇa* is also apparent as the faculty which receives, discriminates, and interprets sense data. Because "*even if one is touched* by anybody *from behind* invisibly, *one knows it* distinctly that this is a touch of the hand, or that this is a touch of the knee; *therefore* the internal organ called mind exists. If there is no mind to distinguish them, how can the skin alone do this? That which helps us to distinguish between perceptions in the mind."[35]

In any act of external perception, four factors are present, the absence of any one of which, therefore, makes it impossible. These are the *ātman*, the *antaḥkaraṇa*, the sense organ, and the object. Of these four elements, the *ātman* alone is immanently luminous, being of the nature of consciousness. In any act of knowing, the object is revealed by the *ātman*, which is conjoined to the former through the mind conjoined with the sense organ.[36] *Advaita* contends that sensible knowledge results from the contact of the sense organs with their appropriate objects. Because it conceives the sense organs as composed of subtle substances, *Advaita* finds no difficulty in claiming that these organs actually reach out to their objects.[37] In reaching out to the objects, the organs are accompanied by the mind, which is also composed of the same subtle substances. The mind assumes a modification (*vṛtti*) which corresponds to the object and which is illumined by the *ātman* as awareness. The result of this entire process is perception.

In the presence of defect-free causal conditions, *pratyakṣa* produces immediate valid knowledge. Invalidity, as we have seen, is the result of extraneous conditions, such as a diseased sense organ or an insufficient medium of light. Except in such instances, perception is unchallengeable in its own field, even by the *Vedas*.

> If you deny an observed fact, saying it is impossible, you would be contradicting experience, a thing which nobody will allow. Nor is there any question of impossibility with regard to an observed fact, because it has actually been observed.[38]

Śaṅkara often rejects an opponent's position if he can point to its disparity with perception.

II. Inference (*Anumāna*)

The Sanskrit term for inference is *anumāna*, which literally means "knowing after." The knowledge arrived at by the application of this method is referred to as *anumiti* (consequent knowledge), from *anu* (after) and *miti* (knowledge). It indicates, therefore, knowledge that is gained from an anterior knowledge. *Anumiti* is the knowledge that is reasoned from the knowledge of an invariable concomitance between what is perceived and what is deduced.[39] The Sanskrit term for this uniform relation is *vyāpti* (extension or pervasion). This universal concurrence of the major term and the minor term in all the loci where the latter is present is held by both *Advaita* and *Nyāya* to be the core of *anumāna* as a *pramāṇa*.[40]

Advaita maintains that *vyāpti* is discerned when it is established by all known cases and when no negative one has been observed. The actual number of observed cases is not important, and *vyāpti* could be detected from one known instance. Repetition is necessary only when there is cause for doubt.[41] The *Advaita* basis, therefore, for determination of *vyāpti* is positive invariable concomitance or agreement in presence (*anvaya*) and non-observation of any exception. The standard example of *anumāna* — where there is smoke, there is fire — illustrates positive invariable concomitance. On this point there is a difference of opinion with *Nyāya*, who insist also on negative invariable concomitance (*vyatireka*) or agreement in absence (where there is no fire, there is no smoke) as a requirement of *vyāpti*.[42] As a consequence of this view, the main fallacy of a syllogism is the contradiction of perception, and Śaṅkara constantly refutes arguments on this basis.

> When a thing is directly recognized as identical, it is improper to infer that it is something else, for when an inference contradicts perception, the ground of such an inference becomes fallacious.[43]

This brings us to a consideration of the syllogistic form which is employed by *Advaita*, and here a comparison with *Nyāya* is advantageous. The terms in Indian logic which correspond to the major, minor, and middle terms of the Western syllogism are *sādhya*, *pakṣa*, and *hetu*. In the standard example, fire (the object to be inferred) is the *sādhya*. The hill (that in which the thing is inferred) is the *pakṣa*, and smoke, the ground of the inference, is the *hetu*. The *hetu* is commonly referred to as the *sādhana* (means of inference) or *liṅga* (mark, sign). The *Nyāya* form of *anumāna* comprises five distinct propositions or stages. These are as follows:

1. *Pratijñā* (proposition to be established) — There is fire on the hill.
2. *Hetu* (reason) — Because there is smoke.
3. *Udāharaṇa* (universal proposition supported by example) — Whenever there is smoke there is fire, as in the kitchen.
4. *Upanaya* (application) — The hill has smoke such as is always accompanied by fire.
5. *Nigamana* (conclusion) — Therefore, there is fire on the hill.

According to *Advaita*, however, the first three or the last three steps of the syllogism are adequate. *Advaita* distinguishes between an *anumāna* meant for oneself (*svārthānumanā*) and one intended for convincing another person (*parāthānumanā*). It is the latter which requires the formal syllogistic form, and this can be constituted of the first three or last three members of the fivefold *Nyāya* procedure.[44]

The necessity of an observed example as an essential part of any *anumāna* points to one of its inherent features. *Anumāna*, basically speaking, is deductive reasoning, since its operation consists in the application of a universal proposition to a particular case. But the support of the universal proposition by at least one example taken from actual experience bestows upon it an inductive feature. Knowledge of *vyāpti* is acquired by observation and generalization. *Anumāna*, therefore, is a combined inductive-deductive process of reasoning.

Inference, dependent as it is on perception for the data of its propositions, is subject to the limitations of being able to deal only with the material that is the proper sphere of perception. They are both, by definition, debarred from authoritativeness with regards to any matter transcending sense apperception. This does not presume, however, that Śaṅkara finds no utility for *anumāna* in his exegesis of the *Vedas*. The task which he apportions to this source of knowledge in relation to *śabda-pramāṇa* will be considered later.

III. Comparison (*Upamāna*)

Upamāna, as an independent source of knowledge, is accepted by *Mīmāṁsā*, *Nyāya*, and *Advaita*. It is defined as "the instrument of the valid knowledge of similarity."[45] The standard example of *upamāna* is provided by the *Vedānta-Paribhāṣā*. Similarity may be known by perception, as in the case of one who, having seen a cow at home, goes into the woods and sees a wild cow (*gavaya*) which resembles his own cow. From this experience, however, he gains the additional knowledge that his cow at home is like the *gavaya*. *Upamāna* is the means by which the judgment of the cow's similarity to the *gavaya* is formed from the perception of the *gavaya's* resemblance to his cow. This resulting knowledge is called *upamiti*. *Advaita* denies that *upamāna* is a case of perception, because the cow is not immediately present before one's eyes. *Upamāna* is also differentiated from *anumāna*. In Indian logic, inference is always syllogistic, and the major premise of a comparative judgment would be formulated as follows: "When A is like B, B is also like A." Such a premise would beg the question. To the argument that *upamāna* is a combination of perception and memory, the *Advaitin* will accept that the elements of comparison may be so derived, the cow through memory and the *gavaya* through perception, but this leaves the question of their integration unanswered. The same objection, moreover, can be raised about inference. Dharmarājā adduces the further evidence that in *upamāna* one has the apperception, "I am comparing [not inferring] the two things."[46] *Advaita* finds it impossible to explain comparative judgments through any of the other *pramāṇas*, and Śaṅkara includes *upamāna* in his detailing of the valid sources of knowledge.

IV. Postulation (*Arthāpatti*)

The term *arthāpatti* is a compound of *artha* (fact) and *apatti* (obtaining). It indicates the assumption of an unperceived or unknown fact in order to explain two facts which are known but contradictory.[47] The standard example is that of a man who fasts during the day but manages to remain fat. These two incompatible facts are reconciled by postulating that he must be eating during the night. Another typical example is that of a person who is alive and not at home. One can assume that he must be somewhere outside, for the fact of being alive and not at home cannot be otherwise explained. It is obvious from these two illustrations that *arthāpatti* is appropriate where there is only one alternative possible. If the options are many, the assumption of one will not irrefutably resolve the contradiction. *Arthāpatti* does not, like a hypothesis, offer a tentative supposition that awaits verification. It arises out of a need for explanation and is intended to carry absolute certainty as the only possible solution. One cannot, for example, postulate the origin of the world in an omnipotent and omnipresent creator, because of the conceivability of alternative explanations. The universe might have come into being from the concerted action of several gods.

Advaitins resist any attempt to reduce *arthāpatti* to a kind of inference. It is argued that any attempt to do so involves begging the question, for the major premise of the syllogism will assume the fact which it is the aim of the inferential argument to prove. A formulation of the standard example in a syllogistic structure will read as follows:

> Devadatta who is stout must eat by day or by night.
> Devadatta does not eat by day.
> Therefore, he eats by night.

Advaita will argue that it is through *arthāpatti* that one arrives at the conclusion of the major premise.[48] Dharmarājā also adds that in *arthāpatti*, one has the apperception of "assuming" and not "inferring."[49]

V. Noncognition (*Anupalabdhi*)

The *Bhāṭṭa* school of *Pūrva-Mīmāṁsā* and *Advaita Vedānta* accept noncognition as an independent *pramāṇa*. According to both schools, the absence of an object or its attributes from any locus is apprehended by its nonperception.[50] The absence of a table from its accustomed position in a room is not known by cognition of its nonexistence, for the organ of vision has no contact with nonexistence, but by the noncognition of its presence.[51]

Indirect knowledge of non-existence can be attained by other means. One can infer, for instance, the absence of a person at his residence from his presence at his place of work. Direct knowledge, however, of the non-existence of perceptible objects and their attributes is available only through *anupalabdhi*. It is considered to be independent because it does not involve any of the processes occurring in *anumāna, upamāna, arthāpatti*, or *śabda*. The attempt to reduce *anupalabdhi* to an inference will result, *Advaita* claims, in a begging of the question. The major premise of such an inference (what is not perceived in a place does not exist there) assumes the very conclusion which is intended to be proved. Moreover, there is still the question of how one arrives at the general proposition.

It must be emphasized that only appropriate nonperception (*yogyānupalabdhi*) can serve as a *pramāṇa* of nonexistence, for not every nonapprehension of an object is evidence of its nonexistence. If the room, for example, in which one does not see the desk is dark, the absence of the desk is not conclusively proved. Nonapprehension could be considered appropriate in a situation where the object would have been perceived if it had been present. If the room is well lit, *anupaladbhi* of the desk is appropriate (*yogya*).[52]

VI. *Śabda-Pramāṇa*

The term *śabda* includes both articulate (*varṇa*) and inarticulate (*dhvani*) sounds.[53] As a means of valid knowledge, *śabda-pramāṇa*, refers to a meaningful, articulate sound, spoken or written, consisting of a single word or group of words.[54] *Śabda-pramāṇa* is accepted by *Sāṅkhya, Nyāya, Pūrva-Mīmāṁsā*, and *Vedānta* schools of Indian philosophy. It must be pointed out, however, that there is no unanimity of interpretation and understanding of the concept in these different systems.

Advaita contends that *śabda-pramāṇa* is a unique method of access to knowledge and cannot be subsumed under any of the other *pramāṇas*. *Śabda-pramāṇa*, for example, cannot be reduced to the process of memory synthesis. The argument that the meaning of a sentence is apprehended by conjoining from memory the meanings of its individual words does not account for the resultant knowledge, which may be entirely new. One can have verbal cognition of something not known before.[55] *Advaita* contends that the comprehension of the significance of a sentence depends upon grasping the relation among the meanings of its individual words. It does not depend only on the cognition of an invariable relation between the individual words and their meanings. For this reason, claims *Advaita*, *śabda-pramāṇa* cannot be reduced to inference, for the latter depends upon the knowledge of invariable concomitance.

Although the *Naiyāyikas* concur with *Advaita* in accepting *śabda* as a *pramāṇa*, there are important differences between both schools with regard to the question of validity.[56] The *Naiyāyikas* accepted *śabda-pramāṇa* on the grounds that it provides information which is not obtained from (even though it may be obtainable from) other sources. The status of *śabda* as a *pramāṇa* is not demolished by the fact that the information which it provides can be obtained from perception or inference. The important point is that the information is novel for the hearer. On the question of validity, however, the *Naiyāyikas*, consistent with their theory of *parataḥ-prāmāṇya-vāda*, argue that it is to be inferred from the trustworthiness of the source. Against this claim, *Advaita* argues that validity is produced and known by the very conditions that generate knowledge. The application of the *Nyāya* theory, according to *Advaita*, leads to infinite regress. It is quite possible to see *Advaita* conceding the importance of the trustworthiness of the source in the production of validity. One imagines, however, that this factor will be understood as one of the intrinsic conditions. The *Advaita* argument, therefore, is that in the absence of any grounds for contradiction or doubt, *śabda*, like any other *pramāṇa*, produces valid knowledge.

With an understanding of this general background of the nature of sources of valid knowledge in *Advaita*, we can now consider how Śaṅkara applies these views in his conception of *śruti* as *śabda-pramāṇa*.

Chapter 2

The *Vedas* as a *Pramāṇa*

Śabda can be seen as a *pramāṇa* for our knowledge of the empirical world as well as ultimate reality. *Advaita*, however, is not primarily concerned with *śabda-pramāṇa* as a vehicle of secular knowledge. As such a medium, *śabda* cannot lay claim to any particular uniqueness, for the knowledge which it conveys is, in most cases, available through other sources.[1] As a *pramāṇa* of the empirical world, it does not have a sphere which is exclusively its own and which, by nature, it alone is capable of transmitting.[2] The special nature of *śabda* for *Advaita*, therefore, lies in its function as a means of knowledge for ultimate reality. In this capacity, *śabda-pramāṇa* is synonymous with the *Vedas* or *śruti*.[3] *Advaita* seeks to justify the view that, because of the very nature of ultimate reality, the *Vedas* alone can transmit accurate knowledge. All of the theories about *śabda-pramāṇa* have emerged as a result of this central concern and the need to defend it against the criticisms of other Indian schools. We hope to show in the discussion below that Śaṅkara posits no alternative to the *Vedas* for our knowledge of *brahman*. His acceptance of the function of the *avatāra* as a teacher and the world, in general, as a revelation of *brahman* does not contradict the necessity for the *Vedas*.

2.1 The *Avatāra* as a Teacher and the World as a Revelation of *Brahman*

Śaṅkara's views on the nature of the *avatāra* and His role as revealer emerge from his commentary on the *Bhagavadgītā*. In his introduction to the text, Śaṅkara states that the Lord, after creating the world and the ancestors of humankind (*prajāpatis*), imparted to them the twofold paths of Works (*pravṛtti dharma*) and Renunciation (*nivṛtti dharma*), meant respectively for worldly prosperity and liberation. By this twofold path, He intended to secure order in the universe. When, however, as a result of unrestrained desire, human discrimination was overwhelmed and religion declined, the Lord incarnated Himself as *Kṛṣṇa*, for the purpose of reintroducing and strengthening the Vedic religion.[4]

> Whenever there is a decay of *Dharma*, O Bharata, and an ascendance of *Adharma*, then I manifest Myself.
>
> For the protection of the good, for the destruction of evildoers, for the firm establishment of *Dharma*, I am born in every age.[5]

Śaṅkara emphasizes that the Lord is by nature eternal, pure, intelligent and free. Through the unimpeded control of His creative power (*māyā*),

He appears as though embodied. Whereas the individual is born under the control of *māyā*, the Lord incarnates through the mastery of *māyā*. It is a voluntary, self-conscious descent, in full awareness of His majesty.

> Though I am unborn, of imperishable nature, and though I am the Lord of all beings, yet ruling over My own nature, I am born by my own *Māyā*.[6]

In the *Bhagavadgītā*, the *avatāra* is not limited by embodiment. Arjuna is limited in knowledge, but *Kṛṣṇa* is conscious of all previous births of them both.[7] Past, present, and future are all spanned in His awareness.[8] The descent of the *avatāra* is not for any personal need or desire born out of a sense of limitation. He is an already fully accomplished being whose actions are not characterized by any motive of personal achievement.

> I have nothing whatsoever to achieve in the three worlds, O son of Pritha, nor is there anything unattained that should be attained; yet I engage in action.[9]

His actions are directed to world welfare and preservation.[10] With reference to His instruction of Arjuna, Śaṅkara writes,

> Without any interest of His own, but with the sole intention of helping His creatures, He taught to Arjuna, who was deeply plunged in the ocean of grief and delusion, the twofold Vedic Religion, evidently thinking that the Religion would widely spread when accepted and practiced by men of high character.[11]

The cardinal point to be noted in Śaṅkara's discussion of the *avatāra* as revealer is that He revivifies and reiterates the doctrines of the *Vedas*. The *Bhagavadgītā*, according to Śaṅkara, "is an epitome of the essentials of the whole Vedic teaching," and is not at variance with it.[12] The instructions of the *avatāra* are in the form of a restatement and do not in any way supersede the primacy of the Vedic revelation. *Kṛṣṇa* does not claim to be instituting a new path to freedom but emphasizing His traditional links and the conventional approach.

> I taught this imperishable *Yoga* to Vivasvat; Vivasvat taught it to Manu; Manu taught it to Ikshvāku.
>
> This, handed down thus in succession, the King-sages learnt. This *Yoga*, by long lapse of time, has been lost here, O harasser of foes.

> That same ancient *Yoga* has been today taught to thee by Me, seeing that thou art My devotee and friend; for, this is the Supreme Secret.[13]

It is clear, therefore, that even in relation to the role of the *avatāra*, the *Vedas* remain the original and authoritative *pramāṇa* of *brahman*.

There are several passages in the commentaries of Śaṅkara in which he suggests that *brahman* is directly and self-evidently revealed in the world and in human beings. In response to an objection that if *brahman* is a completely unknown entity it cannot become the subject of inquiry, Śaṅkara replies "that the existence of *Brahman* is well known from the fact of Its being the Self of all; for everyone feels that his Self exists, and he never feels "I do not exist." Had there been no general recognition of the existence of the Self, everyone would have felt "I do not exist. And that Self is *Brahman*."[14] Earlier on, also, in replying to a query that an unperceived Self cannot become the locus of superimposition, he contends that the Self is well known in the world as an immediately perceived entity. It is nothing but the content of the concept "I."[15] Elsewhere, he remarks that in all cognition, *brahman* as absolute existence is cognized.[16] Each cognition involves a twofold consciousness of the real and unreal. In a cognition such as "This is a post," the object is limited and finite. But the consciousness of existence or "is-ness," which is the persisting substratum of the object, is eternal. From the standpoint of Śaṅkara, the entire universe can be seen as a name and form revealing of *brahman*, with whom it is identical.

The problem with these general forms of revelation, if they can be so termed, is that, through them, we are not made aware of the distinctive nature of *brahman*. Śaṅkara develops his argument about the self-evident manifestation of the *ātman* as the content of the "I" notion, by pointing out that, in spite of this knowledge, the unique nature of the Self remains unknown. As evidence of this, he cites the divergent and mutually contradictory views which different systems hold about the nature of the Self.[17] The point, therefore, is that even though we are not completely debarred from all awareness of ultimate reality, we do not recognize its existence and our understanding is incomplete. What is needed is a valid source of knowledge through which we can apprehend accurately the unique nature of the Self. The *Vedas*, Śaṅkara contends, is just such a *pramāṇa*.

2.2 The Eternity of the Vedic Revelation

It is an important contention of both *Advaita Vedānta* and *Pūrva-Mīmāṁsā* that the *Vedas* are eternal, uncreated, and authorless (*apauruṣeya*). The claim for the infallibility of these texts follows directly from this contention. If a personal author is ascribed to the *Vedas*, they will suffer from the limitations of authorship, and their status as a defect-free source of knowledge will be under doubt. Against the eternity of the *Vedas*, it may be argued that words originate along with or only after the objects which they signify have come into existence. They are as time-bound as their objects and can in no sense, therefore, be eternal. The assumption here is that the *Vedas* can be eternal only if the words of which they are composed are established to be so, and words are as transient as the particular things which they signify. This objection, *Advaita* claims, will be valid if the Vedic words did indeed primarily signify the particular ephemeral objects of the world. To meet this objection and in order to justify the eternity of the *Vedas*, *Advaita* argues that the primary significance of words are universals and not individuals. As universals are eternal, the connection between the word and the object signified is an eternal one.[18] A universal, as conceived by *Advaita*, indicates the essential common characteristics existing in a group of particulars. It signifies both the generic shape (*ākṛti*) and also the generic nature (*jāti*).[19]

The inquiry about whether a word primarily signifies a particular (*vyakti*) or a universal (*jāti*) has elicited a variety of views among the different schools of Indian thought, and the *Advaita* position is better highlighted in relation to some of these views.[20] According to the *Sāṅkhya*, a word signifies a particular only, for it is with individuals alone that we deal in everyday usage and activity. If the primary meaning of a word is its essential common characteristics, how can it be applicable to an individual? When one says "The horse is in the field," one is invariably referring to a particular member of the species. Besides this, there are proper names which are singular and can never refer to a group or class.

The main *Advaita* argument against this view is that if the primary significance of a word is a particular, the word cannot be used more than once. Each individual is unique, and the particular as known at one moment does not persist as the same in the next moment. The fact that the same word can be used repeatedly indicates that its primary significance is not an individual. Śaṅkara adds that objects are limitless in number, and if the primary denotation of a word is an individual, it could not indicate all of them.[21] In isolation, the word "horse" does not indicate any particular animal but rather the essential characteristics of the species. It is the knowledge of the universal which leads to the recognition of the particular. To recognize a particular animal as a horse, one has to first apprehend the universal characteristics of the species, and these are the primary denotations of a word. This fact does not make it impossible for a word to denote a particular object, for the knowledge of the particular is subsumed under the universal. According to Dharmarājā, "the same cognition that comprehends a generic attribute also comprehends the individuals."[22] One may put the argument differently by saying that the individual significance is indirect or implicit, while its universal significance is direct or explicit. It is thus possible, according to *Advaita*, to conceive of words as being prior to all individuals and eternal.

This theory, however, raised a problem for both *Pūrva-Mīmāṁsā* and *Advaita*. The *Vedas* make mention of gods such as *Vasu* and *Indra*, and, according to this view, words cannot primarily indicate an individual. In this case, they will become noneternal, having no referent before the individual's existence and after the individual's destruction. Śaṅkara's view is that Vedic words such as *Vasu* signify distinctive general characteristics, for even gods have forms and species. These general characteristics can be gathered from the *Vedas*. On the other hand, words such as *Indra* indicate certain ranks, like "commander." The conclusion, therefore, that Vedic words are universal in significance is not refuted. The names of gods are not interpreted to be proper names.[23]

The eternal word, according to Śaṅkara, is not of the nature of *sphoṭa*.[24] He holds that "the letters themselves constitute the words."[25] Is it not a fact, however, that letters are noneternal, for they possess no reality before and after their utterance? This is not tenable in Śaṅkara's view, for the letters are recognized to be the same in each new utterance. This recognition is not because of any similarity with a previous utterance, nor is it contradicted by any other means of knowledge. He also rejects the view that this recognition is produced by the fact of the letters belonging to the same species (*jāti*).

> The recognition would have been caused by the species if the letters were cognized as separate entities like individual cows at the time of each fresh utterance. But this is not so, for it is the letters themselves that are cognized to be the same at each fresh utterance, the recognition taking the form, "The word *cow* is uttered twice," but not "There are two words *cow*."[26]

The letters, in other words, are not individuals which constitute a class, as cows comprise a species. He admits a variation in the apprehension of syllables, but ascribes this to differences in pronunciation due to peculiarities of the vocal organs, not to the intrinsic nature of the letters. Differences can also be attributed to variations of tone (*dhvani*).[27] Śaṅkara's conclusion so far seems to be that since letters are recognized to be the same in each new utterance, they are eternal, and the words which they constitute share this nature. In addition to this, words are eternally connected to their referents, which, being universals, are also eternal.[28]

As further evidence of the beginninglessness of the *Vedas*, Śaṅkara remarks that no independent author of the *Vedas* is remembered.[29] This is an argument which was also adduced by Kumārila Bhaṭṭa. He contends that if there was an author of the *Vedas*, he should have been remembered in the long traditional succession of teachers and students, as in the case of, for example, the Buddha. There is no possibility of such an author being forgotten, since religious performances and their effectiveness would be founded solely upon his authority. In reality, however, there are no clear ideas of any composer and some vaguely attribute authorship to "God," *Hiraṇyagarbha*, or *Prajāpati*.[30] In replying to the argument that the *Vedas* must have human authors because some sections are named after certain men,[31] Jaimini explains that this can be accounted for by the fact that such men were foremost in the study and expounding of those portions.[32]

Another important argument introduced by Śaṅkara is the origin of the world from Vedic words. According to him, it is a matter of common experience that when one is intent on creating a desirable object, one first recollects the word signifying it and then produces it. The sequence is the same in the case of the creation of the world. Vedic words occur in the mind of *Prajāpati* when He is intent on creation, and, corresponding to them, He creates the universe.[33] He creates the earth, for example, after the word *bhūḥ* occurs in His mind. This view does not contradict the *Advaita* doctrine of *brahman* as the material cause of creation, for it means simply that "when there is first a word without a beginning and bearing a meaning with which it has an eternal connection, then only is there a possibility of an individual cropping up which can be fit to be referred to by that word. In that sense, it is said to originate from a word."[34] Śaṅkara states that the creation of the world from Vedic words is well known from *śruti* and *smṛti* and he cites several references to support his claim.[35] Śaṅkara would appear to be implying that the universe is cyclically created in conformity with ideas or universals which are eternally present in the creator. One wonders, therefore, whether by *word*, he is really suggesting *idea* rather than the uttered sound or linguistic symbol. A distinction between the two would have been very useful here. The word *śabda* is used to denote both *idea* and *sound symbol*.

Śaṅkara considers another objection to the eternity of the *Vedas*. The objector accepts that the doctrine is maintained if one understands names such as *Indra* to connote eternal species rather than individuals. He contends, however, that the doctrine cannot be argued "in the face of the statements in the *Vedas* and *smṛtis* that the whole creation, consisting of the three worlds, loses its names and forms and gets dissolved without a trace, and it emerges again as a fresh entity."[36] Śaṅkara's reply is that the cyclical creation and dissolution does not refute the eternity of the *Vedas* because the names and forms of each creation are the same as those of the preceding world that was dissolved.[37] The analogy can be drawn between the creation and dissolution of the world and the individual states of deep sleep and waking. In both cases, there is a connection and continuity of activity with earlier states. But is this an appropriate analogy? The individual can easily recollect earlier behavior and activity after emerging from deep sleep, but is such a recall possible after all behavior is eradicated in cosmic dissolution? Śaṅkara concedes that all empirical activity ceases at the time of dissolution (*mahāpralaya*) but argues that because of God's grace, gods like *Hiraṇyagarbha* can recall names and forms of earlier cycles, including the *Vedas*.

> From the fact that ordinary creatures are not seen to recollect their past lives, it does not follow that the fact must be the same in the case of divine beings as well. It is noticed that although as living creatures all are the same, counting from men to a clump of grass, still the obstruction to the manifestation of knowledge, glory, etc. increases successively all through the series at every stage; similarly when it is mentioned more than once in the *Vedas* and *Smṛtis* that knowledge, glory, etc., become increasingly more manifest at each successive stage counting from men themselves up to *Hiraṇyagarbha*, it cannot be brushed aside as nonexistent. From this, it logically follows, on the analogy of a man risen up from sleep, that the recollection of the behavior in the past cycle is possible for beings like *Hiraṇyagarbha*, who had undertaken meditation and work in a superexcellent way in a past cycle, who have emerged at the beginning of the present cycle (as a result of past achievement), and who have been vouchsafed the grace of God.[38]

Another reason justifying the identity of names and forms in successive creations is tendered by Śaṅkara. Each new creation is impelled by the necessity of beings to experience the results of virtuous and unmeritorious acts of the past. It is also a field for the expression of likes and dislikes. It is not a causeless or accidental event and must, therefore, conform to earlier patterns. The new creation is potential in the past ones. It is not possible, according to Śaṅkara, to conceive, for example, a different relation between senses and sense objects in each creation.

It is reasonable to conclude from this discussion that Śaṅkara conceives the eternity of the *Vedas* in the sense of an identical but eternal flow (*pravāha nityatā*). The eternity of *brahman*, on the other hand, is of an absolutely unchanging kind (*kūṭastha nityatā*). It would appear also that Śaṅkara ascribes to the *Vedas* the same empirical (*vyāvahārika*) level of reality as the world, for he admits that the *Vedas*, like the world, are negated in the knowledge of nondual *brahman*.[39]

2.3 *Īśvara* as Revealer of the *Vedas*

Pūrva-Mīmāṁsā uncompromisingly rejects the view that the *Vedas* were ever composed by anyone. *Nyāya*, on the other hand, ascribes authorship to *īśvara*, whose existence they seek to establish inferentially. Śaṅkara occupies a position between these two views.[40] Like the *Mīmāṁsā*, but unlike *Nyāya*, Śaṅkara admits the *Vedas* to be authorless (*apauruṣeya*).[41] He seems, however, to understand this concept very differently, even though he does not offer us a definition anywhere. Commenting on *Brahma-sūtra* 1.1.3, Śaṅkara explains why *brahman* alone can be the source of the *Vedas*.[42] It is a well-known fact, he asserts, that the author of a text on any subject is more informed than the text itself. The grammar of Pāṇini, for instance, represents only a part of the subject known to him. It is obvious, therefore, that the source of texts like the *Vedas*, divided into many branches and illuminating lamp-like a variety of subjects, must be omniscient and omnipotent. This is even more apparent from the effortlessness with which they emerge from God. The *Vedas* compare their own emergence with the ease of breathing.[43] Śaṅkara states very clearly, however, that it is the eternally composed and already existent *Vedas* that are manifest like a person's breath.[44] Elsewhere, he explains that the projection of the *Vedas* should only be understood in the sense of the initiation of a cycle of transmission through a line of teachers and students, for no other kind of projection is possible for a text without beginning and end.[45] *Īśvara*, then, does not produce the *Vedas* but reveals or manifests them as they were in the previous creation. He offers various suggestions to this effect.[46] The general idea is that the *Vedas* are revealed in the same linguistic form at the beginning of each creation to qualified seers.

Further clarification of Śaṅkara's understanding of the concept of *apauruṣeya* is provided by Dharmarājā and Vācaspati. According to Dharmarājā, the *Vedas* are not eternal because they are produced by *brahman*. They are not, however, *pauruṣeya* because they depend on utterance of the same kind. A sentence can be described as *pauruṣeya* only if it is original and not the reproduction of an earlier utterance.

> For instance, in the beginning of the cosmic projection, the Lord produced the *Vedas* having a sequence of words similar to that which had already existed in the *Vedas* in the previous cosmic projection, and not Vedas of a different type. Hence the *Vedas*, not being the object of utterance that is independent of any utterance of the same kind, are not connected with a person. The utterance of the *Mahābhārata* etc., however, is not at all dependent on any utterance of the same kind. Thus two kinds of verbal testimony have been determined, viz., that which is connected with a person and that which is not.[47]

Vācaspati argues along similar lines.[48] *Pūrva-Mīmāṁsakās*, he says, who do not believe in a creation or destruction, advocate a beginningless and unbroken sequence of Vedic study. *Advaita*, however, although differing from them in accepting the supreme Self to be the creator of the eternal

Vedas, does not understand Him to be entirely free in respect of them, since He creates their sequence in conformity to the previous ones.

> Not in any creation is brāhminicide the cause of good nor the horse-sacrifice the cause of evil, any more than fire can wet or water can burn. Just as, in this creation, the study of the *Vedas* in the settled sequence is the cause of prosperity and beatitude, and (studied) otherwise is the cause of evil even as a verbal thunderbolt, even so does it happen in another creation; hence, the creator, who, though omnipotent and omniscient, creates the *Vedas* in accordance with what they were in earlier creations, has not a free hand.[49]

2.4 The Necessity and Justification of the *Vedas* as a *Pramāṇa*

The general justification of Śaṅkara for a special means of knowledge like the *Vedas* is that it provides the knowledge of those things which cannot be known through any of the other available sources of knowledge. More specifically, it informs us of the means of attaining good and avoiding evil, in so far as these cannot be known through perception and inference and are the two ends naturally pursued by us. The *Vedas* are not concerned to provide information about these dual objectives to the extent that they are within the range of human experience. Such knowledge is easily available from perception and inference.[50] One imagines, for example, that a scripture is not necessary for instruction about road safety.

According to Śaṅkara, the two categories of knowledge inaccessible to all other *pramāṇas* and attainable exclusively through the *Vedas* are *dharma* and *brahman*.[51] We are afforded a clear statement of Śaṅkara's view on the knowledge of *dharma* in his commentary on *Brahma-sūtra* 3.1.25.[52] Here he is responding to the objector's claim that the slaying of animals in sacrifices might be responsible for the soul's birth as a plant. He answers that the knowledge of merit (*dharma*) and demerit (*adharma*) is derived solely from the scriptures. From the *Vedas* alone can we know which acts are virtuous and which are not. The reason is that these are supersensuous realities, beyond the capacity of the senses. In addition to this, *dharma* and *adharma* vary with time and place. An act that may be sanctioned at a certain time and place and under some circumstances may not be approved with a change of these factors. It is impossible therefore, to learn of *dharma* from any other source.[53]

It is necessary, however, for the individual to be made aware of the persisting existence of the Self in a future life if one is to be motivated to attain what is good in that life. The materialists (*Cārvākas*), for example, who deny all future existence, do not show any such concern. *Śruti*, therefore, informs us of this future existence and of the particular means of attaining good and avoiding evil in that life.[54] In a typical discussion which illustrates very well his procedure for legitimizing the *Vedas* as a *pramāṇa*, Śaṅkara shows why this knowledge of a future existence is not otherwise attainable. After a series of *Upaniṣad* quotations to show support for the doctrine, a question is tendered.

> *Objection*: Is it not a matter of perception?
>
> *Reply*: No, for we see the divergence of opinion among different schools. Were the existence of the Self in a future body a matter of perception, the materialists and Buddhists would not stand opposed to us, saying that there is no Self. For nobody disputes regarding an object of perception such as a jar, saying it does not exist.
>
> *Objection*: You are wrong, since a stump, for instance is looked upon as a man and so on.
>
> *Reply*: No, for it vanishes when the truth is known. There are no more contradictory views when the stump, for instance, has been definitely known as such through perception. The Buddhists, however, in spite of the fact that there is the ego-consciousness, persistently deny the existence of the Self other than the subtle body. Therefore, being different from objects of perception, the existence of the Self cannot be proved by this means. Similarly, inference too is powerless.
>
> *Objection*: No, since the *śruti* points out certain grounds of inference for the existence of the Self, and these depend on perception, (these two are also efficient means of the knowledge of the Self).
>
> *Reply*: Not so, for the Self cannot be perceived as having any relation to another life. But when its existence has been known from the *śruti* and from certain empirical grounds of inference cited by it, the *Mīmāṁsakās* and logicians, who follow in its footsteps, fancy that those Vedic grounds of inference such as the ego-consciousness are the products of their own mind, and declare that the Self is knowable through perception and inference.[55]

This knowledge of *dharma* and *adharma* is derived from the ceremonial portion (*karmakāṇḍa*) of the *Vedas*.[56] This does not, however, exhaust the authoritative subject matter of the *Vedas*. The *karmakāṇḍa*, authoritative as it is, is not accepted by Śaṅkara as providing a solution to the fundamental problem. It accepts the desires for the enjoyment of the results of various actions but does not question the origin or legitimacy of these desires. This propensity, as maintained by Śaṅkara, is born out of a basic self-ignorance, the perception of oneself as a limited being. As long as this false notion is not removed by the knowledge of one's already-accomplished identity with *brahman*, one continues to search for fullness through the results of limited actions. Actions, however, produce inescapable results, and we are trapped in a futile quest through successive births and deaths (*saṁsāra*). Our ever-accomplished freedom and unlimitedness, the real end of all our actions, perpetually eludes us. The removal of this ignorance (*avidyā*) is the authoritative aim and concern of the *jñānakāṇḍa* (knowledge section) of the *Vedas*.[57] *Śruti* eliminates this ignorance by teaching about the true nature of the Self. It is the intention of all the *Upaniṣads*, Śaṅkara says, to establish the identity between *ātman* and *brahman*.[58]

> We hold that it is the definite conclusion of all the *Upaniṣads* that we are nothing but the *Ātman*, the *Brahman* that is always the same, homogeneous, one without a second, unchanging, birthless, undecaying, immortal, deathless and free from fear.[59]

Śaṅkara is equally emphatic on the absolute inapplicability of all *pramāṇas*, except *śruti*, to the knowledge of *brahman*.[60] He is tireless in explaining the incompetence of sense perception in apprehending *brahman*. Śaṅkara refuses to accept that because *brahman* is an existent entity; like all such realities, it must be the object of other sources of valid knowledge. The senses are naturally capable of grasping and revealing their appropriate objects. *Brahman*, however, remains unapproachable through any of them because of its uniqueness.[61] The organs can only grasp a differentiated object within their range.[62] We have already considered the nature and evolution of the five sense organs.[63] Each organ evolves out of a particular element which enables it to apprehend a quality proper to that element. The eyes, for example, evolve out of the subtle *sattva* aspect of fire and are the organs for perceiving the quality of form which is unique to fire.[64] It is the special relationship, therefore, between sense organ and element which empowers each one to cognize an appropriate quality. Sound, sensation, form, taste, and scent are their respective spheres of functioning. *Brahman*, however, has neither sound, touch, form, taste, or smell. It is without qualities (*nirguṇa*) and outside the domain of the sense organs.[65] *Brahman* is limitless, and to become an object of sense knowledge is to be finite and delimited, to be one object among many objects. A *brahman* that is sense apprehended is, therefore, a contradiction. However perfect or magnified the capacity of a sense organ is imagined to be, it will function only in a limited sphere of activity. Śaṅkara refutes the allegation that there is any contradiction in the *Bhagavadgītā*'s denial of *brahman* as both *sat* and *asat*, by interpreting these terms with reference to the nonavailability of *brahman* as an object of sense knowledge.

> *Objection*: Every state of consciousness involves either the consciousness of existence or that of nonexistence. Such being the case, the Knowable should be comprehended either by a state of consciousness accompanied with the consciousness of existence, or by a state of consciousness accompanied with the consciousness of nonexistence.
>
> *Answer*: No; for being beyond the reach of the senses, it is not an object of consciousness accompanied with the idea of either (existence or nonexistence). That thing, indeed, which can be perceived by the senses, such as a pot, can be an object of consciousness accompanied with the idea of existence, or an object of consciousness accompanied by the idea of nonexistence. Since, on the other hand, the Knowable is beyond the reach of the senses and as such can be known solely through that instrument of knowledge which is called *Śabda*, It cannot be, like a pot, etc., an object of consciousness accompanied with the idea of either (existence or non- existence) and is therefore not said to be *sat* or *asat*.[66]

In addition to the inherent limitations of the sense organs and the absence in *brahman* of any quality that can be apprehended by any one of them, there is the impossibility of objectifying *brahman*. The process of empirical knowledge involves a distinction between the subject and object, the knower and known. We know things by making them the objects of our awareness, and in this way they are available for our scrutiny and analysis. Knowledge of an object presupposes the subject, the knower. *Brahman*, however, is the eternal subject. As awareness, it illumines everything, and the entire universe, including mind, body and sense organs, is its object.[67] It is impossible for the unchanging knower to be made an object of knowledge, like a pot or a thought. It is absurd to conceive of the subject as an objec+, for in its absence there is no subject to know the subject as an object. It is the light even of lights.[68]

> Even in the state of ignorance, when one sees something, *through what* instrument *should one know that owing to which all this is known?* For that instrument of knowledge itself falls under the category of

> objects. The knower may desire to know, not about itself, but about objects. As fire does not burn itself, so the Self does not know itself, and the knower can have no knowledge of a thing that is not its object. Therefore through what instrument should one know the knower owing to which this universe is known and who else should know it?[69]

It is not possible to circumvent this difficulty by positing that the Self can be both subject and object. This might have been tenable if the subject and object were complementary and not opposed. By nature, however, the subject and object are absolutely opposed and such contradictory qualities cannot be posited of the same entity.[70] No division of any kind can be made in the case of the *ātman.*[71]

If perception is unfitted for furnishing us with the knowledge of *brahman*, are any of the other four *pramāṇas* (inference, comparison, postulation, and noncognition) more competent? The general view of Śaṅkara is that these sources are more or less dependent on perception for their data and can have no access to areas from which it is debarred. We have already, for instance, considered the nature of inference as a *pramāṇa.*[72] Inferential knowledge is derived from a knowledge of the invariable relation (*vyāpti*) between a thing inferred (*sādhya*) and the ground from which the inference is made (*hetu*). *Brahman*, however, has no apprehensible or differentiating qualities with which it has an invariable relation and which can form the ground of an inference.[73] It is impossible, therefore, to infer the existence of *brahman.*

There is no hint, however, of the skeptic in Śaṅkara. He is unwavering in his position that *brahman* is knowable and that *śabda-pramāṇa* is the only valid means. In a discussion in which he is concerned to establish that *brahman* is changeless and indivisible in spite of being the material cause of the creation, his views are unequivocal.

> There is no violation of the texts about partlessness, since partlessness is accepted on account of its very "mention in the *Upaniṣads*," and the *Upaniṣads* are the only authority about it, but not so are the senses etc. Hence it has to be accepted just as it is presented by the *Upaniṣads*. The *Upaniṣads* prove both the facts for *Brahman* — the nontransformation of *Brahman* as a whole and partlessness. Even the things of this world like gems, incantations, herbs, and so on, are seen to possess many powers capable of producing incompatible effects under a variety of space (environment), time, and cause. And even these powers can be known not from mere reasoning but from such instructions

> as "Such a thing has such kinds of potency with the aid of such things, on such things, and for such purposes." So what need has one to argue that the nature of *Brahman*, whose power is beyond all thought, cannot be ascertained unless it be through the *Vedas*? So also it has been said by an author of the *Purāṇa*, "Do not bring those things within the range of argumentation which are beyond thought. The nature of a thing beyond thought consists in its being other than the things within Nature." Hence a supersensuous thing is truly known from the Vedic source alone.[74]

It is not possible, according to Śaṅkara, to even guess about *brahman* without the assistance of the *Vedas.*[75] He leaves no room for any doubt about this conclusion. *Brahma-sūtra* 1.1.2, for instance, reads "That (is *Brahman*) from which (are derived) the birth etc. of this (universe)." The following *sūtra* (1.1.3) reads, "Because of being the source of the scriptures" (*śāstrayonitvat*). Śaṅkara sees another possibility in the Sanskrit compound of the latter and reads it also as "Since the scriptures are its valid means."[76] He justifies this reading on the ground that since *sūtra* 1.1.2 made no explicit mention of the scriptures, one might construe that an inferential argument is being presented for establishing *brahman* as the source of the world. Any such doubt ought to be removed, and it must be made clear that *brahman* is known as the source of the universe from the scriptures alone. They are the only valid means of this knowledge.[77] We can briefly note that Śaṅkara also dismisses independent reasoning as a suitable means of arriving at accurate knowledge of *brahman.*[78]

One has to be extremely cautious in examining Śaṅkara's exegesis of *Upaniṣad* verses treating the unknowability of the Self. He never accepts any of these passages literally, and there is no basis for concluding, as some have done, that in Śaṅkara's view, none of the *pramāṇas* can give us knowledge of *brahman.*[79] There are basically two ways in which Śaṅkara interprets these statements. First of all, the Self is unknowable in the sense and manner of an object. The knowing process generally involves the knowledge of an object different from oneself. As the eternal knower, the witness of every cognition, *brahman* can never be known in this manner.

> *Teacher*: If you think "I have known *Brahman* well enough," then you have known only the very little expression that It has in the human body and the little expression It has among the gods. Therefore *Brahman* is still to be deliberated on by you.
>
> *Disciple*: I think *Brahman* is known. I do not think I know *Brahman* well enough; (i.e. I consider) not that I do not know: I know, and I do not know as well.

> *Teacher*: He among us who understands that utterance, "Not that I do not know: I know and I do not know as well," knows that *Brahman*. It is known to him to whom It is unknown; he does not know to whom It is known. It is unknown to those who know well, and known to those who do not know."[80]

Secondly, *brahman* is unknown in the sense of being undisclosed through any other *pramāṇa* but *śabda-pramāṇa*. *Bṛhadāraṇyaka Upaniṣad* 3.6.1, for example, consists of a discussion between Gārgī and Yājñavalkya. Beginning with earth and ending with the world of *Hiraṇyagarbha*, Gārgī questions him about the successive pervasiveness of each factor. According to Śaṅkara, the inference suggested here is that "whatever is an effect, limited and gross, is respectively pervaded by that which is the cause, unlimited and subtle, as earth is pervaded by water."[81] When Gārgī, however, asks, "By what is the world of *Hiraṇyagarbha* pervaded?," Yājñavalkya refuses to proceed with the discussion.

> "Do not, O Gārgī, push your inquiry too far, lest your head should fall off. You are questioning about a deity that should not be reasoned about. Do not, O Gārgī, push your inquiry too far." Thereupon Gārgī, the daughter of Vacaknu, kept silent.

Śaṅkara does not construe Yājñavalkya's refusal as an indication of the impossibility of any further knowledge. On the contrary, he charges Gārgī with disregarding the proper method of inquiry. Yājñavalkya terminates the discussion, according to Śaṅkara, because of Gārgi's attempt to establish *brahman* inferentially, whereas it is to be known only from the *Vedas*. The idea is that *brahman* is not unascertainable but must be approached through the apposite *pramāṇa*.[82] *Kena Upaniṣad* 1.3 is a classic declaration of the predicament of conceptualization and instruction about *brahman*.

> The eye does not go there, nor speech, nor mind. We do not know (*Brahman* to be such and such); hence we are not aware of any process of instructing about It.

Śaṅkara does not reiterate this sense of perplexity and impotence. Concluding his remarks on this verse and introducing the following one, he writes

> The contingency of the total denial of any process of instruction having arisen from the text, "We do not know *Brahman*, and hence we are not aware of any process of instructing about It," an exception to this

> is being stated in the next verse. True it is that one cannot impart knowledge of the highest with the help of such means of valid knowledge as the evidence of the senses; but the knowledge can be produced with the help of traditional authority. Therefore traditional authority [*āgama*] is being quoted for the sake of imparting instruction about It.[83]

It is palpable, therefore, that Śaṅkara presents an argued and developed rationale for *śabda-pramāṇa* as the only source of *brahmajñāna*. Radhakrishnan's view that it is difficult to find support in Śaṅkara for the claim that inquiry into the *Vedas* is the only avenue to the knowledge of *brahman* is absolutely without basis.[84] Unsubstantial also is Devaraja's argument that Śaṅkara's reliance on *śruti* is an expression of his "ultra-orthodox mood."[85] It is not at all possible to dismiss Śaṅkara's affirmation of the *śruti* as simply an attempt to clothe his views with a sanction of a traditional authority. One may perhaps dispute his exegesis of particular scriptural passages but not his endorsement of *śruti* as the only credible *pramāṇa* of *brahmajñāna*.

2.5 The Authority and Infallibility of the Vedic Revelation

The authority of the *śruti* within the sphere of its own subject matter is, according to Śaṅkara, independent and self-evident. Its function in relation to the revelation of *brahman* is comparable to the perception of an object through the eye.[86] This independent authoritativeness is underscored by his analogy with the sun. The *Vedas*, he says, are as trustworthy with respect to their own subject matter as the sun is with regard to the objects which it illumines.[87] The suggestion here seems to be that while objects depend for their revelation on the light of the sun, the sun itself is self-illuminating. Similarly, the authoritativeness of the *śruti* is independent and self-evident. The validity of the *Upaniṣad* does not await inferential verification.[88] There are no misgivings about *śruti*'s infallibility with respect to its subject matter. "Knowledge of Reality springs from the *Upaniṣad* texts alone."[89] "Truth is the fact of being in accordance with the scriptures."[90] Vedic statements, he affirms, unlike those of men, are not delusive, equivocal, or deceptive about their theme.[91] They admit of no doubt and are productive of accurate knowledge.[92] In this respect, there is no difference between ritualistic texts and those informing us of the nature of *brahman*.

> That rites like the new and full moon sacrifices produce such and such results, and have to be performed in a certain definite way, with their parts following each other in a particular order, is a supersensuous matter beyond the range of our perception and infer-

> ence, which we nevertheless understand as true solely from the words of the *Vedas*. Similarly it stands to reason that entities like the Supreme Self, God, the deities, etc., of which we learn also from the words of the *Vedas* as being characterized by the absence of grossness, etc., being beyond hunger and thirst and the like, and so on, must be true, for they are equally supersensuous matters. There is no difference between texts relating to knowledge and those relating to rites as regards producing an impression. Nor is the impression conveyed by the *Vedas* regarding the Supreme Self and other such entities indefinite or contrary to fact.[93]

In the main, however, Śaṅkara's principal justification of the reliability and authoritativeness of the *Vedas* is an epistemological one. The *śruti* fulfills the criteria of being a *pramāṇa*. It has the capacity to generate certain and fruitful knowledge.

> Is or is not certain and fruitful knowledge generated by passages setting forth the nature of the Self, and if so, how can they lose their authority? Do you not see the result of knowledge in the removal of the evils which are the root of transmigration, such as ignorance, grief, delusion and fear? Or do you not hear those hundreds of *Upaniṣad* texts such as, "Then what delusion, and what grief can there be for one who sees unity?" (IS.U. 7).[94]

In addition to its fruitfulness, this knowledge can neither be produced nor nullified by any other *pramāṇa*, for there is none superior to the Vedic texts.[95] Sureśvara suggests four reasons when a *pramāṇa* may be disregarded:[96] (i) if it reveals something already revealed by another authoritative source of knowledge; (ii) if its revelations are contradicted by another source of knowledge; (iii) if it reveals ambiguous or doubtful knowledge. (iv) if it reveals nothing. The *Vedas*, however, according to him, reveal *brahman*, which is beyond the scope of all other *pramāṇas*. Their revelations are neither ambiguous nor contradicted by any other *pramāṇas*. In addition, they are productive of fruitful knowledge.[97] A similar view has been tendered by Vācaspati. He argues that the authoritativeness of a *pramāṇa* consists in generating knowledge which is unsublated, not already understood, and indubitable. This capacity is an intrinsic one and not dependent on any other *pramāṇa*.[98]

At this stage, we can underline a conclusion which was only hinted at earlier. *Advaita* does not attempt to establish the authority or infallibility of the *Vedas* from the fact of *īśvara's* omniscience. The reason is that *Advaita* finds it impossible to demonstrate the existence of God by any kind of independent reasoning. In the absence of such a proof, all arguments become helplessly circular, "omniscience being proved from the authority of the scriptures and the (authority of the) scriptures being proved from the knowledge of the omniscience of the author."[99] In Indian philosophy, *Nyāya* champions the rational theology and seeks to establish God's existence by a syllogistic inference. This argument, as we have seen, is based on a knowledge of the invariable relation (*vyāpti*) between the object perceived (*hetu*) and the object inferred (*sādhya*). The *Nyāya* argument takes the following form: All created or produced objects, for example, pots, have sentient beings as their makers, who are aware of the material cause and purpose of creation. The universe is a created object because it is a compound of insentient parts which could not have assembled themselves. From this fact, it is inferred that the world has a creator. In brief, the *Vedas* are authoritative because they are derived from God, who is reliable and trustworthy.[100] Śaṅkara accepts that the world is an effect but argues that it cannot be certified by inference that *brahman* is the cause. While the universe is an object of perception, *brahman* is not, and an invariable relation (*vyāpti*) cannot be established between them.[101] Śaṅkara also advances other strong arguments against the conclusions of a purely rational theology.[102] It is difficult, he contends, to explain the inequalities of creation unless we ascribe to God the possession of likes and dislikes. If in order to avert this charge, one argues that God is impelled by the merits and demerits of beings, the defect of a circular argument arises. God acts in accordance with *karman* and *karman* produces results when impelled by God. To suggest that this mutual dependence is beginningless does not avert this difficulty. Moreover, *Nyāya* themselves admit that the impulse to act is an indication of the defect of likes and dislikes. The *Yoga* concept of God as a special indifferent *puruṣa* does not help. *Nyāya* maintains that God is distinct from matter and individual souls. How then does God control them? God, matter, and souls being omnipresent and partless, neither can be related by conjunction nor inherence. Those who resort to inference argue that God molds matter (*pradhāna*) even as a potter with clay. But this is not possible because *pradhāna* is conceived of as being formless and beyond the range of perception. How is it possible to work upon such a material? We are thrown into enormous difficulties if perceptual experience is used as the basis for inferences about God. We will be forced to conclude that God possesses a body like us and is consequently subject to all of our limitations. Finally, *Nyāya* argues that God, matter, and soul are eternal and infinite. In this case, Śaṅkara says, God will be unable to measure the limits of all three, and God ceases to be omniscient. On the other hand, if God knows the limits of all three, they cannot be infinite and will come to an end, depriving God of rulership.

Unlike the rationalists, however, the *Advaitin* is not constrained into dependence upon observed facts for the knowledge of God. *Śruti* is the source for ascertaining the nature of the cause. For this reason, one has no difficulties in accepting *brahman* to be both efficient and material cause, although we find no such analogy in experience. Conscious agents are not generally material causes.[103] To the argument that in conformity with experience, it is not admissible for *brahman* to create without organs, Śaṅkara rejoins,

> This supreme and sublime *Brahman*, is to be known from the *Vedas* alone, but not from reasoning. Moreover, there cannot be any such rule that since somebody is seen to have some power in some way, another should also have it in the same way. Moreover, this also has been stated that even though all distinctions are denied in *Brahman*, still It can have accession of all powers owing to the presence of a variety of aspects conjured up by ignorance. In support of this is the scripture, "He moves and grasps even though he is without feet and hands, he sees without eyes and hears without ears" (SV.U. 3.19), which shows the possession of all kinds of power by *Brahman*, even though It is devoid of organs.[104]

One should not conclude from the above argument that Śaṅkara finds no use for inferential arguments about God's existence. The problem with these kinds of arguments is that they merely suggest possibilities; they are not conclusive. Once, however, the reality and nature of God are ascertained from the *śruti*, he attempts as far as possible to show that the conclusions of *śruti* conform to reason. In this attempt, he unhesitatingly uses inferential arguments and analogies.[105]

Before concluding this section of our discussion, it is necessary, on the basis of our ascertained conclusion, to refute some of the widely accepted interpretations of Śaṅkara's orientation to the authority of the *Vedas*.[106] Having seen that he does not try to establish authoritativeness on the basis of an inference from God's omniscience, there is no basis whatsoever for the view that *śruti* is acceptable to him because it embodies the records of the religious experiences of ancient mystics. The uniqueness of *śruti* is that its authority is not personal or derived. It is, as we have seen, *apauruṣeya*. We cannot emphasize strongly enough the purely conjectural character of the view that the *Vedas* are merely meant for inferior aspirants who are incapable of directly discovering revealed assertions, or that these assertions are discoverable through some other source. Śaṅkara has not left his matter open to speculation, and such conclusions are entirely indefensible. The overwhelming evidence of his major commentaries affirms that he saw *śabda-pramāṇa* as the only definitive source of *brahmajñāna*. His unambiguous justification of this *pramāṇa* is the impossibility of knowing *brahman* otherwise. The view that the *Vedas* "contain truths which man could, by the exercise of his own faculties, discover" is entirely irreconcilable with Śaṅkara's vindication of their authority.[107] The nature and detail of his justification of the *Vedas* as the only *pramāṇa* of *brahman* do not lend any support to the view that his aim was merely to seek the approval of their authority for his conclusions.

2.6 The Limitations of *Śruti* and Its Relation to *Smṛti*

The word *smṛti* is derived from the root *smṛ* (to remember). It is generally used to indicate authoritative texts other than the *Vedas.*[108] *Smṛtis* are also a form of *śabda-pramāṇa*, but unlike the *śruti*, they are of human origin (*pauruṣeya*) and, therefore, less authoritative. Śaṅkara uses the analogy of perception and inference to describe the relationship between *śruti* and *smṛti*. *Smṛti* is dependent on *śruti* even as inference is reliant on perception for its data. *Smṛtis* are not, therefore, independently authoritative.[109] Compared to the direct and independent validity of the *Vedas*, the authority of *smṛti* is remote because it "depends on some other source of knowledge and since the memory of the speaker intervenes."[110]

Smṛtis are authoritative only when they conform to Vedic texts. They are to be discarded in those cases where they directly contradict the sense of the *Vedas*. This is the method, according to Śaṅkara, of reconciling and deciding between mutually opposed *smṛti* texts.[111] One need not reject an entire *smṛti* text because some parts are opposed to Vedic doctrines. *Advaita*, for example, shares some doctrines in common with *Sāṅkhya* and *Yoga*. Although they are both dualists, *Sāṅkhya* subscribes to the quality-less nature of the Self and *Yoga* emphasizes the value of detachment. These views are compatible with and acceptable to*Advaita.*[112] Śaṅkara also acknowledges the authority of Kapila and his followers with respect to the nature, functions, and products of the *guṇas.*[113]

How should we view *smṛti* texts which do not contradict Vedic ones, but for which we can find no corroboration in the *Vedas*? In such cases, according to Śaṅkara, we are to infer the existence of the *śruti* text upon which the *smṛti* is based.[114]

The *śruti* shares with all other *pramāṇas* the characteristic of having a circumscribed concern and sphere of authority. As we noted earlier, it is intended for the revelation of *dharma* and *brahman*, both of which are incapable of being known through any other *pramāṇa*. Its purpose is not to disclose matters within the range of human experience, ascertainable through any of our ordinary means of knowledge. If a *śruti* statement contradicts a well-established fact of our everyday experience, it cannot be considered authoritative because such a matter would be outside its authority.

> *Śruti* is an authority only in matters not perceived by means of ordinary instruments of knowledge such as *pratyaksha* or immediate perception; — i.e., it is an

> authority as to the mutual relation of things as means to ends, but not in matters lying within the range of *pratyaksha*; indeed, *śruti* is intended as an authority only for knowing what lies beyond the range of human knowledge.... A hundred *śrutis* may declare that fire is cold or that it is dark; still they possess no authority in the matter.[115]

If, however, *śruti* did describe fire as being cold or dark, we should construe its meaning figuratively.[116] Vedic texts are not meant for creating things anew or reversing the nature of anything. They are revelatory and are concerned with simply expressing things as they are. They do not misrepresent facts.[117] In order to accomplish its purpose, the *śruti* uses conventional words and meanings and cites examples from our everyday world. By these examples, "the scriptures seek to tell us about some other thing which does not contradict them. They would not cite an example from life if they wanted to convey an idea of something contradictory to it. Even if they did, it would be to no purpose, for the example would be different from the thing to be explained."[118]

As conceived by Śaṅkara, one *pramāṇa* does not contradict another. Each *pramāṇa* only reveals knowledge that cannot be obtained by another.[119] Clarification has been provided on this point by Sureśvara.[120] According to him, two *pramāṇas* whose spheres are entirely different cannot be contradictory. The eye, which perceive forms, and the ears, which apprehend sounds, are not opposed. It is only when two *pramāṇas* deal with the same object and are contradictory that they are opposed.

> If a thing is perceived by the senses it cannot be revealed by the *Veda*; if a thing is genuinely revealed by the *Veda* it cannot be an object of sense-perception. A perception (purporting to bear on a revealed subject is only) a semblance of a perception; and a revealed text (bearing on what is subject to perception is only) a mere semblance of a revelation.[121]

Sureśvara goes on to add that *pramāṇas* do not have to cooperate with each other to produce knowledge as the various members of a syllogism do. Each is authoritative within its own sphere and independently capable of giving rise to valid knowledge.

In Śaṅkara's view, then, the knowledge of the *Vedas* is not opposed to fact. He denies, for example, that there is any conflict between *śruti* and perception with regard to the nature of the Self. The claim of the *śruti* that the Self is free from all limitations is not opposed to our perceptual experience. The latter has for its object the Self as identified with various limiting adjuncts (*upādhis*). *Śruti*, however, points to a Self free from all erroneous identification.[122] Similarly, Śaṅkara denies that there is any contradiction between perception and the unity of *brahman*.[123] We should remind ourselves, however, of Śaṅkara's position that not everything revealed by *śruti* is explicable on the analogy of our everyday experience. The nature of *brahman* as both efficient and material cause cannot be inferred from any of our experiences of creation.[124] If, after the meaning of a *śruti* text is well ascertained, a conflict arises with any other *pramāṇa*, *śruti* must be accorded primacy.[125]

Śaṅkara mentions some very specific topics which it is not the function of the *śruti* to reveal. It is not the purpose of the *śruti* to inform us of the details and order of the creation of the world. We neither observe, nor are told by the texts that the welfare of humanity depends upon this kind of knowledge. In fact, when the texts are properly analyzed, we find that such passages are intended for instruction about *brahman*. They are not independent passages but are subservient and linked to those discussing *brahman*. Accounts of creation, which involve analogies of clay, iron, sparks, etc., are only meant for showing the nondifference of effects from cause and upholding the unity of *brahman*.[126]

Similarly, *śruti* is not concerned to provide information about the individual self (*jīvātman*).

> The individual soul, present in everybody as the agent and experienced in association with such limiting adjuncts as the intellect, is known from common experience itself, and so it is not mentioned in the *Upaniṣads* for its own sake. But as God is not thus familiarly known from common experience, He is intended to be declared in the *Upaniṣad* for His own sake. Hence it is not proper to say that any mention of Him is uncalled for.[127]

Finally, not only is *śruti* limited with reference to its content, but its injunctions have a limited applicability. The one who has gained *brahmajñāna* stands outside the pale of injunctions. Directives to act or to refrain from action are relevant to one who is in search of appropriate means for gaining some desirable object or avoiding an undesirable one. Injunctions somehow appear superfluous to the *brahmajñāni* who has no unfulfilled personal wants.

> That man, verily, who rejoices only in the Self, who is satisfied with the Self, who is content in the Self alone, — for him there is nothing to do.
>
> For him, there is here no interest whatever in what is done or what is not done. Nor is there in all beings any one he should resort to for any object.[128]

The point seems to be that the *brahmajñāni*, having shed self-centered wants, spontaneously becomes a source and example of right action. The directives which aim at bringing about this effortless ideal are redundant once it is discovered. It is *śruti*'s own tribute to her ideal. As Śaṅkara remarks,

> If man who has realised the identity of the Self and *Brahman* has still to bow down to injunctions, even though he is beyond all mandates, then there will remain none who is outside the pale of scriptural direction; and so all actions will become fit to be undertaken by all and sundry at all times. But that is undesirable. Nor can he be directed by anybody, for even the scriptures emanate from him. Not that anyone can be impelled by any sentence issuing out of his own wisdom. Nor is a well-informed master commanded by an ignorant servant.[129]

The conclusions I have reached in this discussion about Śaṅkara's understanding of the nature of the authority of the *śruti* differ radically from some of the opinions I summarized in our Introduction. I terminate the discussion here by reflecting on these.

It is indisputable that there is a profound epistemological basis for Śaṅkara's dependence on *śruti* as the only authoritative source of *brahmajñāna*. There is no dearth of evidence to support the view that he saw the *śruti* as the only valid source of this knowledge. His way of justifying the necessity for a *pramāṇa* in the form of words completely belies the argument that his recourse to *śruti* was motivated merely by the wish to gain the support of an authoritative tradition for his personal views. *Śabda-pramāṇa*, contrary to the view of current opinion, is perceived by him as a unique source of knowledge about *brahman*, justified by the fact that, as human beings, we cannot otherwise know *brahman*. *Śruti* would not satisfy the criterion of novelty if the knowledge which it provides could be obtained from any other source. I have also highlighted his argument that the *śruti*, like all other valid sources of knowledge, does not need the confirmation or verification of any other *pramāṇa*. It is a self-valid source of fruitful knowledge.

I have not found any evidence in the commentaries of Śaṅkara to support the conclusion that he accepted the *śruti* as authoritative and infallible because it embodied the self-certifying experiences of ancient mystics. The grounds of his argument for *śruti*'s infallibility are very different. When Śaṅkara does not even seek to establish the authority of the *śruti* on the basis on *īśvara's* omniscience, it is difficult to conceive that he would derive it from human authority. In this matter, his views are closely allied with those of *Pūrva-Mīmāṁsā*. I have noted the connection between his arguments for the uncreated, eternal, and impersonal (*apauruṣeya*) nature of the *śruti* and its infallibility.

While Śaṅkara advances various arguments for the validity of the *śruti*, it appears to me that he ultimately falls back upon the claim that the *śruti* fulfills the criteria of being a *pramāṇa*. It provides a knowledge which is not available through any other source and which is not contradicted by another valid *pramāṇa*. In addition, this knowledge is seen to be fruitful in the elimination of *saṃsāra* and its attendant — evils such as grief, fear, and delusion. It would seem that the onus is rather thrust upon the one who does not accept *śruti* as a *pramāṇa* to disprove its validity.

Having thus examined Śaṅkara's understanding of the status and justification of *śruti* as a *pramāṇa* of *brahman*, we can now consider how he sees *brahmajñāna* as unfolded through this medium.

Chapter 3

The Method of *Brahmajñāna*

In the previous chapter, I discussed Śaṅkara's conception of the *Vedas* and sought to establish his evident conclusion that the *Vedas* are our only authoritative means for the knowledge of *brahman*. I also attempted to unfold the rationale underlying this view. In brief, his argument is that because *brahman* possesses no characteristics or distinguishing marks which can be apprehended by any of our ordinary means of knowledge, it can be known only through *śabda-pramāṇa*.

The case for *śabda-pramāṇa* in Śaṅkara, however, cannot end there. If *brahman*, by definition, excludes the applicability of all other sources of knowledge, it also poses special difficulties for *śabda-pramāṇa*. There is clear evidence in Śaṅkara's commentaries of his acute awareness of these problems. *Śabda-pramāṇa* is a means of knowledge in the form of words, and the words of the *Vedas* are the conventional words of everyday usage.[1] If the words employed by the *Vedas* are unfamiliar, the texts become useless as a *pramāṇa*.[2] The problem, however, is that conventional words and meanings are employed in designating known and familiar objects. When employed in the *śruti*, they must serve as the medium of informing us about an unknown entity (*brahman*) which possesses none of the distinguishing marks of ordinary objects. A language which is conditioned by the world of objects which it describes must somehow define a unique and entirely dissimilar entity. Words, according to Śaṅkara, can define their objects in four ways. They do this through categories denoting genus, actions, quality, or relation. Words such as *horse* and *cow* imply genus, *cook* and *teacher* suggest action, *white* and *black* indicate qualities, and *wealthy* or *cattleowner* point to a relation or possession. *Brahman*, however, belongs to no genus. It is devoid of qualities (*nirguṇa*), actionless, and not related to anything.[3]

It seems obvious, therefore, that if conventional words are to be employed in informing us accurately of *brahman*, they will have to be employed in a very special manner, as part of a unique method of instruction. The feasibility of *śabda-pramāṇa* as a vehicle of *brahmajñāna* becomes credible only when some method can be demonstrated for overcoming the natural limitations of language. This is a difficulty which also partly explains the attempt, in contemporary interpretations, to suggest an alternative to *śabda-pramāṇa* in Śaṅkara, and it is important, therefore, that we examine his treatment of this problem. We can do this more effectively, however, by first examining the precise problem which *śabda-pramāṇa* aims to resolve. Its adequacy or inadequacy can only be assessed in relation to this problem.

3.1 The Fundamental Problem of *Avidyā* and Its Resolution

The *Vedas*, according to Śaṅkara, do not reveal the *ātman* in the sense of illumining its existence. Being of the nature of consciousness (*cit*), *ātman* is self-revealing. It is absolute awareness in whose light everything stands revealed.

> There the sun does not shine, neither do the moon and the stars; nor do these flashes of lightning shine. How can this fire? He shining, all these shine; through His lustre all these are variously illumined.[4]

There are several important and interesting discussions in Śaṅkara's commentaries which are relevant to this issue. In his introduction to the *Brahma-sūtra*, an objection is raised against the superimposition (*adhyāsa*) argument.[5] The objector's view is that superimposition is possible only on something that is available for sense perception. In the mistaken apprehension of the rope for a snake, for example, the form of the snake is seen. How can anything, however, be superimposed on the *ātman*, which is not an object of the senses? Śaṅkara's reply is to suggest that even though the Self is not an object of perception, it is not entirely unknown, and *adhyāsa* is possible.

> The Self is not absolutely beyond apprehension, because It is apprehended as the content of the concept "I"; and because the Self, opposed to the non-Self, is well known in the world as an immediately perceived (i.e., self-revealing) entity. Nor is there any rule that something has to be superimposed on something else that is directly perceived through the senses: for boys superimpose the ideas of surface (i.e., concavity) and dirt on the space (i.e., sky) that is not an object of sense perception. Hence there is nothing impossible in superimposing the non-Self on the Self that is opposed to it.[6]

Elsewhere, the objector asks whether *brahman* is known or unknown.[7] The point of the query here is that if *brahman* is known, there is no need for a means of knowledge or an inquiry to ascertain its nature. If, on the other hand, *brahman* is entirely unknown (i.e., not even the object of a desire to know), it cannot become the subject of any kind of inquiry (*jijñāsā*). Śaṅkara, however, denies that *brahman* is entirely unknown.

> Besides, the existence of *Brahman* is well known from the fact of Its being the Self of all; for everyone feels that his Self exists, and he never feels "I do not exist." Had there been no general recognition of the existence

> of the Self, everyone would have felt, "I do not exist." And the Self is *Brahman*.[8]

If the *ātman* is known, is not inquiry into the *śruti* redundant?

> No, for there is a conflict about Its distinctive nature. Ordinary people as well as the materialists of the *Lokāyata* school recognize the body alone to be the Self possessed of sentience. Others hold that the mind is the Self. Some say that it is merely momentary consciousness. Others say that it is a void. Still others believe that there is a soul, separate from the body, which transmigrates and is the agent (of work) and the experiencer (of results). Some say that the soul is a mere experiencer and not an agent. Some say that there is a God who is different from this soul and is all-knowing and all-powerful; others say that He is the Self of the experiencing individual. Thus there are many who follow opposite views by depending on logic, texts, and their semblances. If one accepts any of these views without examination, one is liable to be deflected from emancipation and come to grief. Therefore, starting with the presentation of a deliberation on *Brahman*, here is commenced an ascertainment of the meaning of the texts of the *Upaniṣads* themselves, for the purpose of leading to emancipation (through knowledge).[9]

Śaṅkara's reference to the absence of distinctive or particular knowledge (*viśeṣa-jñāna*) suggests that the kind of knowledge of the *ātman* which we possess is of a general nature only (*sāmānya-jñāna*). In fact, superimposition occurs where knowledge is of a general nature and lacks specificity. In the rope-snake analogy, an object is perceived as existing, but its particular (*viśeṣa*) nature is incorrectly ascertained. The qualities of a snake are then attributed to the rope. In the case of the *ātman*, that "I exist" and "I know" are self-revelatory. This knowledge, however, is of a general (*sāmānya*) nature only. Upon this existence (*sat*) and awareness (*cit*), mortality and finitude are superimposed. That one exists in all three periods of time is unknown. Bliss (*ānanda*) is manifest in various experiences, but its identity with the Self is not known. It is generally understood to be a quality of sense objects. Where the *ātman* is concerned, therefore, the problem is a lack of *viśeṣa-jñāna*, and this makes superimposition possible. The result is the ascription of the qualities of the non-Self upon the Self. If the *ātman* is fully known or entirely unknown, it cannot become the locus of any kind of superimposition. It is clear, therefore, that from Śaṅkara's standpoint, the problem does not involve the knowledge of an entirely unknown, unrevealed or remote Self. It is one of incomplete or erroneous knowledge of an ever-available and self-manifesting *ātman*.

Śaṅkara introduces his commentary on the *Brahma-sūtra* by arguing that the Self (subject) and the non-Self (object) are so radically different from each other that identity between them is impossible. Nevertheless, he says, owing to the absence of discrimination, their natures and attributes are mutually confused and superimposed.[10] He concludes his introduction by illustrating the forms which this transposition takes.

> One superimposes the characteristics of the body when one has such ideas as "I am fat," "I am thin," "I am fair," "I stay," "I go," or "I scale." So also one superimposes the attributes of the senses and organs when one thinks, "I am dumb," "I am deaf," or "I am blind".... Similarly one superimposes the attributes of the internal organ, possessed of the idea of ego, on the Self, the witness of all the manifestations of that organ; then by an opposite process, one superimposes on the internal organ, etc. that Self which is opposed to the non-Self and which is the witness of everything.[11]

The function of the *śruti* in this context lies primarily in the negation of attributes imposed through *avidyā* on the Self. The *śruti* does not reveal an unknown entity.[12] One of the most important reasons for emphasizing the immediate availability of the Self and clarifying the nature of *avidyā* pertaining to it is that it establishes the possibility of *śabda-pramāṇa* giving rise to immediate and direct knowledge. It is very simple, when words like *search*, *quest*, *achieving*, *accomplishing*, and *attaining* are used, to think of the object of inquiry as being remote and immediately unavailable. In fact, from the perspective of *Advaita*, the seeker's difficulty arises from not having appreciated oneself as the object of all quests. The seeker is the ever-available sought. The challenge is not one of creating anything new but of erroneous understanding of oneself. In fact, if the Self to be known is not always available and manifest, the implication would be that it is somehow limited.

It is extremely significant that Śaṅkara opens his commentary on the *Brahma-sūtra* with an introduction on superimposition. It is necessary to posit superimposition (*adhyāsa*) before nonduality and liberation (*mokṣa*) can be established. Since *adhyāsa* is a product of *advidyā*, it can be negated by *jñāna*. It is as absurd to employ any other means as it is to use a stick for protecting oneself against the snake perceived in place of the rope. Śaṅkara's emphasis on *jñāna* as the only direct means to *mokṣa* has to be understood in light of his definition of bondage. His standpoint is that if bondage is real (i.e., existing in all three periods of time without change), it cannot be eliminated by *jñāna* or indeed by any other means. If it is entirely nonexistent, for example, like the son of a barren woman, there is no need for any means to bring about freedom. An apparent bondage, however, with its basis in incomplete and erroneous knowledge, can be overcome by *jñāna* born out of *śabda-pramāṇa*.

This is the true context also in which his refutation of action (*karman*) as a direct means to *mokṣa* has to be placed.[13] *Karman* becomes a direct means where the attainment involved is one of accomplishing something not yet accomplished. If one admits, Śaṅkara contends, that *mokṣa* is to be effected through *karman*, then the action necessary, whether physical, mental, or vocal, should be any one of four kinds.[14] These are creation, modification, attainment, and purification. If, however, *mokṣa* is regarded as the product of an act of creation (e.g., like the creation of a pot from clay) or modification (e.g., milk into curds), it becomes finite and noneternal. The result of any action is conditioned by the nature of the act, and action is always finite and limited. In any event, *brahman* is an already existing entity and beyond all change. Is *brahman* an already-existing entity but separate from the individual (*jīva*)? Can we consider *mokṣa* to be the result of an act of attainment or reaching? *Brahman*, being the very nature of one's Self, there is no question of its accomplishment through an act of reaching or any movement.

> Even if *Brahman* be different from oneself, there can be no acquisition, for *Brahman* being all-pervasive like space, It remains ever attained by everybody.[15]

Is it possible to view *mokṣa* as the result of an act of purification? The latter, Śaṅkara points out, can be effected either by the addition of some excellence to what is to be purified or by the removal of some blemish. *Mokṣa*, however, is of the nature of *Brahman* to which no excellence can be added.[16] *Brahman* is, by definition, eternally pure, and there is no question of the removal of any blemish from it. A final possibility is envisaged and refuted by Śaṅkara.

> *Objection*: May it not be, that though liberation is inherent in oneself, it remains covered and it becomes manifest when the Self is purified by action, as the brilliance of a mirror does when cleaned by the act of rubbing?
>
> *Vedāntin*: No, since the Self cannot reasonably be the sphere of any action, for no action can take place without bringing about some change in its locus. But if the Self changes through action, It will be subject to impermanence and that will militate against such texts as, "It is said to be immutable..." (B.G. 2:25) Hence

> the Self can have no action occurring on Itself. And action, taking place on something else, cannot purify the Self which is not an object thereof.[17]

If action is the appropriate mode for realizing the accomplishment of the unaccomplished, *jñāna* is adequate for the accomplishment of the already accomplished. The accomplishment of the accomplished is a paradoxical description, but it is quite clear from Śaṅkara's metaphysics that he conceives *mokṣa* to be an attainment of this kind. Such an attainment is involved where the loss is entirely notional or apparent and the gain is in the form of knowledge. Śaṅkara uses a number of illustrations to describe a problem of this kind and its solution. The story of the tenth person has become a classic parable of *Advaita*, and its implications have been contemplated in detail.[18] Ten disciples were on their way to a pilgrimage site when they encountered a river in flood. In the absence of the boatman, they decided to swim across. On reaching the opposite shore, the leader took a count to ensure that everyone was safe. To her dismay, one seemed to be missing. Every other member of the group did likewise, but ended up with the same result. They were all deeply grieved after concluding that the tenth man had drowned. A passerby, who was attracted by their loud lamentations, inquired about the problem. After patiently listening and observing, he assured them that the tenth man was indeed available and requested the leader to count again. When the disciple stopped at nine and looked bewildered, the stranger smilingly said, "You are the tenth person." The error was immediately appreciated by everyone. Each had omitted herself from her count. The already accomplished and immediately available tenth person is denied in *avidyā* and again accomplished in *jñāna*. Similarly, the limitless, which is the object of the seeker's quest, is not different from one's own ever-accomplished, always-shining, Self. Being unaware of this, one assumes the guise of finitude and like the tenth person is subject to all its attendant sorrows. *Śruti* is like a mirror in which one sees one's true image.[19]

> The attainment of the Self cannot be, as in the case of things other than It, the obtaining of something not obtained before, for here there is no difference between the person attaining and the object attained. Where the Self has to obtain something other than Itself, the Self is the attainer and the non-Self is the object attained. This, not being already attained, is separated by acts such as producing and is to be attained by the initiation of a particular action with the help of auxiliaries. And the attainment of something new is transitory, being due to desire and action that are themselves the product of a false notion, like the birth of a son, etc., in a dream. But this Self is the

very opposite of that. By the very fact of Its being the Self, It is not separated by acts such as producing. But although It is always attained, It is separated by ignorance only.[20]

3.2 The Independent Authoritativeness of the *Vedānta* Sentences

The aim of the previous section was to establish Śaṅkara's conception of the nature of *avidyā* as it relates to the *ātman*, and its appropriate resolution. The function of the *śruti* does not lie in establishing or revealing the existence of the *ātman* but in removing ignorance and in negating the attributes and qualities which are erroneously ascribed to an ever-manifest, but imperfectly known Self. One may say that the problem is not a lack of experience of *ātman* but one of incorrect knowledge. Someone, for example, searching for a certain Mr. Smith encounters a stranger and has a lengthy conversation with him. At the end of the exchange, he inquires about Mr. Smith, and the stranger declares, "I am Smith." One may say that prior to this revelation, the seeker had the experience of Smith but lacked knowledge. Similarly, *ātman* as *sat* (existence), *cit* (awareness), and *ānanda* (bliss) is not completely unknown but is erroneously understood. We also sought to understand the notional nature of bondage and the rationale of Śaṅkara's conclusion that *jñāna* is the only direct means to freedom.

We must now consider some relevant aspects of his exegesis of the Vedic texts. His exegetical position was developed, in a large measure, in response to the interpretations of *Pūrva-Mīmāṁsā*. Although some of the issues and arguments appear archaic, we can examine those still-important arguments which shed further light on his conception of the nature of *jñāna* and the role of *śruti* as a *pramāṇa*.

In brief, the *Mīmāṁsā* exegesis, in so far as it is relevant to Śaṅkara, contends that the *Vedas* have their purport only in the inculcation of *dharma*.[21] The latter is defined by Jaimini as, "that which, being desirable, is indicated by Vedic injunction."[22] On the basis of this view, *Pūrva-Mīmāṁsā* argues that only injunctions (*vidhi*) inculcating the performance of acceptable acts and prohibitions (*niṣedha*) instituting restraint from acts opposed to *dharma* are direct and independent in authority.[23] The authority of all other texts is indirect and dependent for their meaningfulness on a connection with the injunctions. They are not viewed as having any independent end in themselves. Many Vedic texts, for example, including *Vedānta* sentences (*Vedānta-vākyas*), are seen as having their purposefulness only in praising what has been enjoined in the injunctions.[24] *Pūrva-Mīmāṁsā* argues that if such sentences are taken by themselves, they are absolutely meaningless because they neither impel us to activity or restrain us from a prohibited action.[25] Their view is that the *Vedānta-vākyas* are merely an appendage to the main body of injunctive statements. Their utility lies only in praising the prescribed action or in providing some useful information such as knowledge of the deity or agent for the performance of a particular rite. If they are statements about already-accomplished entities, then they are without fruit, for they neither prompt the performance of *dharma* nor the avoidance of *adharma*. Against the independent authority of the *Vedānta-vākyas*, *Pūrva-Mīmāṁsā* contends that knowledge about already-accomplished things is obtainable from other *pramāṇas*. The knowledge of *dharma* and *adharma*, however, is not otherwise obtainable.[26]

This *Mīmāṁsā* exegesis is obviously incompatible with Śaṅkara's justification of the role of the *Vedas*. It is irreconcilable with his view that the *Upaniṣads* are an independent *pramāṇa* for *brahman*. He seeks therefore, to refute from various standpoints the *Mīmāṁsā* thesis and to establish that the *Vedānta-vākyas* are not subservient to any other texts but have an independent meaningfulness and authority in the revelation of *brahman*.

Śaṅkara does not accept that sentences cannot have a factual referent or significance.[27] He points out that even though a sentence might have its ultimate purport in initiating some activity, it does not necessarily cease to communicate valid factual information. Even as a person travelling to some destination perceives the existence of leaves and grass at the side of the road, a statement might have its aim in activity, but its factual content is not thereby invalidated.[28] In response to the *Mīmāṁsā* exaltation of injunctions Śaṅkara reminds them that injunctions are valid not simply because they are injunctions, but because they are revealed in an authoritative *pramāṇa*, the *Vedas*.

> When a thing has been known to be true from the *Vedas*, a person will perform it, should it admit of being performed, but will not do it if it is not a thing to be done.[29]

Another proposition of *Mīmāṁsā* is that if Vedic statements are understood to independently signify already-existent things, they become redundant. Existent things are knowable through ordinary sources of knowledge. While agreeing that most existent things can be so known, Śaṅkara contends that *brahman* is unique. Possessing no characteristics apprehensible through any other *pramāṇa*, it can be cognized through *śabda-pramāṇa* alone. Its existence cannot be denied just because its nature precludes all other sources of knowledge.[30]

In reply to the claim that mere factual statements which neither persuade us into activity nor dissuade us from it are fruitless, Śaṅkara asserts that "the test of the authority or otherwise of a passage is not whether it states a fact or an action but its capacity to generate certain and fruitful knowledge. A passage that has this is authoritative and one that lacks it is not".[31] He never tires of continuously affirming the independent fruitfulness of the *Vedānta-vākyas*. Even as a simple statement of fact, "This is a rope, not a snake," is fruitful in removing the fear occasioned by the error of taking a rope for a snake. *Vedānta-vākyas*, by helping to discriminate the Self from the non-Self, release us from the sorrow of taking ourselves to be incomplete and finite beings.[32] It contravenes experience to maintain that *brahmajñāna* is unproductive because knowledge brings about no change in the life of someone who knows *brahman*.

> For one who has realized the state of the unity of the Self and *Brahman*, it cannot be proved that his mundane life continues just as before; for this contradicts the knowledge of the unity of *Brahman* and the Self arising from the *Vedas*, which are a valid means of knowledge. From noticing the fact that a man can have sorrow, fear, etc., as a result of identifying himself with the body, etc., it does not follow that this very man will have sorrow, etc. contingent on false ignorance, even when his self-identification with the body etc., ceases after the realization of the unity of *Brahman* and the Self, arising from the *Vedas*, which are a valid source of knowledge. Just because a householder, who had been rich and prided himself on that account, had been seen to be sorrowing for the theft of his wealth, it does not follow that this very man will be miserable for any loss of that wealth even after he had become a monk and given up the idea of being wealthy.[33]

Besides, Śaṅkara states, if one contends that only statements prompting activity are meaningful, Vedic prohibitions (*niṣedha*) will be deprived of all authority. A sentence such as "A *Brāhmaṇa* should not be killed," is neither directly nor indirectly connected with an action. It is the aim of a *niṣedha* to influence us to desist from a particular action.[34] Finally, our attention is drawn to the contradiction involved in asserting that the *Vedānta-vākyas* are subsidiary to the injunctive texts. *Vedānta* texts, which proclaim the reality of the nondual *brahman*, deny the absolute truth of the duality of agent, instrument, and result implied in activity. In the light of such a clear repudiation of duality, it is impossible to maintain that they can in any way subserve injunctions.[35]

From a hermeneutical point of view, the most important basis for Śaṅkara's affirmation that *Vedānta-vākyas* are independently authoritative and fruitful is his contention that by right correlation (*samanvaya*) it can be shown that these sentences have their purport (*tātparya*) only in the revelation of *brahman*.

> Besides, when the words in the Upaniṣadic sentences become fully ascertained as but revealing the nature of *Brahman*, it is not proper to fancy some other meaning; for that will result in rejecting something established by the *Vedas* and accepting some other thing not intended by them.[36]

In order to discover the purport of any scriptural passage, *Advaita* makes use of the sixfold criteria (*ṣaḍliṅga*) formulated by *Pūrva-Mīmāṁsā* exegetists.[37] These very important exegetical canons are as follows:

1. *Upakramopasaṁhara* (the beginning and the end). This means the presentation at the beginning as well as the end of the subject matter treated in a particular section. A unity of the initial and concluding passages is considered to be a good indication of the intention of the *śruti*. For example, CH.U. 6.2.1, begins with the text, "In the beginning, my dear, this was being only, one without a second." The section ends (6.16.3), "All this is identical with That; That is the Self; That Thou Art, O Shvetaketu."

2. *Abhyāsa* (repetition). The purport of the *śruti* is also suggested by the frequent repetition of a theme in the course of a discussion. In CH.U. 6, the sentence "That Thou Art" is uttered nine times.

3. *Apūrva* (novelty). The idea here is that if the subject under discussion is knowable through other *pramāṇas*, it cannot be the purport of *śruti*. As a *pramāṇa*, the main function of *śruti* is to inform us of things which are inaccessible through any other means of knowledge. *Brahman* is considered to be a subject unknowable through any means but the *Vedas*.

4. *Phala* (fruit). The purport of a passage is also indicated by the clear mention of an independent result. The fruitfulness of the *Vedānta-vākyas* is an argument which Śaṅkara returns to again and again. CH.U. 6.14.2 mentions *mokṣa* as the *phala* of *brahmajñāna*. In other words, if in a particular passage there is an unambiguous mention of its own independent fruit, such a passage cannot be seen as being merely subservient to some other parts of the text. A distinct result gives a good indication of a different purport. By arguing that there is a clear mention of a different end in the *jñānakāṇḍa* (i.e., *mokṣa*), Śaṅkara distinguishes its purport from the *karmakāṇḍa* section of the *Vedas*.

5. *Arthavāda* (commendation). This is the praise of the subject matter in the course of the discussion. "Have you ever asked for that instruction by which one hears what has not been heard, one thinks what has not been thought, one knows what has not been known?" (CH.U 6.1.3) is seen as a praise of *brahmajñāna*.

6. *Upapatti* (demonstration). This indicates the use of arguments to suggest the reasonableness of the subject presented. CH.U. 6.1.4–6 uses

a variety of illustrations to demonstrate the nondifference of cause and effect and to explain *brahman* as the material cause of the universe.[38]

Advaita contends that by the application of the *ṣaḍliṅga*, it can be proved that the *Vedānta-vākyas* are not ancillary to any other texts but have an independent purport (*tātparya*) in revealing the nondual *brahman*.

Śaṅkara's refutation of the *Mīmāṁsā* exegesis of the significance of the *Vedānta-vākyas* highlights and reinforces salient features of his own outlook. It underlines the nature of *brahman* as an ever-available entity and emphasizes the role of *Vedānta-vākyas* in producing fruitful knowledge of an existent thing. That *brahman* is existent does not at all imply its attainability through other *pramāṇas*. *Brahmajñāna* is fully revelatory in character, for it does not accomplish its end by instigating engagement in any activity. Like the case of the tenth person, *śabda-pramāṇa* can produce fruitful results where the problem involved is a mistaken notion of an existent reality.

Having highlighted Śaṅkara's arguments for the autonomy of the *Vedānta-vākyas*, we can conclude by summing up his conception of the subject matter and purport of the *Vedas* as a whole. The first section (*karmakāṇḍa*) informs us of approved means for attaining desirable but yet unaccomplished ends.[39] The second section (*jñānakāṇḍa*) constitutes the *Upaniṣads* and informs us of the nature of *brahman*.[40] The two sections are clearly distinguishable from each other in four ways:[41]

1. *Viṣaya* (subject matter). *Karmakāṇḍa* is concerned with the revelation of *dharma*, while the *jñānakāṇḍa* has *brahman* as its subject.
2. *Adhikārī* (aspirant). The aspirant after the ends of the *karmakāṇḍa* is one who has not yet grown to understand the limitations of any result achievable by *karman*. The *adhikārī* of the *jñānakāṇḍa* has appreciated the noneternity of *karman*-accomplished ends and seeks an unaccomplished limitless end.[42]
3. *Phala* (result). The *karmakāṇḍa* has prosperity as its result. The result of the *jñānakāṇḍa* is *mokṣa*.[43]
4. *Sambandha* (connection). The knowledge which is revealed in the *karmakāṇḍa* informs us of an end which is not yet existent. Its actualization depends upon being effected by an appropriate action. Knowledge here is not an end in itself. The *jñānakāṇḍa*, on the other hand, reveals an already existent *brahman*. *Brahmajñāna* is an end in itself. The connection here is between a revealed object and a means of revelation. *Jñānakāṇḍa* fulfills itself in its informative role, while the *karmakāṇḍa* impels us to activity.

Śaṅkara makes frequent reference in his *bhāṣya* to the criticism that the nondual *brahman* of the *jñānankāṇḍa* renders invalid the entire *karmakāṇḍa* with its dualistic presuppositions. His general response is that the *śruti* is realistic and practical in its awareness of the human condition and provides solutions which are appropriate to human needs and demands. *Śruti* does not, he points out, instruct us at birth about the duality or unity of existence and then about rites or the knowledge of *brahman*. In fact, he says, the notion of duality does not have to be instructed. It is initially accepted as naturally true by all of us. The scripture, he argues, in full awareness of this fact and in recognition of the multifarious desires in us, prescribes, in the *karmakāṇḍa*, appropriate rites for securing these ends.[44] In doing this, the *śruti* does not comment on the reality or otherwise of these actions.

> Moreover, actions, their factors, and their results are things we naturally believe in: they are the creation of ignorance. When, through their help, a man who desires to gain something good or to avoid something evil proceeds to adopt a means of which he has only a vague, not definite idea, the *śruti* simply tells him about that; it says nothing either for or against the truth of the diversity of actions, their factors, and their results — which people have already taken for granted. For the *śruti* only prescribes means for the attainment of desired ends and the avoidance of untoward results.[45]

Śruti stands helplessly in its confrontation with insatiable human desires. To exercise forceful restraint is utterly futile. It simply instructs in accordance with capacity. Śaṅkara explains the stance of the *śruti* in one of his clearest statements on this issue.

> People have innumerable desires and various defects, such as attachment. Therefore they are lured by the attachment, etc., to external objects, and the scriptures are powerless to hold them back; nor can they persuade those who are naturally averse to external objects to go after them. But the scriptures do this much that they point out what leads to good and what to evil, thereby indicating the particular relations that subsist between ends and means; just as a lamp, for instance, helps to reveal forms in the dark. But the scriptures neither hinder nor direct a person by force, as if he were a slave. We see how people disobey even the scriptures because of an excess of attachment, etc. Therefore, according to the varying tendencies of people, the scriptures variously teach the particular relations that subsist between ends and means. In this matter people themselves adopt particular means according to their tastes, and the scriptures simply re-

> main neutral, like the sun, for instance, or a lamp. Similarly, somebody may think the highest goal to be not worth striving after. One chooses one's goal according to one's knowledge, and wants to adopt corresponding means.[46]

When, however, an individual appreciates the limited nature of all the results that can be achieved through *karman* and seeks the enduring factor of existence, *śruti* imparts *brahmajñāna*. It is only for this person that the validity of duality, presupposed in the *karmakāṇḍa*, is negated.[47] Therefore, Śaṅkara concludes, the texts that teach the unity of *brahman* are not antagonistic to those enjoining rituals. Nor do the ritualistic texts deprive the *Upaniṣads* of authority. Each is authoritative in its own sphere.[48]

3.3 The Distinctive Method of Word Manipulation as Mode of Instruction

I have already emphasized the need for cautious approach to Śaṅkara's explanation of *śruti* statements treating the unknowability of *brahman* and discussed the chief ways in which he reads such passages.[49] That *brahman* is knowable and that *śabda-pramāṇa* is the only vehicle of this knowledge are the unmistakable conclusions of his commentary. In his altercation with *Pūrva-Mīmāṁsā*, we have seen his labor to argue the independent significance and efficacy of the *Vedānta-vākyas*. The task of such statements is not to demonstrate *brahman*'s existence but to correct and complete our muddled and partial understanding.

As an entity which has to be defined by a *pramāṇa* in the form of words, *brahman* presents unique difficulties. It possesses none of the characteristics of genus, quality, relation, and activity through which words are normally able to describe a subject. Therefore, along with his emphasis on the possibility of *brahmajñāna*, Śaṅkara also draws attention to a traditional method of instruction. With all of their limitations, there is no means of evading the use of words, since they constitute the very nature of the indispensable *pramāṇa*. If limited words are to discard their finite references and reveal the infinite, they must be skillfully and deliberately wielded. It is this necessity for skillful instruction which explains the *Advaita* conception of the role and qualifications of the traditional teacher. There is no lack of emphasis in Śaṅkara on the imperative of the *guru*. "*Brahman*," he says, "can only be known through such a traditional instruction of preceptors and not through argumentation, nor by study (or exposition), intelligence, great learning, austerity, sacrifices, etc."[50] Śaṅkara describes such a teacher as a rare one among many.[51] In the *Chāndogya Upaniṣad*, the certain acquisition of knowledge by the person fortunate to have a teacher is described in an illustration, which is often cited by Śaṅkara.

> Just as, my dear, someone, having brought a man from the *Gandhāra* regions with his eyes bound up, might leave him in a desolate place, — and that man would shout towards the East, or towards the North, or towards the South, or towards the West — "I have been brought here with my eyes bound up and left here with my eyes bound up."
>
> And as someone might remove his bandages and tell him — the *Gandhāra* regions lie towards this direction, go in this direction — whereupon, asking his way from village to village, and becoming informed and capable of judging for himself, he would reach the Gandhāra regions; — in the same manner, in this world, that person knows who has a teacher; and for him the delay is only so long as I am not liberated and become merged.[52]

The qualified teacher is one who has thoroughly mastered the *śruti* (*śrotriyam*) and who abides in *brahmajñāna* (*brahmaniṣṭham*). Such a teacher should be reverentially approached and is under an obligation to instruct the well-qualified student (*śiṣya*).[53]

> To him who approaches duly, whose heart is calm and whose outer organs are under control, that man of enlightenment should adequately impart that knowledge of *Brahman* by which one realises the true and immutable *Pursua.*[54]

The skillful teacher instructs in accordance with the receptivity of the student and his/her capacity for assimilation. The method of teaching is referred to in *Advaita* as *arundhatī-darśana-nyāya* (the method of indicating *arundhatī*). *Arundhatī*, a very small star, is difficult to perceive. In order to point it out, a proximate, larger star is indicated as *arundhatī*. This large star is dismissed when it is seen, and *arundhatī* is then shown.[55] The aim of imparting *brahmajñāna* is accomplished by a combination of several approaches. Only for the sake of convenience can we try to distinguish among them. In *śruti* and in the actual teaching process, they are employed together and presuppose each other.

I. The Method of *Adhyāropa* (Superimposition) and *Apavāda* (De-Superimposition)

One of the finest examples of this method of instruction is to be found in the *Bhagavadgītā* 13:12–14.[56] We can understand Śaṅkara's conception of the nature of this process of instruction by following his *bhāṣya* on these verses.

> That which has to be known I shall describe; knowing which, one attains the Immortal. Beginningless is the Supreme *Brahman*. It is not said to be *sat* or *asat*.[57]

Śaṅkara advances two reasons for not accepting that the *Bhagavadgītā*'s description of *brahman* as neither *sat* (existent) nor *asat* (nonexistent) is contradictory.[58] His argument here is that only something which can be perceived by the senses can be an object of consciousness accompanied by the idea of existence or nonexistence.[59] *Brahman* is beyond all sense apprehension and is knowable through *śabda-pramāṇa* alone. In addition to this, no word can define *brahman*, which lacks all characteristics (viz., genus, quality, action, relation) denoted by words. The assertion, however, Śaṅkara says, that *brahman* is not definable by the word *sat* may lead one to the unacceptable conclusion that *brahman* has no reality. The next verse averts this by attributing to it the organs of a living being.

> With hands and feet everywhere, with eyes and heads and mouths everywhere, with hearing everywhere, that exists enveloping all.[60]

The superimposition (*adhyāropa*) of sense organs and organs of action on *brahman* is a purely pedagogic device for indicating its existence. In reality all such attributions (*upādhis*) are false. Once its existence is indicated, the *apavāda* immediately follows in the next verse.

> Shining by the functions of all the sense organs, yet without the senses; unattached, yet supporting all; devoid of qualities, yet enjoying qualities.[61]

This paradoxical method of *adhyāropa* and *apavāda* is one way by which the finite limitations of language can to some extent be overcome to indicate *brahman*. The *śruti* abounds with examples of this kind of verbal juxtaposition.[62] The *adhyāropa-apavāda* procedure is a unique method of indicating the immanent and transcendent aspects of *brahman*. *Adhyāropa* definitions are possible because the entire universe is dependent on *brahman*, and nothing is apart from it. In the actual process of instruction, initial attention must necessarily be drawn to *brahman* through its association with the world and the individual.[63]

> That from which all these beings take birth, that by which they live after being born, that toward which they move and into which they merge. That is *Brahman*.[64]

> That which man does not comprehend with the mind, that by which, they say, the mind is encompassed,

> know that to be *Brahman* and not what people worship as an object.[65]

Definitions of the first kind reveal the world's dependence on and identity with *brahman* by presenting the latter as both its material and efficient cause.[66] Definitions of the second type reveal *brahman* as the *ātman*. *Brahman* is indicated as the Self through its nature as illumining awareness (*caitanya*) in relation to the body, sense organs, and mind. They serve as the indicators through which *brahman* can be pointed out, even as one points out the star *arundhatī*. When these aspects of *brahman* are fully grasped by the student, then all false attributions (*upādhis*) must be negated because of their finite implications and because of the nonessential nature of the characteristics associated with *brahman*. Having accomplished their purposes, these definitions are withdrawn, and *apavāda* negates from *brahman* all anthropomorphic semblances. Both procedures are complementary and indispensable. Language is employed by revealing its limitations.

II. The Method of Negation (*Neti, Neti*)

The method of pure negation is another means by which words can be detached from their primary, limited denotations. Purely negative definitions of *brahman* are intended to distinguish it from the known and limited referents of all words. Such negative descriptions are exceedingly common in the *Upaniṣads*.

> The wise realize everywhere that which is invisible, ungraspable, without family, without caste, without sight or hearing, without hand or foot, immortal, multiformed, and all pervasive, extremely subtle, and undiminishing; and which is the source of all.[67]

> One becomes freed from the jaws of death by knowing that which is soundless, touchless, colorless, undiminishing, and also tasteless, eternal, odourless, without beginning and end, distinct from *Mahat* and ever constant.[68]

Very often the negation employed by the *śruti* is twofold. Contrary attributes are side by side denied in order that the negation of one attribute does not lead to the supposition that *brahman* is characterized by its opposite.

> Tell (me) of that thing which you see as different from virtue, different from vice, different from this cause and effect, and different from the past and future.[69]

> It is neither gross nor minute, neither short nor long, neither red color nor oiliness, neither shadow nor darkness, neither air nor ether, neither savor nor odor, without eyes or ears, without the vocal organ or mind, nonluminous, without the vital force or mouth, not a measure, and without exterior or interior. It does not eat anything, nor is It eaten by anybody.[70]

Words are so saturated with the content of finitude, that no single word can directly signify *brahman*. One is initially surprised to encounter Śaṅkara's statement that even terms like *ātman* and *brahman* are incompetent to directly denote it. Commenting on BR.U. 1.4.7, Śaṅkara points out that the use of the particle *iti* (thus) along with the word *ātman* signifies that the truth of the *ātman* is beyond the scope of the term and concept *ātman*. If it were otherwise, the *śruti* would have said, "One should meditate upon the *Ātman*." This would have wrongly implied, however, that the term and concept *ātman* were acceptable with reference to the Self.[71] The essential aim of the negative method is to deny all specifications which are the result of superimposition. *Neti, neti* (not this, not this) can also be seen as a rejection of *brahman* as a known objectified entity and as a positive hinting of its nature as the knower. The negative method, according to Śaṅkara, is our only option when we wish to describe *brahman* free from all known and finite specifications.

> By elimination of all differences due to limiting adjuncts, the words [*neti, neti*] refer to something that has no distinguishing marks such as name, or form, or action, or heterogeneity, or species, or qualities. Words denote things through one or the other of these. But *Brahman* has none of these distinguishing marks. Hence It cannot be described as "It is such and such," as we describe a cow by saying "There moves a white cow with horns." *Brahman* is described by means of name and form and action superimposed on It, in such terms as "Knowledge, Bliss, Brahman [*vijñānam, ānandam, brahman*]" (BR.U. 3.9.28) and "Pure Intelligence [*vijñānaghana*]" (BR.U. 2.4.12), "Brahman," and "Ātman." When, however, we wish to describe Its true nature, free from all differences due to limiting adjuncts, then it is an utter impossibility. Then there is only one way left, viz., to describe It as "Not this, Not this," by eliminating all possible specifications of It that have been known.[72]

It is obvious, therefore, that the method of negation, as understood by Śaṅkara, is more a unique positive way of defining *brahman* rather than the suggestion of an inability to formulate a concept of *brahman*. In association with the other methods of teaching, it is remarkably suitable for indicating the nonobjectivity of *brahman* and its freedom from all limiting characteristics.

III. The Method of *Lakṣaṇā* (Implication)

The two methods of teaching about *brahman* which we have so far considered are essentially negative in character. They highlight the problems of language in relation to *brahman* and point to the latter as being beyond the ordinary signification of any words. These methods are successful if they alert us to the difficulties involved in speaking about *brahman*. They prepare us for and are made complete by the positive method of definition through *lakṣaṇā*.[73]

Although references to this method can be found in various places throughout the writings of Śaṅkara, his most detailed discussion occurs in his *bhāṣya* on *Taittirīya Upaniṣad* 2.1.1. In this verse, we have what is perhaps the most important definition of *brahman* in *Advaita Vedānta*.

> *Satyam, jñānam, anantam, brahma* (*brahman* is reality, knowledge, and infinite).[74]

In the light of Śaṅkara's view that the *Upaniṣads* impart positive knowledge of *brahman* and his clear contention that ordinary words cannot directly signify it, it is important to understand how such an apparently positive definition can inform us decidedly about *brahman*'s essential nature.[75]

According to Śaṅkara, the sentence "*satyam, jñānam, anantam, brahma*" is meant as a definition of *brahman*. All three words, which have the same case endings and are in apposition, serve as distinguishing adjectives of *brahman*. When qualified by these three terms, *brahman* becomes distinguished from all other substantives. The method is the same as when a lotus is differentiated from all other lotuses by being described as "big, blue, and fragrant."

Śaṅkara formulates a likely objection to this view of *satyam, jñānam, anantam, brahma*. It is argued that a substantive can be differentiated when there is a possibility of negating alternative attributes. The adjective "white," for instance, negates "red" or "blue" from the particular lotus. Adjectives are useful when there are many substantives belonging to the same genus and there is a possibility of qualification by several adjectives. They are not similarly purposeful where there is a single, unique entity and no possibility of any other substantives with alternative attributes. Like the sun, there is one *brahman*. Unlike the blue lotus, which can be distinguished from the red or white one, there are no other *brahmans* from which it can be distinguished.

In this case, Śaṅkara responds, the adjectives are meant for defining and not for qualifying *brahman*. He explains that while an adjective might distinguish a noun from others of the same genus, a definition distinguishes it from all other things. As an example, Śaṅkara gives the definition of *ākāśa* as that which gives space. The sentence *satyam, jñānam, anantam brahma* is meant as a definition of *brahman*. The three terms are not mutually related, since they are meant for subserving the substantive. Each term is independently related to *brahman*, and the sentence ought to be read in this way: *satyam brahman, jñānam brahman, anantam brahman*.

The term *satyam* (reality) indicates the nondeviation of an object from its established nature. The opposite is *anṛtam* (unreality). Changeability is thus equivalent to untruth or unreality. *Satyam*, therefore, distinguishes *brahman* from all changing and therefore, unreal things. On the basis of the word *satyam* alone and its implications, one might conclude that *brahman* is an insentient material like earth. To avert this conclusion, Śaṅkara says, the term *jñānam* is introduced. *Jñānam* means knowledge or consciousness. It conveys the abstract notion of the verb *jñā* (to know). It does not refer to the agent of knowing (*jñānakarta*) because of its use in conjunction with *satyam* and *anantam*. Reality and infinity cannot be attributed to the agent of knowledge, since agency implies change. Knowership also implies the division of knower and known and cannot be described as infinite in accordance with Vedic texts, such as "Wherein one sees nothing else, — that is the Infinite; wherein one sees something else, hears something else, and understands something else, — that is Finite. That which is Infinite is immortal; that which is Finite is mortal" (CH.U. 7.24.1).[76] *Jñānam*, therefore, along with *satyam* and *anantam* denies agency and insentience in *brahman*. The term *anantam* (infinite) following *jñānam*, also serves to negate the idea that because all human knowledge is finite, *brahman* is similarly limited.

Śaṅkara explains that the word *jñānam* in its ordinary sense cannot define *brahman*. The word *jñāna* normally indicates a modification of the intellect and is subject to change. When the word is applied to *brahman*, however, it is used as identical with *brahman* and eternal.

> But the Consciousness of *Brahman* is inherent in *Brahman* and is inalienable from It, just as the light of the sun is from the sun or the heat of fire is from fire. Consciousness is not dependent on any other cause for its (revelation), for it is by nature eternal (light). And since all that exists is inalienable from *Brahman* in time or space, *Brahman* being the cause of time, space, etc., and since *Brahman* is surpassingly subtle, there is nothing else whether subtle or screened or remote or past, present or future which can be unknowable to it. Therefore *Brahman* is omniscient.... Just

> because *Brahman*'s nature of being the knower is inseparable and because there is no dependence on other accessories like the sense-organs, *Brahman* though intrinsically identical with knowledge, is well known to be eternal. Thus, since this knowledge is not a form of action, it does not also bear the root meaning of the verb. Hence, too, *Brahman* is not the agent of cognition. And because of this, again, It cannot even be denoted by the word *jñāna*.[77]

Śaṅkara explains, however, that *brahman* can be implied by the word *jñānam* even though the latter cannot directly signify it.[78] Similarly, Śaṅkara points out, the word *satya*, which refers to external reality in general, can only by implication refer to *brahman*.

> Thus the word truth, etc., occurring in mutual proximity, and restricting and being restricted in turns by each other, distinguish *Brahman* from other objects denoted by the words truth, etc., and thus become fit for defining It as well.[79]

The clear contention of Śaṅkara, then, is that any single term drawn from general usage can be misleading if applied directly to *brahman*. When, however, carefully chosen expressions are skillfully juxtaposed, they mutually qualify and eliminate from each other their finite associations. Such terms are then capable of defining *brahman* by implication. Other striking examples of this kind of exegesis are adduced by Śaṅkara. The word *ātman* ordinarily refers to the empirical Self (*jīvatman*), identified with the body and subject to the notions of differentiation. When, however, by the process of elimination, the body, etc., are rejected as the Self, the word *ātman* can then indirectly signify the Self.

> For instance, when an army with the king is seen marching along, with umbrellas, flags, standards, — even though the king is actually hidden by all this paraphernalia and hence, not visible, yet the expression is used "the king is seen"; and when it is asked "which is the king?" and people come to look for the particular person who is the king, — everyone of the other persons that are actually visible being rejected (as not being the king), there follows (as a result of elimination) that the person who is not visible is the king, — and thus the idea of the "king" is secured; — exactly similar is the case in question.[80]

Similarly, *ānanda* (bliss), when used as a definition of *brahman* cannot be understood as pleasure born out of contact between a sense organ and object. Such as joy is transient; when associated with *brahman* it is eternal.[81] When used along with *brahman, ānanda* has to be understood as signifying *brahman*'s very nature. It does not suggest that the bliss of the Self is cognised.[82]

The kind of implication involved in the exegesis of positive defining words such as *satyam, jñānam, anantam* is of the exclusive – nonexclusive type (*jahadajahallakakṣaṇā*).[83] It is not nonexclusive (*ajahallakṣaṇā*) because the word meaning is not entirely retained. It is not exclusive implication (*jahallakṣaṇā*) because the word meaning is not entirely rejected. By the rejection of the ordinary meaning and the retention of the implied meaning, the word denotation is freed of its finite associations. It is then acceptable for defining *brahman*. Recourse to implication in the case of sentences such as *satyam, jñānam, anantam, brahman*, is necessitated by a frustration of both the logical connection of the words and the purport (*tātparya*). The direct meanings of the words are incompatible with each other and incapable of defining *brahman*. The purport in any context is discovered by the application of the sixfold criteria (*ṣadliṅga*). By arguing that *brahman* can only be defined at the implied level of meaning, Śaṅkara is able to accept *śruti* statements such as "Failing to reach which (*brahman*) words, along with the mind turn back" (TA.U. 2.4.1) and still maintain the adequacy and effectiveness of the *śruti* as the *pramāṇa* of *brahmajñāna*. The essentially negative methods of *adhyāropa – apavada* and *neti, neti* do not culminate in nihilism and are not understood in an absolutely literal sense by Śaṅkara.

> As for the statement that *Brahman* is beyond speech and mind, that is not meant to imply that *Brahman* is nonexistent. For it is not logical to deny that very *Brahman* after establishing It with a great show of girding up one's loins, in such sentences of the *Upaniṣads* as "The knower of *Brahman* attains the highest," "*Brahman* is Truth, Knowledge, Infinity" (TA.U. 2.1.1); for as the popular saying has it, "Rather than wash away the mud, it is much better to avoid its touch from a distance." As a matter of fact the text "Failing to reach which, words turn back with the mind" (TA.U. 2.9.1) presents only a process of propounding *Brahman*. The idea expressed is this: *Brahman* is beyond speech and mind; It cannot be classed with objects of knowledge; It is one's inmost Self; and It is by nature eternal, pure, intelligent, and free.[84]

One cannot overestimate the importance of *lakṣaṇā* as a method of defining *brahman*. It is integral to Śaṅkara's rationale for the *Vedas* as a *pramāṇa* of *brahman*. After his justification of the *Vedas* as a source of knowledge by showing the limitations of all other *pramāṇas* with regard to *brahman*, the problem of the latter's inexpressibility through words, which are unavoidably finite in their reference, still remains. In response to this dilemma, Śaṅkara proposes *lakṣaṇā* as the method of surmounting *brahman*'s inexpressibility. It complements his case for the necessity of *śruti* by demonstrating its competence and capability to effect *brahmajñāna*.

3.4 The *Lakṣaṇā* Exegesis of "That Thou Art" (*Tat Tvam Asi*)

The *lakṣaṇā* method can be demonstrated further by a consideration of the *Advaita* exegesis of the *mahāvākya* (great sentence), "That Thou Art" (*tat tvam asi*).[85] The text first occurs in CH.U. 6.8.7, during a conversation between the teacher Uddālaka and his son Śvetaketu.[86]

The term *tat*, according to Śaṅkara, indicates Being, the ground of the entire universe. It is that which is real, eternal, and immortal.[87] The word *tvam* indicates Śvetaketu, the son of Uddālaka, the one who was exposed to the teaching, pondered over it, and requested to be taught again.

> This represents the person who, being entitled to be the hearer, the ponderer, and the knower, — did not, before he was taught by his father, had not reached the true nature of his own Self, as Being, the Self of all as distinct from all aggregates of causes and effects, — which — as the Supreme Deity, — had entered into the *aggregate of causes and effects made up* of Fire, Water, and Food, for the differentiating of Names and Forms, — just as a man enters the mirror, as his own reflection, or the sun enters into the water and other reflecting surfaces, as its own reflection; — now, however, having been enlightened by his father by the teaching "That Thou Art," through a number of illustrations and reasons, — he understood from his father that "I am Being itself."[88]

The result of this instruction, according to Śaṅkara, is the elimination of the notion of doership and enjoyership in respect of the Self. The knowledge imparted by the *mahāvākya* is incompatible with Śvetaketu's previous notions of himself and displaces the latter.[89] Although Śaṅkara does not specifically mention a *lakṣaṇā* interpretation here, the latter is obvious from the context of his discussion and from his assertion that no word can directly indicate *brahman*. It is *tvam*, stripped of all finite attributes, which is identical with *brahman*.[90]

This best known of *Advaita mahāvākyas*, therefore, is to be understood just like the sentence, "This is that Devadatta." Here the identity is not posited between the primary meanings of "this" and "that." These indicate present and past spatial and temporal conditions and are clearly incompatible. The qualities associated with space and time are negated and the identity of Devadatta is asserted by the implied meanings of both terms. The rejection here of ordinary for implied meanings is, of course, an instance of *jahadajahallakṣaṇā*. The primary meaning of *tat* is consciousness in association with the attributes of omnipotence, omniscience, creatorship, etc., in other words, *īśvara* or *saguṇa brahman* (*brahman* with qualities). Consciousness unassociated with these *upādhis* (*nirguṇa brahman*) is the implied meaning of *tat*. Similarly, consciousness associated with individual ignorance and the qualities of limited knowledge and powers of action is the primary meaning of *tvam*, in other words, the individual (*jīva*). The implied meaning is again pure consciousness.[91] Like in the sentence, "This is that Devadatta," the primary meaning of *tat* and *tvam* are incompatible. Omniscience and omnipotence are opposed to limited knowledge and powers of creation. This conflict of primary meaning leads to the positing of identity at the level of pure consciousness, free from the superimpositions of *jiva*-hood and *iśvara*-hood. The exegesis involved here is not *jahallakṣaṇā* as in the sentence, "The village is on the Ganges," where the express meaning of the sentence is entirely abandoned. In the case of *tat tvam asi*, the contradiction is in part of the meaning only. Nor is it a case of *ajahallakṣaṇā*, because there is an incompatibility involved and part of the meaning has to be dropped. The identity between *ātman* and *brahman* is affirmed through *jahadajahallakṣaṇā*.

Śaṅkara categorically denies any interpretation of *tat tvam asi* other than the absolute identity of *ātman* and *brahman*.[92] The sentence is not comparable in meaning to the attribution of the idea of *Viṣṇu* on a *mūrti* and the contemplation of the latter as if it were *Viṣṇu*. The *mahāvākya* does not ask us to look upon *ātman* as if it were *brahman* but asserts a definite identity. Nor is it to be conceived figuratively (*gauṇa*), as in the sentence, "You are a lion." If identity were a mere figure of speech, *jñāna* alone could not lead to the discovery of oneness with *brahman* and the gain of *mokṣa*. *Tat tvam asi* is also not a mere eulogy (*stuti*). Śvetaketu is not an object of worship in the discussion, and it is no praise to *brahman* to be identified with Śvetaketu. A king is not complimented by being identified with his servant. Apart from these interpretations, Śaṅkara concludes, there is no other way of understanding the *mahāvākya*.

In Chapter 2, my aim was to highlight the deliberate case which Śaṅkara makes out for *śruti* as the only *pramāṇa* of *brahman*. In the light of the current opinions presented in the Introduction, it was necessary to clearly demonstrate, by citing crucial arguments from Śaṅkara's commentaries, that his recourse to *śruti* is not adventitious or dispensable. His rationale is firmly grounded in the argument that because of the very nature of *brahman*, knowledge through any other *pramāṇa* is inconceivable.

The discussion in the present chapter supplements these arguments and affords further insights into the way he regarded the *śruti* and its capacity to produce *brahmajñāna.* It was necessary to treat his understanding of the nature of *avidyā* because the capacity of the *śruti* to resolve this problem becomes credible in the light of this approach. Words can liberate where the problem is only a notional one of incorrect understanding. In this sense, the words of the *śruti* are not unlike those of the passerby who "produced" the tenth person. We cannot overemphasize the connection between Śaṅkara's arguments for the effectiveness of *śruti* as a *pramāṇa* and his view of the *ātman* as always available and accomplished. This all-important connection seems to have been entirely missed in current studies of the role of *śruti* in Śaṅkara. Śaṅkara clearly accepts that the knowledge derived through words is not an end in itself, if the object about which we are informed is as yet unaccomplished or not immediately available. If the object is available but simply misapprehended, correct knowledge through the words of a valid *pramāṇa* is all that is needed.

The significance of this distinction is further highlighted by one of the key grounds for his distinction between the *karmakāṇḍa* and the *jñānakāṇḍa.* The former does not fulfil itself in the knowledge or information which it provides. It tells us of the means for the achievement of ends not yet actualized. The *jñanakāṇḍa*, on the other hand, fulfills itself in its informative or revelatory role, for its object (the *ātman*) is already available. Its fruit (*phala*) is immediate. It was useful and necessary to focus on Śaṅkara's differences with the *Pūrva-Mīmāṁsā* over the status of the *Vedānta-vākyas*, for the points of divergence illuminated his understanding of *śruti* as a *pramāṇa.* The dispute clearly showed that he differentiates the *Vedānta-vākyas* from sentences which prompt engagement in action for the accomplishment of their end. The *Vedānta-vākyas* are not redundant just because they inform us of an immediately available entity. They have a sufficient and fruitful purport in eliminating our misunderstandings about the *ātman.* This end is accomplished through the grasping of the purport (*tātparya*) of the words which constitute the *pramāṇa.* There is no suggestion here that Śaṅkara conceives the knowledge gained from inquiry (*jijñāsā*) into the words of the *śruti* as provisional or hypothetical. There is no indication that it can or needs to be confirmed by any other source of knowledge. Śaṅkara's case for the competence of the *śruti* as a *pramāṇa* includes a view about the particular methods employed by *śruti* for overcoming the limitations of the words it is constrained to use. *Śruti* is unfolded by specific traditional methods of teaching, and I sought to highlight some of these in the concluding sections of the discussion. Words must be wielded in a manner which frees them from their limited denotations.

The significance of some of these arguments will be further developed in the next chapter, where we examine the nature of *brahmajñāna* and the process and context of its acquisition.

Chapter 4

The Nature of *Brahmajñāna* — The Process and Context of Its Acquisition

We have already considered, from different standpoints, Śaṅkara's vindication of the *śruti* as a *pramāṇa* of *brahman*. We have seen his responses to a total denial of its authority. We have also examined his arguments against those who accept the overall authority of the *Vedas* but forbid any independent purport to the *Vedānta-vākyas*, assigning them a subsidiary role to the ritualistic texts.

One of the primary concerns in the previous chapter was to explore, in the context of the inherent limitations of language, the problems confronting *śabda-pramāṇa* in its aim to inform us accurately of *brahman*. The methods of negation deny *brahman* to be a limited object of our knowledge and caution us about the difficulties of defining *brahman*. The result, however, is not a mere negativism. When we have seen that no word in its direct significance can define *brahman*, we are shown that definition is possible by the method of implication (*lakṣaṇā*). By a deft handling of rightly chosen and placed words, the latter can to some extent shed their finite apparel and become pointers of the infinite. This is one of the important reasons for Śaṅkara's emphasis on the role of the teacher and the traditional methods of instruction. The argument in Śaṅkara for the *lakṣaṇā* method of definition is a crucial one, for *śabda-pramāṇa* is of no avail unless we can properly apprehend the object of our investigation through it.

By considering Śaṅkara's conception of the nature of knowledge along with the mode and conditions of its attainment, I aim, in the present discussion, to clarify further the relationship between *śabda-pramāṇa*, *brahmajñāna*, and *mokṣa*.

4.1 The Character of Knowledge (*Jñāna*) and Its Differentiation from Activity (*Karman*)

Śaṅkara's distinction between the nature and aim of the *karmakāṇḍa* and *jñānakāṇḍa* is central to his entire Vedic exegesis. Another differentiation with wide implications is the one he makes between knowledge and activity.[1] An action (*karman*), secular or religious, as Śaṅkara understands it, is dependent on the individual (*puruṣatantram*) in the sense of involving options. It may or may not be done, or could be done in alternative ways. In moving from one place to another, for example, one may walk, use a vehicle, or perhaps not go at all. Options are sometimes even provided by the *Vedas* in respect to ritualistic activity. In the *atirātra* sacrifice, for instance, the sixteenth cup may or may not be used. Oblations can be offered before or after sunrise. It is only with reference to an action that is yet to be accomplished that the injunctions (*vidhi*) and prohibitions (*niṣedha*) as options, general rules, or exceptions are possible. Injunctions and prohibitions, possible in the case of activity, imply the existence of alternatives. They are redundant where an alternative is not possible. The distinctive features of any action, then, for Śaṅkara, are the presence of options, the possibility of injunctions and prohibitions, and its dependence on the individual person (*puruṣatantram*).

Knowledge, on the other hand, according to Śaṅkara, which involves an already accomplished object, does not involve options dependent on the human intellect. It must entirely conform to the nature of the object and is, therefore, solely dependent on the thing itself (*vastutantram*). Knowledge is centered on the object and is as true as the object. It does not involve any choice as far as the nature of its object is concerned. Fire, for instance, cannot be known as either hot or cold. The valid knowledge of a post, for example, cannot be of the form "This is a post, a man or some unknown object," "This is a post" is valid knowledge because it is dependent on the object and conforms to its nature. *Brahman* is no exception to this fact. Being an already accomplished object, *brahmajñāna* is also dependent on *brahman*.

> An exception can be made with regard to some part of an action, where the general rule would otherwise apply. For example, in the dictum, "Killing no animals except in sacrifices" (CH.U. 8.15.1), the killing of animals prohibited by the general rule is allowed in a special case, viz. a sacrifice such as the *Jyotiṣṭoma*. But that will not apply to *Brahman*, the Reality. You cannot establish *Brahman*, the one without a second, by a general rule, and then make an exception in one part of It; for It cannot have any part, simply because It is one without a second. Similarly, an option also is inadmissible. For example, in the injunctions "One should not use the vessel *Ṣoḍaśi* in the *Atirātra* sacrifice" and "One should use the vessel *Ṣoḍaśi* in the *Atirātra* sacrifice"; an option is possible, as using or not using the vessel depends on a person's choice. But with regard to *Brahman*, the Reality, there cannot be any option about Its being either dual or monistic, for the Self is not a matter depending on a person's choice.[2]

Following from this general distinction between knowledge and activity is Śaṅkara's very important distinction between knowledge and mental activity. In this context, his definition of an action is significant.

> An action is in evidence where the injunction about it occurs independently of the nature of the thing concerned and where it is subject to the activities of the human mind.[3]

As an illustration of a mental action, Śaṅkara gives examples such as, "When the priest is about to utter *vauṣat*, he shall meditate mentally on the deity for whom the libation is taken up" or "One should mentally meditate on (the deity identified with) evening."[4] Even though these forms of meditation (*dhyāna*) are mental, Śaṅkara contends they are still dependent on the human person (*puruṣatantram*) for they involve the options of being done, not done, or done in a different way. Knowledge (*jñāna*), on the other hand, is generated entirely by a *pramāṇa* which has for its object the thing as it exists. It cannot be effected in a way different from the object of its inquiry. Śaṅkara does not deny that *jñāna* is mental but argues for its difference from *dhyāna* (meditation). Another example which he offers helps to clarify his distinction.[5] The injunction, "O Gautama, a man is surely a fire" (CH.U. 5.7.1), "O Gautama, a woman is surely a fire" (CH.U. 5.8.1), is a mental action where a choice is involved. There is no concern here for the real nature of fire. If, however, fire is to be known as fire, this is a case of *jñāna* which can only be the result of a valid *pramāṇa* and does not involve any human option. The real nature of the object cannot be disregarded. *Brahmajñāna* must conform to the nature of *brahman*, and the *pramāṇa* involved is *śabda-pramāṇa*.[6]

It is clear from Śaṅkara's discussion that when he speaks of a mental action, he is identifying it with what is termed as *upāsanā* or *dhyāna* (meditation), and he clearly denies *brahman* as an object of this kind of activity.[7] It is important to pursue this distinction in some detail, for it is germane to our consideration of the role of *anubhava*. The latter is generally presented as the culmination of an act of meditation or contemplation and seen as the true *pramāṇa* of *brahman*.

There are several points in his commentaries where Śaṅkara defines *upāsanā*.[8] This *Bṛhadāraṇyaka Upaniṣad bhāṣya* definition is typical.

> Meditation is mentally approaching the form of the deity or the like as it is presented by the eulogistic portions of the *Vedas* relating to objects of meditation and concentrating on it, excluding conventional notions, till one is completely identified with it as with one's body, conventionally regarded as one's Self.[9]

Śaṅkara mentions four kinds of meditations.[10]

1. *Sampad upāsanā*: This is an imaginary identification between two dissimilar objects with some similar attributes. For example, the mind has endless modifications and the *viśvedevas* (gods) are innumerable. On the basis of this resemblance, the mind is contemplated upon as the *viśvedevas*.

The result of this particular meditation is that the *upāsaka* (meditator) attains infinite worlds.[11] In another example, the bricks (*yājuṣmati*) used for building the altar for the *agnihotra* are three hundred and sixty in number. This is equal to the number of oblations, which are daily offered throughout the year. By meditating upon the resemblance between the bricks, the oblations and the days of the year, one attains identity with Fire, the *Prajāpati* called the year.[12] In *sampad upāsanā*, the inferior factor (e.g., the mind) is contemplated as the superior one (e.g., *viśvedevas*), and primacy is accorded to the latter. In the case of the opponent's argument that *brahmajñāna* involves *sampad upāsanā*, the parallel is that because of a similarity of consciousness (*caitanya*), *brahman* is merely imagined in the *jīva*.

2. *Adhyāsa upāsanā*: In this form of meditation, there is no necessary similarity between the two factors. "One should meditate thus: 'The mind is *Brahman*' " (CH.U. 3.18.1) and "The instruction is: 'The sun is *Brahman*' " (CH.U. 3.19.1) are examples of *adhyāsa upāsanā*. The difference between *sampad* and *adhyāsa upāsanā* is that in the latter, primacy is accorded to the locus (*ālambana*) and not to the superimposed object.[13] In the case of *brahmajñāna*, the opponent's contention is that *brahman* is only superimposed on the *jīva* and the latter is contemplated as *brahman*.

3. *Kriyāyoga upāsanā*: This meditation is based upon some mode of activity. Here the two factors are distinct but are contemplated as one, owing to a similarity of action. *Chāndogya Upaniṣad* 4.3.1–4, for example, describes *Vāyu* as the great absorber at the time of cosmic dissolution. Similarly, at the time of sleep, all organs of the individual are said to merge in the vital air (*prāṇa*). Because of this resemblance in activity, *prāṇa* is contemplated as *Vāyu*. Similarly, the *jīva* is contemplated as *brahman* because of its association with the act of causing to grow (i.e., because of a common root-meaning of "causing to grow").

4. *Saṁskāra upāsanā*: In the *upaṁśu* sacrifice, there is the injunction that the sacrificer's wife should look at the ghee for its purification. The purification of the ghee is a subsidiary action to the performance of the sacrifice. Similarly, the opponent's argument here is that as a subsidiary purificatory rite, the *jīva* ought to contemplate himself as *brahman* before the commencement of any ritual. Such a meditation purifies the agent of the specific ritual.

Śaṅkara emphatically argues against the idea that the *Vedānta-vākyas* are meant for meditation of any of the above four kinds.[14] To suggest this, he adds, would do violence to the purport of the *mahāvākyas* whose clear intention is to declare the real identity obtaining between the *jīva* and *brahman*. A sentence such as "One who knows *Brahman* becomes *Brahman*" (MU.U. 3.2.9), declaring the simultaneity of *jñāna* and identity, cannot be reconciled with the view that *Vedānta-vākyas* are meant for meditation. This view also, Śaṅkara adds, contradicts the clearly mentioned result of the knowledge of the already obtaining identity between *jīva* and *brahman*.[15]

The significance of Śaṅkara's careful distinction between knowledge and meditation can never be overestimated in the context of the function of the *śruti* in giving rise to *brahmajñāna*. It is perhaps a conveniently overlooked distinction, which repudiates the view that the *Vedānta-vākyas* merely afford an indirect knowledge to be then contemplated upon in order to produce an experience (*anubhava*) giving direct insight into the nature of *brahman*. Along with all the other evidence we have considered, it lends support to the direct relationship which Śaṅkara sees in respect of the *śruti*, *brahmajñāna*, and *mokṣa*. The substance of Śaṅkara's distinction between *jñāna* and *upāsanā* is that the action of *upāsanā* is possible where the real nature of the contemplated object is irrelevant and where the action is directed towards the production of a hitherto nonexistent result.[16] Where there is a question of knowing the nature of an object as it is, for which all that is required is the appropriate *pramāṇa*, then it is a question of *jñāna*. Meditation is nowhere elevated by Śaṅkara to the status of a *pramāṇa*. New knowledge is not produced by contemplating, as if they were identical, two known and distinct entities. *Upāsanā* does not produce the identity of the contemplated objects and if, as in the case of *jīva* and *brahman*, the identity is an already obtaining but unknown one, a *pramāṇa* is required for its revelation. If the identity is not an already existing fact, it cannot be produced by knowledge alone. It is exceedingly clear that in Śaṅkara's view, the relationship between *śruti* and *brahman* is that obtaining between a means of revelation and revealed object.[17] *Upāsanā*, however, is not entirely futile in the process of acquiring *brahmajñāna*. Rightly practiced, it purifies the mind and develops its powers of concentration. These are important prerequisites for the acquisition of *brahmajñāna*.[18]

4.2 The Simultaneity of Knowledge and Freedom

The general understanding that *śabda-pramāṇa* has only mediate or provisional validity as a means to the accomplishment of *mokṣa* is also clearly refuted when assessed alongside very important, but generally ignored, passages from Śaṅkara's commentaries concerning the coincidence of *brahmajñāna* and *mokṣa*.

It is his often-repeated contention, supported by numerous scriptural references, that release is simultaneous with the gain of knowledge. He is emphatic in his denial of the necessity of any intervening action between the two. In fact, from the standpoint of Śaṅkara, it is not even accurate to say that *mokṣa* is the fruit or effect of *jñāna*. *Mokṣa*, being identical with *brahman*, is ever-accomplished and eternal. The function of *jñāna* lies in the removal of obstacles to the appreciation of the ever-liberated Self.[19]

The relationship is comparable, Śaṅkara says, to that obtaining between standing and singing where no other action intervenes.[20]

> In connection with the subject matter of injunctions are to be found certain acts which are like the *Agnihotra* to be performed subsequent to the understanding of the text, through a combination of numerous accessories, to wit, the agent, etc. Unlike this, nothing remains to be performed here within the domain of the higher knowledge; but all actions cease simultaneously with the comprehension of the meaning of the sentences, inasmuch as nothing remains to be done apart from continuance in mere knowledge revealed by the words.[21]

In fact, adds Śaṅkara, the absence of any intervening action constitutes the very beauty and glory of *brahmajñāna*. The gain of knowledge alone leads to the fulfillment of all human desires.[22] Even the gods cannot frustrate the fruit of *brahmajñāna* (i.e., the attainment of *brahman*), since the latter consists merely in the cessation of *avidyā*. Even as in our everyday world a form is revealed to the eyes as soon as it is properly illumined in light, similarly *avidyā* and its effects are negated once *brahmajñāna* is gained.

> They [the gods] succeed in their efforts to put obstacles only in the case of one who seeks a result which is other than the Self and is separated by space, time, and causation but not with regard to this sage, who becomes their Self simultaneously with the awakening of knowledge, and is not separated by space, time, and causation, for there is no room for opposition here.[23]

We have already considered the significance of Śaṅkara's distinction between knowledge and meditation. In denying the necessity for any intervening action between *jñāna* and *mokṣa*, he is very explicit about the redundancy of *upāsanā*. His *bhāsya* on *Bṛhadāraṇyaka Upaniṣad* 1.4.7 includes a fascinating discussion in which he considers several related objections from the proponents of meditation.[24] Here the opposing view is that knowledge and meditation are synonymous. The argument is that in response to its injunctions concerning sacrifices, the *Vedas* supply the relevant information about the nature of the rituals, the materials, and the methods to be used. Similarly, in response to the injunction to meditate, we are told that the *ātman* is to be the object of meditation through the mind by means of the practice of renunciation, continence, etc. All the *Upaniṣad* texts dealing with the *ātman*, it is contended, should be seen as part of this meditative injunction. This meditation, it is argued, generates a special kind of knowledge about the *ātman* which eliminates *avidyā*. Ignorance is not eliminated merely by the *Vedānta-vākyas* revealing the nature of the Self. The resemblance, if not identity, between this objection and the more modern interpretations that the mediate knowledge of the *Vedānta-vākyas* must be converted into *anubhava* is remarkable.[25] Śaṅkara's unhesitating reply is forceful and unequivocal.

> Except the knowledge that arises from the dictum setting forth the nature of the Self and refuting the non-Self, there is nothing to be done, either mentally or outwardly. An injunction is appropriate only where, over and above the knowledge that arises immediately from hearing a sentence of the nature of an injunction, an activity on the part of a man is easily understood, as in sentences like "One who desires heaven must perform the new and full moon sacrifices." The knowledge arising from a sentence enjoining these sacrifices is certainly not the performance of them. This depends on considerations such as whether a person is entitled to perform them. But apart from the knowledge arising from such passages delineating the Self as "Not this, not this," there is no scope for human activity as in the case of the new and full moon sacrifices, etc., because, that knowledge puts a stop to all activity.[26]

Sentences such as, *tat tvam asi*, Śaṅkara adds, do not suggest the necessity for any action over and above the knowledge of *brahman* which they impart. The ritual analogy is inappropriate here. Unlike the ritual, where, after it is enjoined, one wishes to know its nature, materials, and method, once the meaning of the texts defining *brahman* is understood, there is no further curiosity.[27]

Brahmajñāna, because it is identical with the nature of *brahman*, which is eternal and unchanging, is independent of time, place, and circumstances.[28] Its function is neither to create anything anew nor to alter the nature of an existent entity. Like other valid *pramāṇas*, its role is entirely informative and revelatory. Because bondage is only a notional problem resulting from a mental confusion of mutually superimposing the Self and non-Self, the *Vedānta-vākyas* are self-sufficiently adequate to the task of removing ignorance. This is itself the long-desired freedom, for bondage and limitation were always only imagined on the ever-free, full, and joyful *ātman*.

4.3 The Fourfold Means (*Sādhana-catuṣṭaya*)

There is no lack of definitive statements in the writings of Śaṅkara on the relationship between *brahmajñāna* and *mokṣa*. The *Vedānta-vākyas* themselves, without any physical or mental accessories, liberate; knowledge is itself freedom. *Brahmajñāna*, however, although mental like other kinds of knowledge, is nonpareil. Generally, our knowledge is involved with the apprehension of objects other than the knower.[29] It is the knowledge of things which can be objectified. In the case of *brahmajñāna*, the knower is the subject of inquiry and investigation. *Brahman*, the entity to be known, is unique. It is full, complete, without lack or want, eternally peaceful, and of the nature of joy. *Brahmajñāna* is not the vague awareness of a remote *brahman* to be of this nature. If it were, the inquiry (*jijñāsā*) would have little relevance to the inquirer's problem. Narada's angst in the *Chāndogya Upaniṣad* is quite typical of the sort of predicament and unaccountable anguish which motivates the inquirer towards *brahmajñāna*. After listing his accomplishments and mastery of various subjects, he declares his helplessness before the teacher, Sanatkumāra.

> It has been heard by me from persons like your reverence that one who knows the Self passes beyond sorrow; — I am in sorrow;-please Sir, make me pass beyond that sorrow.[30]

Brahmajñāna is the appreciation of oneself to be of the unique nature of *brahman*, and the receptacle of this knowledge is the mind (*antaḥkaraṇa*).[31] If *brahmajñāna* is to be meaningfully and successfully attained, it is imperative that the mind enjoys a certain disposition. If the *ātman* to be known is all peace and fullness, such a knowledge cannot occur in a mind which is in perpetual agitation and which entertains countless desires. The beauty and joy of a Self which shines in everything cannot be discovered in a mind lacking in compassion and love. The significance of *brahmajñāna* will be lost to one who has not risen above the yearning and pursuit after limited ends. It is vital here, therefore, that the receptacle of knowledge relatively conforms to the nature of the object which it seeks to know. Such an identification is not generally required where other kinds of knowledge are concerned. Another reason for emphasizing the indispensability of the right mental disposition is that *brahmajñāna*, once successfully accomplished, must be continuously retained. Outside of certain contexts and times, there is no need for a constant remembrance of knowledge centered on objects other than the Self. There is no necessity, for example, to be continuously aware and attentive of one's knowledge of geology. *Brahmajñāna*, however, is not rewarding unless it is fully integrated and assimilated. Even as one naturally and effortlessly assumes oneself to be limited and identified with the body and its manifold dispositions, so one should spontaneously know oneself to be limitless and complete. For this, the vision of oneself must be held uninterruptedly in one's awareness, and this demands certain mental qualities.

It is the lack of these qualities which renders *brahmajñāna* difficult of attainment.[32] Knowledge itself, once it has emerged, requires no accessories for giving rise to *mokṣa*. Its emergence, however, is dependent on various factors.[33] Śaṅkara emphasizes that even inquiry with the aid of the right *pramāṇa* does not produce knowledge in one who lacks self-control and austerity and who is arrogant.[34]

> Though the intellect in all beings is intrinsically able to make the Self known, still, being polluted by such blemishes as attachment to external objects, etc., it becomes agitated and impure, and does not, like a stained mirror or ruffled water, make the reality of the Self known, though It is ever at hand. The favorableness of the intellect comes about when it continues to be transparent and tranquil on having been made clean like a mirror, water, etc., by the removal of pollution caused by the dirt of attachment, springing from the contact of the senses and sense object.[35]

It is important to clarify and emphasize this neglected aspect of *brahmajñāna* because the role generally assigned to *anubhava* is partly influenced by the wish to demonstrate that *jñāna* is not only a process at the cognitive level but involves a transformation of will and emotion. It is perhaps felt that a cognitive change alone is inadequate for the commitment to a new understanding of oneself. It is the search for a level of verification beyond the authority of the *Vedānta-vākyas.* It is not necessary, however, to misrepresent Śaṅkara's understanding of the *śruti* in order to make this point. The meaningful emergence of *brahmajñāna*, as we are seeking to demonstrate, is dependent on a transformation and involvement of intellect, will, and emotion.

There are references to these virtues and their roles as prerequisites throughout the writings of Śaṅkara. Commenting on *Brahma-sūtra* 1.1.1, "Hence (is to be undertaken) thereafter a deliberation on *Brahman*," Śaṅkara argues that the word *atha* (thereafter) should be understood in the sense of "immediate succession" only.[36] The problem then, he says, is to determine what is that which immediately precedes the inquiry into *brahman* as a prerequisite of its success. He denies that the inquiry into *brahman* (*brahmajijñāsā*) must be preceded by a knowledge of rituals acquired by an inquiry into the first part of the Vedic texts (*karmajijñāsā*). Between *brahmajijñāsā* and *karmajijñāsā* there are differences of subject matter, result, aspirant, and connection between texts and results.[37] The predispositions for *brahmajijñāsā* have been classified by Śaṅkara under four headings:

1. *Viveka*
2. *Vairāgya*
3. *Śamādisādhanasampatti*
4. *Mumukṣutvam*

Before considering each factor separately, it is important to note the close interrelationship which exists among these dispositions. The acquisition of one often presupposes and implies the other. As far as the aspirant is concerned, it is not the perfection of these qualities which is demanded. In fact, such a perfection is not possible without *brahmajñāna*, when these qualities are spontaneously manifest. What is required is a disposition toward and a relative mastery of the fourfold means. As the inquiry proceeds and understanding grows, the qualities emerge in a new depth and profundity.

1. *Viveka*: This is defined by Śaṅkara as the discrimination between the real (*nitya*) and unreal (*anitya*).[38] As a prerequisite of the inquiry into *brahman*, Śaṅkara's definition cannot be taken as an example of an accomplished understanding of reality. In that case, there is no further need for inquiry. It is perhaps better understood as the capacity to undertake the investigation which leads to the distinguishing of the real from the unreal. Various forms of reasoning are employed by both teacher and *śruti*, and the qualified student (*adhikārī*) should be able to quickly assess and assimilate the impact of these. The quality of *viveka* underlines the necessity for focusing our capacity for rational thought and analysis upon our quest for *brahmajñāna*. The deliberation upon *brahman* is in the form of an inquiry (*jijñāsā*), during which doubts about the validity of the means of knowledge and about the object investigated are aroused. Such doubts are to be resolved by proper application of the prescribed forms of investigation (e.g., *ṣaḍliṅga*). The student also has to contend with the views of rival Vedic and non-Vedic systems. The structure of Śaṅkara's commentaries in the form of rival view (*pūrvapakṣa*) and refutation (*siddhānta*) is an excellent example of the subtlety, detail, and fervor of traditional debates.[39] The necessity for an alert and discriminating intellect is emphasized both in the *Upaniṣads* and by Śaṅkara.[40] While the inquirer will not have a full grasp of the nature of the real at the initiation of the inquiry, one must have understood, to some extent, the limitations of the noneternal. This partly explains the motivation to seek out a teacher and is a sufficient incentive for continuation of the inquiry.

2. *Vairāgya*: This is defined by Śaṅkara as nonattachment to the enjoyment of the results of one's actions here or hereafter. The dispassion, which is a necessary prerequisite of *brahmajijñāsā*, is aroused by the appreciation of the limitations of noneternal pursuits. It bears a direct relationship, therefore, to *viveka*. The student will not yet know that the fullness which is sought through innumerable desires and activities is

not different from the Self. One will have discovered, however, that one continues to want and to feel insufficient inspite of the struggles to fulfill successive desires. One has a deep intimation that there is some lasting and reconciling purpose in existence. Naciketā, the exemplar of *vairāgya* in the *Upaniṣad*, approaches the teacher Yama for *brahmajñāna*.[41] As an appraisal of his competence and resolve, Yama tries to dissuade him from yearning for knowledge by luring him with the offer of unmitigated sensual pleasures. Naciketā, as Śaṅkara says, was as unperturbed as a vast lake.

> O Yama, ephemeral are these, and they waste away the vigour of all the senses that a man has. All life, without exception, is short indeed. Let the vehicles be yours alone; let the dances and songs be yours.
>
> Man is not satisfied with wealth. Now that we have met you, we shall get wealth. We shall live as long as you will rule it. But the boon that is worth praying for by me is that alone (i.e., *brahmajñāna*).[42]

Śaṅkara sums up very well the dispassionate state of mind which is a precondition for approaching the teacher.

> In the universe there is nothing that is *akṛta*, a non-product, for all the worlds are effects of *karma*; and being products of action, they are impermanent. The idea is that there is nothing that is eternal. All actions are productive of transitory things, since all effects of actions are only of four kinds — they can be produced, acquired, purified, or modified; over and above these, action has no other distinctive result. But I am desirous of the eternal, immortal, fearless, unchanging, unmoving, absolute Entity and not of its opposite.[43]

Vairḡya, therefore, presupposes a certain degree of reflection and analysis upon one's experiences. *Brahmajñāna* is of the nature of a solution which becomes relevant only when the problem that informs it is intensely experienced.

It is important to note that the dispassion mentioned by Śaṅkara extends also to results that may be enjoyed in heavenly worlds. The transitoriness of the results of actions is absolute. Even the fruits of meritorious actions, which lead to the attainment of heavenly worlds, are limited. Upon their exhaustion, one is plunged back into the world of mortality.

> They, having enjoyed that spacious world of *Svarga*, their merit exhausted, enter the world of mortals; thus following the *dharma* of the Triad, desiring (objects of) desires, they attain the state of going and returning.[44]

Vairāgya, as a prerequisite of *brahmajñāna*, is not an attitude of escapism born out of a fear of life. It is associated with a serious reflection upon the nature of one's fundamental pursuit in life and the inherent limitations of finite activities to lead directly to that result. *Kaṭha Upaniṣad* describes the human choice as one between the good (*śreyaḥ*) and the pleasurable (*preyaḥ*). Good befalls the discriminating one who opts for *śreyaḥ*. The shortsighted, who aspire for *preyaḥ*, fall short of the supreme human purpose.[45]

3. *Śamādisādhanasampat*: These six accomplishments are: *śama, dama, uparati, titikṣā, samādhāna*, and *śraddhā*. *Śama* is generally defined as mental control.[46] It is a disposition closely allied to the acquisition of *viveka* and *vairāgya*. A mind which has shed a multiplicity of personal desires, having come to appreciate their limitations, is more disposed to quietness and restraint. Desires for various objects of enjoyment are, according to Śaṅkara, the principal causes of mental agitation. *Vairāgya*, therefore, is conducive to *śama*.

> By convincing oneself of the illusoriness of sense-objects through an investigation into their real nature, and by cultivating indifference to worldly objects, the mind can be restrained from sense-objects and brought back to the Self wherein to abide firmly.[47]

Śama is a discovery which accompanies the unfolding of *brahmajñāna* rather than a forceful restraint. It is vital for the deep attentiveness necessary in a sustained inquiry. In a person of firm knowledge, it is a natural quietness and mental restfulness consequent upon the fulfillment of all desires in the knowledge of the Self.[48]

Dama is the control or restraint of the sense organs and the organs of action. It reflects and presupposes the acquisition of *śama*. It is the natural tendency of the sense organs to be attracted to their respective sense objects, but it is possible by discrimination to turn the attention inward for the knowledge of the Self.[49] The relationship between *śama* and *dama* or between intellect, mind, and sense organs is beautifully described in the chariot analogy of the *Kaṭha Upaniṣad*.[50]

Uparati (withdrawal) seems to differ little from *śama* and *dama* but would seem to indicate the actual state of accomplishment achieved by the practice of both. Sadānanda offers an alternative definition of *uparati* as indicating the formal renunciation of obligatory duties in accordance with the injunctions of *śruti*.[51]

Titikṣā (fortitude) is the patient endurance of suffering. It is the cheerful accommodation of the many unpleasant experiences in our relations with our environment and the refusal to unnecessarily linger or lament over them. In the *Bhagavadgītā*, it is presented as the tolerance of opposites, and the one who achieves success in it is said to be fit for immortality.[52]

In terms of human relationships, it expresses itself in an unwillingness to seek redress or revenge. *Titikṣā* is a quality born out of an awareness of the profundity of one's inquiry and a refusal to be diverted. A mind that is easily troubled in the face of the unpleasant, or aroused to heights of excitement in encountering the pleasant, lacks the poise and composure necessary for *brahmajijñāsā*.

Samādhanā is single-pointedness of mind. It is the ability to focus one's attention upon the object of inquiry until the end is attained. It is an expression of commitment and determination in pursuit of the ideal.

Śraddhā is faith in the authority of the *pramāṇa* and the teacher who unfolds it. Its importance as a prerequisite is constantly emphasized by Śaṅkara.

> Though when a certain fact has been established by reasoning and scriptural authority, it is always understood to be so (and true), — yet, in the case of extremely subtle things, a man who has his mind taken up by external things, and follows the natural bent of his activities, could find it difficult to understand if he were not imbued with a large degree of faith.[53]

4. *Mumukṣutvam* is a burning desire for *mokṣa*. It is the flame which is fed by all the aforementioned qualities. Unless there is a deep earnestness and sincerity of purpose, efforts will be mediocre.[54]

Equipped with these qualities, the student is ready to undertake *brahmajijñāsā* and fit to be instructed.[55] It is the qualification of the aspirant by virtue of possessing these prerequisites which ensures that *brahmajñāna* is immediate in its results and is not a mere theoretical possibility unable to effect a total transformation of vision. In their absence, the declarations of *śruti* seem indirect, and there is perhaps the suspicion that something over and beyond the *pramāṇa* itself is required for effecting *jñāna*. As noted in the Introduction, *anubhava* is presented as that additional *pramāṇa* which is required for converting the theory of the *śruti* into realized fact. But this denies the direct connection which Śaṅkara affirms between the *Vedānta-vākyas* and the results they aim at, and it undermines their status as a self-sufficient *pramāṇa*. Śaṅkara clearly distinguishes *Vedānta-vākyas*, whose results are immediate, from statements which impel the individual into action for the production of a result. To claim that he advocates a further verification for the *Vedānta-vākyas* is to deny the clear evidence of his commentaries and to miss the significance and subtlety of his conception of *śruti* as a *pramāṇa*. It is also inconsistent with his metaphysics about the nature of *brahman* and the problem of *avidyā*. Śaṅkara does not conceive *brahmajñāna*, as unfolded by the *śruti* and the teacher, as a hypothesis needing the aid of another *pramāṇa* for its certification. It is a means of knowledge which, in the absence of obstacles, is immediate in its results. *Sādhana-catuṣṭaya* is meant for eliminating some of these obstacles and preparing the way for *jñāna*.

4.4 *Karmayoga* as Preparation for *Brahmajñāna*

The collective aim of *sādhana-catuṣṭaya* is the attainment of what is termed in *Advaita* as *citta-śuddhi* (mental purity). *Karmayoga*, in Śaṅkara's view, is intended for the accomplishment of the same end.

The successful attainment of *jñāna* requires that the *antaḥkaraṇa* should relatively assume the nature of *brahman*. To know *brahman*, which is absolute peace, the mind should enjoy an alert poise and equanimity. One obstacle to the discovery of this serenity is the helpless subjection to likes and dislikes. These opposites are termed in the *Bhagavadgītā* as *rāga* and *dveṣa*, and their mastery is always mentioned as a precondition of *brahmajñana*.

> Love and hate lie towards the object of each sense; let none become subject to these two; for, they are his enemies.[56]

> He should be known as a perpetual renouncer who neither hates nor desires; for, free from the pairs of opposites, O mighty-armed, he is easily set free from bondage.[57]

Conversely, the description of the *jñāni* in the *Bhagavadgītā* always includes reference to the triumph over *rāga* and *dveṣa*.

> He who, without attachment anywhere, on meeting with anything good or bad, neither exults nor hates, his knowledge is steady.[58]

> He attains peace, who, self-controlled, approaches objects with the senses devoid of love and hatred and brought under his own control.[59]

The subjection to *rāga* and *dveṣa* is most apparent in one's response to the results of various activities. Hoping to find a joy that is ever evasive, the human being entertains desires of every description and engages in action for their accomplishment. If the result of the action is favorable, one is elated. If it is not, one is dejected and disappointed. One is, therefore, constantly tossed between these pairs of opposites.

> The very desire and aversion which are opposed to each other like heat and cold, which, arising in connection with pleasure and pain and their cause, occur to every being in its turn, are known as pairs (*dvandva*).

> Now, when desire and aversion arise on the occurrence of pleasure and pain or of the causes thereof, they cause delusion in all beings and create obstruction to the rise of a knowledge of the Supreme Reality, the Self, by subjugation to themselves the intelligence of those beings. To one whose mind is subject to the passions of desire and aversion, there cannot indeed arise a knowledge of things as they are, even of the external world; and it needs no saying that to a man whose intellect is overpowered by passion there cannot arise a knowledge of the Innermost Self, inasmuch as there are obstacles in this way.[60]

The solution does not lie in the abandonment of actions, as this is clearly impossible. Withdrawal from pursuits, as Kṛṣṇa points out (B.G. 3:5-6), without genuine mental detachment is self-deceptive.

> None, verily, even for an instant, ever remains doing no action; for everyone is driven helpless to action by the energies of Nature.
>
> He who, restraining the organs of action, sits thinking in his mind of the objects of the senses, self-deluded, he is said to be one of false conduct.

It is not possible also to perform actions without expecting a result, even though *karmayoga* is often spoken of as motiveless action. It is obvious that action, even of the simplest kind, presupposes a motive and the expectation of a result.

Karmayoga, as envisaged by Śaṅkara, is a method of neutralizing *rāga* and *dveṣa* while remaining in the field of activity. It involves the recognition that while we have to perform actions, the results are beyond our control.[61] Those results are determined by *īśvara* in His role as distributor of the fruits of actions (*karmadhyakṣa* or *karma-phala-dātā*). Therefore, whether the results are favorable or unfavorable, they are acceptable as coming from Him. *Karmayoga* is best described as *prasāda-buddhi*. Even as the sacramental food (*prasāda*), distributed after the performance of a ritual, is gladly accepted with no regard to its actual nature because it is visualized as coming from God, so also are the results of ordinary actions seen. This reverential acceptance of results implies the dedication of the action to *īśvara*. In this sense, therefore, *karmayoga* presupposes, and is in fact indistinguishable from, *bhaktiyoga*. Without an attitude of surrender and devotion, it is not possible to gladly accept all results as determined by God, and Śaṅkara does not particularly attempt to distinguish *karmayoga* and *bhaktiyoga*. The worship attitude becomes the all-pervasive factor in everything.

> He offers all actions to *Isvara*, in the faith that "I act for His sake" as a servant acts for the sake of the master.... The result of actions so done is only purity of mind, and nothing else.[62]

By this outlook, actions which can normally be an obstacle to the pursuit of freedom become, as a means of mental purification (*citta-śuddhi*), an indirect aid to its accomplishment.

> When a man who is qualified for (*Karmayoga*) performs obligatory works without attachment and without a longing for results, his inner sense (*antaḥkaraṇa*) unsoiled by desire for results and regenerated by (the performance of) obligatory works, becomes pure. When pure and tranquil, the inner sense is fit for contemplation of the Self.[63]

> Though the Religion of Works, — which, as a means of attaining worldly prosperity, is enjoined on the several castes and religious orders, — leads the devotee to the region of the *Devas* and the like, still, when practiced in a spirit of complete devotion to the Lord and without regard to the (immediate) results, it conduces to the purity of mind (*sattva-suddhi*). The man whose mind is pure is competent to tread the path of knowledge, and to him comes knowledge; and thus (indirectly) the Religion of Works forms also a means to the Supreme Bliss.[64]

The psychological end result of *karmayoga* is the absence of egotistic elation at the successful accomplishment of an action and dejection in failure. *Rāga* and *dveṣa* are thus effectively neutralized, and the mind abides in a quiet joyfulness even as it does in the culmination of every act of worship. It becomes receptive and competent for *jñāna*. It is obvious, therefore, that *karmayoga* is not envisaged by Śaṅkara as a method for its own sake. It is intended primarily as a preparation relevant to one who has the acquisition of *jñāna* in view but is not yet fit to embark directly upon *brahmajijñāsā*. *Karmayoga*, according to Śaṅkara, was recommended to Arjuna because of his incompetence for *jñāna*[65]. As a preparatory attitude, it is redundant after knowledge is gained.[66] This does not imply that the *jñāni* is debarred from engagement in action. Being free from personal desires, one can act, like *īśvara*, for the welfare of others and in order to set an example of right action. In the case of the active *jñāni*, however, there is no delusion about the Self and actions are not accompanied by any sense of doership.[67] The *karmayogi* is still acting in the hope of attaining freedom; the *jñāni* acts out of his already accomplished freedom.

Karmayoga does not, in Śaṅkara, describe a specific type of action. It is essentially an attitude with reference to the performance of all actions. It is, in itself, not a direct means to *mokṣa* for, like meditation, it is not a *pramāṇa*. Any aid to *jñāna* can only serve it indirectly by facilitating its emergence.

This chapter has highlighted salient aspects of Śaṅkara's understanding of the relationship between *śruti*, *brahmajñāna*, and *mokṣa*. We consider Śaṅkara's distinction between *jñāna* (knowledge) and *karman* (activity), which is totally overlooked in contemporary discussions, to be fundamental to a correct understanding of his conception of *śruti*, and its direct role in producing *brahmajñāna*. This distinction is the basis of his differentiation between *upāsanā* or *dhyāna* (meditation) and *jñāna*. In *dhyāna* or *upāsanā* one is not concerned with gaining correct knowledge of an object. In the examples Śaṅkara has given, the object meditated upon may be imagined or conceived in a manner different from its real nature. When, on the other hand, a decision is made to obtain knowledge (*jñāna*), there is no choice or question of conceiving the object differently from what it is. *Jñāna* of any kind is produced only by an appropriate *pramāṇa*, and in the case of *brahman*, the *Vedānta-vākyas* constitute the only valid *pramāṇa*.

We wish to strongly reiterate Śaṅkara's clear conviction that the sentences of the *Upaniṣads* are concerned with imparting *jñāna* of an already available *brahman* and are not at all meant for *dhyāna* or *upāsanā* of the kinds mentioned by him. The simple point, perhaps missed because of this very simplicity, is that these sentences fulfil their purpose in being correctly understood. Whereas meditation is a mental activity concerned with the production of a hitherto nonexistent result, *jñāna* informs us of already existing things. The *Vedānta-vākyas* tell us something about *brahman*, and that information, correctly understood, constitutes their aim. This conclusion is a challenge to the view that Śaṅkara understands knowledge gathered from the *śruti* as merely hypothetical. *Śruti* is not a *pramāṇa* if it fails to engender *pramā* (valid knowledge). We find it impossible, therefore, to support the conclusion of de Smet and others that even after grasping the purport of the *śruti* and eliminating all doubts, *jñāna*, in Śaṅkara, still awaits further verification.[68] This is a very central and crucial issue on which we differ radically. De Smet, after a detailed and lucid discussion of Śaṅkara's methods of exegesis, has missed the cardinal implication of his acceptance of *śruti* as the *pramāṇa* of *brahmajñāna*.[69]

I find further support for my conclusions in the numerous passages in which Śaṅkara affirms the simultaneity of *jñāna* and *mokṣa*. His position is that between *jñāna* (conceived as a clear comprehension of the purport of the *Upaniṣads*) and *mokṣa*, there is no necessity for any kind of intervening activity. I wish here to emphasize his refutation of the contention that it is meditation, over and above the understanding of the meaning of the *Vedānta-vākyas*, which gives rise to knowledge capable of destroying *avidyā*. I have pointed to the identity of this contention with current views. Nothing more that the understanding of the nature of the Self and non-Self is required.

I suspect that one reason for the positing of *anubhava* as the *pramāṇa* of *brahman* is the wish to show that *jñāna* is not only a cognitive transformation but also carries the conviction of will and emotion. It is not necessary, however, to overturn Śaṅkara's epistemology to make this point. The discussion on *sādhana-catuṣṭaya* was introduced to demonstrate that the successful attainment of *jñāna* implied a transformation of intellect, will, and emotion. These qualities are the prerequisites for inquiry into the *śruti* and for the successful gain of *jñāna*. It is in the absence of these prerequisites that *śruti*-derived knowledge lacks conviction and immediacy. *Śraddhā* (faith) in the *pramāṇa* and in the teacher is a very significant attitude. One can be faithful to Śaṅkara's epistemology and also demonstrate that *jñāna* implies a profound transformation of one's entire vision. Fitness to inquire into the *śruti* demands and presupposes a high level of moral attainment in the aspirant. *Bhagavadgītā* 13:6–11, enumerates a selection of such qualities, and summing up his commentary on these virtues, Śaṅkara writes,

> Knowledge of truth results from the mature development of such attributes as (humility 13:7), which are the means of attaining knowledge. The end of this knowledge is *moksa*, the cessation of mortal existence, of *samsara*. The end should be kept in view; for, it is only when one perceives the end of knowledge of truth that one will endeavour to cultivate the attributes which are the means of attaining that knowledge. These attributes — from "humility" to "perception of the end of the knowledge of truth" — are declared to be knowledge because they are conducive to knowledge. What is opposed to this — viz., pride, hypocrisy, cruelty, impatience, insincerity, and the like — is ignorance, which should be known and avoided as tending to the perpetuation of *samsara*.[70]

Chapter 5

The Triple Process —

Śravaṇa (Listening), *Manana* (Reflection), and *Nididhyāsana* (Contemplation)

The triple process in relation to the acquisition of *brahmajñāna* is described in the *Bṛhadāraṇyaka Upaniṣad* in the course of Yājñavalkya's instruction to his wife, Maitreyī.[1] In the Introduction, I have noted the contemporary view that the task of *śravaṇa* is to acquaint us with the declarations of *śruti*. Knowledge gained during *śravaṇa*, however, is not self-certifying and, therefore, is incapable of conferring freedom. It is indirect (*parokṣa*) and lacks conviction. In *manana*, it is argued, we remove all doubts which might have arisen about the validity of what we have apprehended during *śravaṇa*. The assumption, however, seems to be that even at this stage of the process, knowledge is still inadequate. The removal of all doubts is somehow not doubtless, immediate (*aparokṣa*) knowledge. It is only after *manana* that we can undertake the practice of *nididhyāsana*, which eventually provides us with a direct experience of what we have gathered as a possibility in *śravaṇa* and reasoned over in *manana*. This experience (*anubhava*), it is claimed, offers us a direct insight, and it is held up as the true *pramāṇa* of *brahman*. The theory of the *śruti* is realized, even as we realize our knowledge of a foreign place when we reach there.

On the cumulative evidence of our analysis so far, however, it is not possible to reconcile Śaṅkara's views with this seemingly well-ordered division. There are many areas of obvious contradiction which cannot be easily dismissed. Besides important questions which arise about the very nature of the experience which *nididhyāsana* is supposed to produce, its elevation to the status of the ultimate *pramāṇa* of *brahman* runs counter to all of the laborious arguments of Śaṅkara to legitimatize and advocate the *śruti* as the singular and exclusive means of knowledge about *brahman*. The logic and detail of this justification does not lend support to the view that Śaṅkara's only motive was to secure the prestige of traditional authority in support of his views. Śaṅkara has left no doubts about his view of the *pramāṇa* for our knowledge of *brahman*. The argument that *śruti* needs the confirmation of *anubhava* which *nididhyāsana* affords is not reconcilable with the cardinal epistemological theory of *svataḥ-prāmāṇya* (the self-validity of knowledge). The view that the dependence of one *pramāṇa* upon another for its validity leads to infinite regression is relevant in this context. Within the framework of Śaṅkara's view, the *śruti* is no longer a valid *pramāṇa* if it cannot independently give rise to valid knowledge. That *śabda-pramāṇa* is only capable of giving rise to an indirect form of knowledge is also contrary to the main trends of Śaṅkara's arguments. In any assessment of the triple process in *brahmajñāna*, Śaṅkara's dismissal of the argument that *Vedānta-vākyas* are meant for meditation is centrally significant. The incompatibility and tensions between both viewpoints are even further evidenced when we look at some of the direct references in Śaṅkara on *śravaṇa, manana*, and *nididhyāsana*.

In his *Brahma-sutra bhāsya*, Śaṅkara considers an objection that *jñāna* is a mental action, the fruit of which is *mokṣa*.[2] This mental action, it is argued, is enjoined in *śruti* declarations such as "The Self, my dear Maitreyī, should be realised — should be heard of, reflected on, and meditated upon" (BR.U. 2.4.5.). We have already examined part of Śaṅkara's response in our analysis of the significance of his distinction between knowledge and meditation.[3] Briefly, he has argued there that an action is something with reference to which an injunction is possible, even without regard to the nature of the object, and is dependent on the activity of a person (*puruṣatantram*). It may be done, not done, or done in a different manner. Knowledge, on the other hand, is generated by a *pramāṇa* which has for its object the nature of the thing as it exists. It is not subject to our choice, for the knowledge of an object, once gained, cannot be dismissed or known in a different way. It is entirely dependent on the object (*vastutantram*). An injunction instigating an action is possible where there exists the chance of acceptance or rejection. As the Self, however, *brahman* can neither be accepted nor rejected and cannot be the object of any injunction.

> Though verbs in the imperative mood, etc., are seen (in the *Upaniṣad*) to be used with regard to this knowledge, they become infructuous like the sharpness of a razor, etc., striking against stone, etc., for they are aimed at something beyond the range of human effort inasmuch as that knowledge has for its object something (i.e., *Brahman*) that is neither acceptable nor rejectable.[4]

If such texts do not enjoin an action in respect of the acquisition of *brahmajñāna*, what function do they serve? Śaṅkara sees the purpose of such statements in challenging our attention from its preoccupations with the natural pursuit of sense objects and turning it towards *brahmajñāna*.

> As for expressions like "(The Self) is to be seen" (BR.U. 2.4.5), which are met with in the context of the supreme knowledge, they are meant mainly for attracting one's mind towards Reality but do not aim mainly at enjoining any injunction about the knowledge of Reality. In ordinary parlance also, when such directive sentences as "Look at this," "Lend ear to

> that," etc., are uttered, all that is meant is "Be attentive to these," but not "Acquire this knowledge directly." And a man, who is in the presence of an object to be known, may sometimes know it, and sometimes not. Hence a man who wants to impart the knowledge of the thing has to draw his attention to the object of knowledge itself. When that is done, the knowledge arises naturally in conformity with the object and the means of knowledge. It is not a fact that any knowledge (of a given thing), contrary to what is well known through other means of valid knowledge, can arise in a man even when acting under some direction. And should the man, under the belief "I am directed to know this in such a way," know it otherwise, this cannot be true knowledge.[5]

The clear implication of Śaṅkara's argument here is that the text does not enjoin a mental action over and above *jñāna*. *Nididhyāsana*, as a mental action, does not produce *jñāna*.[6]

Śaṅkara terminates his discussion on the fourth *sūtra* by returning again to a consideration of the roles of *śravaṇa*, *manana*, and *nididhyāsana*.[7] Here the objector appears to accept that there is no injunction (*vidhi*) in *śravaṇa*. His argument, however, is that since *manana* and *nididhyāsana* are mentioned subsequent to *śravaṇa*, these must be understood as actions enjoined for a result different from the knowledge of *brahman* gained in *śravaṇa*. *Brahman*, therefore, still becomes subsidiary to the injunction of reasoning and contemplation. Śaṅkara unequivocally denies that *manana* and *nididhyāsana* are meant for accomplishing anything different from the knowledge of *brahman* gained during *śravaṇa*. All three processes, he argues, have the same aim of *brahmajñāna* in view. It is only, he points out, if *brahman*, known from the *śruti*, was meant for some other purpose (i.e., beyond the goal of its knowledge) that is could become the object of an injunction. The argument here again is clear. *Brahmajñāna*, revealed by the *śruti*, is the end in itself. *Manana* and *nididhyāsana* do not seek to produce a result which is in any way different from the knowledge of *brahman* gained during *śravaṇa*.

If these three processes are not different in aim but are meant for bringing about the knowledge of *brahman* which is revealed in the *Upaniṣads*, we can now turn our attention to the specific function and contribution of each to this end. It is important that these functions be consistent with the general trends of Śaṅkara's arguments so far outlined.

5.1 *Śravaṇa* (Listening)

Śravaṇa indicates the acquisition of knowledge by listening. It suggests, of course, the indispensable role of the teacher in transmitting this knowledge and the oral nature of traditional Vedic learning. It is defined as "the ascertainment through the six characteristic signs [i.e., *ṣaḍliṅga*] that the entire *Vedānta* philosophy establishes the one *Brahman* without a second."[8] *Śravaṇa* is essentially an exegetical investigation of the purport (*tātparya*) of the *Vedānta* texts conducted on the student's behalf by the teacher. As the first of the three processes, it emphasizes the primacy of *śruti* as the source of *brahmajñāna*. It is during *śravaṇa* that the teacher seeks to establish that the *Upaniṣads* have *brahman* as an independent subject matter and are not subservient to the texts enjoining rituals. It is an attempt to show that *brahmajñāna* is not baseless but grounded in the authority of the *śruti*. It is during *śravaṇa* also that the teacher seeks to unfold the nature of *brahman* by applying the exclusive-inclusive method of implication to words and sentences defining *brahman*. *Mahāvākyas* like *tat tvam asi* are carefully analyzed to show that the identity imparted is at the level of awareness alone. *Śravaṇa*, therefore, incorporates the entire process of Vedāntic instruction and encompasses all the traditional methods (e.g., *adhyāropa-apavāda; neti, neti*) employed by the teacher in gradually unfolding *brahman*.

Brahman is an already accomplished and ever-available entity, identical with the *ātman* and only wrongly apprehended by us. *Brahmajñāna* is its own end and does not require us to do anything. We are called upon to simply know. It is entirely reasonable and consistent with Śaṅkara's arguments to suggest that the act during which we eliminate our misapprehensions and correctly comprehend the nature of *brahman* must be the principal one in the process of *brahmajñāna*. As the direct inquiry into the only *pramāṇa* of *brahman*, *śravaṇa* must be granted primary significance. This accords with both Śaṅkara's epistemology and his metaphysics as it relates to the fully notional problem of *avidyā*. The view that *śravaṇa* is capable only of affording a speculatory or hypothetical knowledge of the *ātman* raises two kinds of questions. First, it implies, contrary to the main thrust of Śaṅkara's reasoning, that something over and above the knowledge of *ātman* gained from the *Vedānta-vākyas* is required. It also, of course, undermines Śaṅkara's concept of the *śruti* as a *pramāṇa*. Second, and very interestingly, it raises doubts about the method of teaching which such an understanding suggests. How does the teacher unfold *brahman*, the self-manifest awareness of the student, in an entirely conjectural manner? The subject matter is not a remote entity to be reached or created, and the aim of the *Advaita* teacher is to produce immediate liberating knowledge. The problem that confronts the teacher is akin to the tenth-person analogy. The limitless *ātman* mistakenly attributes on itself the qualities of finitude, even as the alive tenth person erroneously denies herself. If the teacher's exegesis follows the texts of the *Upaniṣads* there is little scope for indirect instruction, for the hearer must be made to appreciate *brahman* as one's very Self. It is impossible to putatively exegesize texts like the following from the *Kena Upaniṣad.*

> That which is not uttered by speech, that by which speech is revealed, know that to be *Brahman*, and not what people worship as an object.
>
> That which man does not comprehend with the mind, that by which they say, the mind is encompassed, know that to be *Brahman* and not what people worship as an object.
>
> That which man does not see with the eye, that by which man perceives the activities of the eye, know that alone to be *Brahman* and not what people worship as an object.[9]

The exegesis of passages like these can only proceed by helping the student to appreciate the nonobjectivity of the knower. In other words, passages like these are direct in their instruction of the Self as *brahman*, and they aim at complete knowledge. There is no evidence that Śaṅkara understands their function in any other way. To the skillful teacher and the qualified student, *śravaṇa* can never mean the hypothetical instruction which it is made out to suggest in current opinions.

If *śravaṇa*, therefore, does not produce *brahmajñāna*, the explanation does not lie in its conjectural nature or in the fact that *brahmajñāna* is not its aim. There might be several possible obstacles. For example, in spite of being exposed to the instruction of the teacher, the listener might be unconvinced. One could be troubled by doubts about various aspects of the teaching. There may be doubts concerning the validity of the *pramāṇa* or the nature of *brahman.* According to Śaṅkara, the knowledge that leads to *mokṣa* must be free from all doubts.[10] It is to deal with this impediment to *jñāna* that the second of the threefold process is suggested.

5.2 *Manana* (Reflection)

Manana is defined as "the constant thinking of *Brahman*, the one without a second, already heard about from the teacher, by arguments agreeable to the purport of the *Vedānta*."[11] There are numerous references in Śaṅkara to the possibilities and limitations of reason in relation to the *brahmajñāna*, and it is important that they be properly correlated so that we can accurately evaluate the contribution of *manana* to the acquisition of knowledge.

Śaṅkara is certain that independent reasoning cannot lead to *brahmajñāna*. This conclusion emerges very clearly from several discussions in his commentaries. In his *bhāṣya* on *Brahma-sūtra* 2.1.11, he says that reasoning, which is not rooted in the *Vedas* and springs from mere conjecture, lacks conclusiveness.[12] Human conjecture has no limits. The thoughts of one group of clever persons, he points out, are falsified by others, and these are also in turn eventually contradicted. Intellectual opinions differ, and arguments are indecisive. We cannot hold fast to the views of eminent thinkers like Kapila and Kaṇada, for even they are seen to contradict each other.[13]

To this view, the rationalist responds by arguing that not all reasoning is inconclusive, for this conclusion is arrived at by reasoning alone. Besides, if we were to adopt the view that all reasoning is inconclusive, ordinary life becomes impossible. Future plans for securing happiness and avoiding pain, the rationalist demonstrates, are made on the supposition that nature is uniform in the past, present, and future. Even with regard to divergent interpretations of Vedic passages, reasoning is applied in order to arrive at the correct meaning. The tentative nature of reasoning, he contends, is its advantage. Faulty reasonings can be discarded in favor of sound ones. Even as one should not be considered a fool because one's ancestors were foolish, so also, all reasoning should not be discarded because some forms are defective. Śaṅkara's reply, which sums up very well his views on the limits of reason in relation to *brahmajñāna*, is worth quoting in full.

> Although reasoning may be noticed to have finality in some contexts, still in the present context it cannot possibly get immunity from the charge of being inconclusive; for this extremely sublime subject matter, concerned with the reality of the cause of the Universe and leading to the goal of liberation, cannot even be guessed without the help of the *Vedas*. And we said that It cannot be known either through perception, being devoid of form, etc., or through inference, etc., being devoid of grounds of inference, etc.
>
> Besides, it is the accepted view of all who stand by liberation that freedom from bondage comes from true illumination. And that true enlightenment has no diversity, since its content is the thing-in-itself. That content of knowledge is said to be the most real, since it ever remains the same; and in the world, the knowledge of that kind is said to be right knowledge, as for instance, the knowledge about fire that it is hot. This being the case, people should have no divergence

> when they have true knowledge, whereas the difference among people whose knowledge is based on reasoning is well known from their mutual opposition. For it is a patent fact of experience, that when a logician asserts "This indeed is true knowledge," it is upset by somebody else. And what is established by the latter is disproved by still another. How can any knowledge, arising from reasoning, be correct, when its content has no fixity of form?... It is not also possible to assemble all the logicians of past, present, and future at the same place and time, whereby to arrive at a single idea, having the same form and content, so as to be the right source of knowledge. But since the *Vedas* are eternal and a source of knowledge, they can reasonably reveal as their subject matter something which is (well established and) unchanging; and the knowledge arising from them can be true, so that no logician, past, present, or future can deny it.[14]

Śaṅkara's conclusions in passages like these do not imply the complete rejection of every form of reasoning. Indian philosophy generally employs two kind of reasoning.[15] The first type is the syllogistic inference or *anumāna* as illustrated by the establishment of fire from the perceived smoke. We have seen, however, that because *brahman* possesses no perceptible characteristics, this kind of reasoning is inapplicable. The second type is termed *sāmānyato-dṛṣṭanumāna* and is equivalent in modern logic to analogical reasoning. It is also designated as *yukti* or *tarka.* This type of reasoning is not itself a *pramāṇa* but operates as an ancillary to a *pramāṇa.* Its function is to produce a belief in the possibility of a thing. In relation to *brahmajñāna*, the aim of all such *tarkas* is to strengthen the teaching of the *Upaniṣads.* The *Nyāya* argument that the world as an effect must have as its source a sentient being is viewed by *Advaita* as an example of this kind of reasoning. This argument cannot conclusively establish *īśvara's*, existence, but it demonstrates the reasonability of God's revelation in the *śruti.*

Reasoning in harmony or conformity with the *śruti* is what the Śaṅkara repeatedly emphasizes.

> It was also argued that by enjoining reflection over and above hearing, the (*Bṛhadāraṇyaka*) *Upaniṣad* shows that logic is also to be honored. But through such a subterfuge, empty logic cannot find any scope here; for logic, conforming to the *Upaniṣads*, is alone resorted to here as a subsidiary means helping realization.[16]

Śruti has to be supplemented by such kinds of *tarka* because of the variety of contradictory views which are held about the distinctive nature of *brahman*.[17] These arguments fortify the *Vedānta-vākyas*.

> The realization of *Brahman* results from the firm conviction arising from the deliberation of the (Vedic) texts and their meanings, but not from other means of knowledge like inference, etc. When, however, there are Upaniṣadic texts speaking of the origin, etc. of the world, then even inference, not running counter to the Upaniṣadic texts, is not ruled out in so far as it is adopted as a valid means of knowledge reinforcing these texts; for the *Upaniṣads* themselves accept reasoning as a help.[18]

The meaning of *śruti* should be tested in the light of arguments, for it is only when they are both combined that they can show the unity of the *ātman* "as clearly as a bael fruit on the palm of one's hand."[19]

Even when Śaṅkara seems to suggest that *Advaita* can be established by *tarka* alone, close examination reveals that the reasoning employed is only of the analogical type in conformity with *śruti* (*srutyanugṛhīta tarka*). In his introduction to *Bṛhadāraṇyaka Upaniṣad* 4.5.1, he says that the Yājñavalkya section of the text illustrates the establishment of *brahmajñāna* by *tarka*. Yet, the arguments which Śaṅkara uses in this section are not of an independent kind. At one point, he argues that the sun and the moon, which are like two lamps giving light to all beings, are held in place even as a kingdom under the unbroken and orderly rule of a king. He says that even as we infer the existence of the lampmaker from a lamp, the sun and moon "must have been created for the purpose of giving light by a Universal Ruler who knows of what use they will be to all, for they serve the common good of all beings by giving light."[20] We cannot construe this as an independent argument for the establishment of the Self, because it is the very kind of argument which Śaṅkara criticizes *Nyāya* for independently using to verify *īśvara's* existence.[21] Similarly, in his *Māṇḍūkya Upaniṣad Kārikā bhāṣya*, Śaṅkara says that nonduality can be demonstrated on logical grounds.[22] That these are not independent logical grounds becomes obvious when he concludes his commentary on the *Kārikā* by pointing out that nonduality is to be known only from the *Upaniṣads* and that this doctrine was not the same as that unfolded by the Buddha, in spite of certain similarities.

> That the nature of the supreme Reality is free from the differences of knowledge, the known, and the knower and is without a second, this thing was not expressed by Buddha; though a near approach to nondualism was implied in his negation of outer objects and his

> imagination of everything as consciousness. But this nonduality, the essence of the ultimate Reality, is to be known from the *Upaniṣads* only. This is the purport.[23]

It will be useful to further clarify the nature of reasoning employed in *Advaita* by looking at some examples. The *Upaniṣad*, for example, declares the Self to be *ānanda* (joy).[24] This conclusion may seem doubtful to the aspirant because of the general tendency to pursue joy by striving after acquisitions other than the *ātman* and the common experience of sorrow (*duḥka*). In order to demonstrate the reasonableness of the *śruti* revelation, arguments of the following kind are employed. If the joy which is assumed to be the content of the pursued object was an objective quality of it, the object should universally make any person happy. It is impossible, however, to find a single object which can satisfy this criterion. An object which appears to be a source of delight to one is very often a cause of pain to another. This is not only valid in relation to different individuals. A single object at different periods of time could be a source of joy and sorrow to the same individual. Reasoning, therefore, suggests that our belief in the presence of joy in objects other than the Self is not unquestionable. *Ānanda* appears to be related to desirability. In deep sleep, there is an experience of joy without any object or sense of possession. *Advaita* suggests that this joy is identical with the Self. It explains that in the fulfillment of a desire, we only temporarily eliminate the sense of want and inadequacy, entertain a thought of fullness, and identify with a joy that is not different from the Self. We mistakenly, however, attribute the source of this joy to the object outside. Arguments of this kind, therefore, strengthen and make reasonable the *śruti* declaration that *ātman* is *ānanda*.

Another example of acceptable reasoning, suggested by Śaṅkara himself, concerns the analysis of our three states of experiences.[25] *Śruti* informs us that the *ātman* is changeless, and this is found to be consistent with our own experiences. In the waking state (*jāgarita avasthā*), all our experiences are illumined by awareness (*cit*). As the knower , *ātman* is the witness of the entire waking world. In the dream state (*svapna avasthā*), the waking world is temporarily negated and a world of subtle experiences projected. The Self as awareness, however, also illumines and makes these experiences known. The entire dream experience is enveloped in the light that is awareness. The state of deep sleep (*suṣupti avasthā*) negates both the waking and dream worlds, but even here, *Advaita* contends, the experience is known. Statements like, "I had an undisturbed, pleasant sleep," indicate the presence of awareness. Thus, the three states and their experiential content vary and mutually negate each other, but the common unchanging factor is the Self.[26] The *Bhagavadgītā* uses the argument of unchanging awareness in the states of childhood, youth, and old age to illustrate the immortality of the Self.[27] States and experiences differ, but

"I know" is common to all states and life experiences. Arguments such as the difference of the knower from the known are used to reinforce the *śruti's* revelation of the distinction of the Self from the body, sense organs, and mind. Each one is progressively distinguished by showing that it is subject to objectification and, therefore, different from the knower.

The same function of creating certainty in the *śruti* is served by a profuse use of analogies in the texts themselves and by Śaṅkara. The rope-snake analogy, so frequently resorted to by Śaṅkara, illustrates a creation of ignorance as a result of incomplete knowledge and its immediate negation by right knowledge. The story of the tenth person aptly illustrates the notional loss and gain of something that is already available. It also reveals very well the sense of sorrow which can accompany a fictitious loss and the joy and freedom which knowledge brings. The crystal ball example shows how the *ātman*, while remaining pure and unaffected, seems to assume the characteristics and qualities of adjuncts (*upādhis*) with which it becomes associated.

> Just as before the perception of distinction, the transparent whiteness, constituting the real nature of a crystal, remains indistinguishable, as it were, from red, blue, and other conditioning factors; but after the perception of distinction through the valid means of knowledge, the crystal in its latter state is said to attain its true nature of whiteness and transparency, though it was exactly so even earlier; similarly in the case of the nature of the individual soul, remaining indistinguishably mixed up with such limiting adjuncts as the body, etc., there springs up a discriminating knowledge from the *Upaniṣads* constituting his rising from the body (consciousness); and the result of the discriminating knowledge is the attainment of the real nature, its realization of its nature as the absolute Self.[28]

Brahman as both instrumental (*nimitta kāraṇa*) and material cause (*upādāna kāraṇa*) of the creation is made comprehensible when compared with the spider's projection of its web.[29] The nondifference of cause and effect is illustrated by the analogy of clay or gold and their many products. Differences are the creation of name alone.[30] The example of space is often cited. It illustrates the purity of the Self in spite of its association with the body, as well as the accommodation of all change by the changeless Self.[31] *Brahman* appears divided even as the space within pots is only seemingly broken up.[32] Analogies, however, are useful only as a method of teaching.

> Since the Self is by nature Consciousness Itself, distinctless, beyond speech and mind, and can be taught

> by way of negating other things, hence in scriptures dealing with liberation an illustration is cited by saying that it is "like the sun reflected in water."[33]

An interesting objection is raised against the above analogy. Both the sun and water are limited entities remotely placed from each other. It is possible, therefore, for the sun to be reflected on the latter. The Self, however, is unlimited and all-pervasive. There is nothing remote or separate from it. The comparison, therefore, is inappropriate.[34] In responding to this, Śaṅkara explains that between the illustration and the thing illustrated, there is similarity only in some respects. It is this similarity that is the focus of attention. If both objects were identical in all respects, the analogy would not be possible. He points out the particular aim of this analogy.

> "A participation in increase and decrease," inasmuch as the reflection of the sun in water increases with the increase of water, and decreases with its reduction, it moves when the water moves, and it differs as the water differs. Thus the sun conforms to the characteristics of the water; but in reality the sun never has these. Thus also from the highest point of view, *Brahman*, while remaining unchanged and retaining Its sameness, seems to conform to such characteristics as increase and decrease of the limiting adjunct (body) owing to Its entry into such an adjunct as the body. Thus, since the illustration and the thing illustrated are both compatible, there is no contradiction.[35]

The primary function of *manana*, therefore, is to demonstrate the tenability of *śruti*'s declaration. It is neither an independent means to *brahmajñāna* nor an alternative to the *śruti*. Contrary to the sharp distinctions we have examined in the Introduction, *manana* is not necessarily exercised only after *śravaṇa*. It is an integral part of *śravaṇa* itself. The application of the sixfold canons of interpretation in determining the purport of the *Vedānta-vākyas* is an exercise of reasoning and critical evaluation. It is important to remind ourselves that *upapatti* (intelligibility in the light of reasoning) is one of those canons. Reasoning is also necessary for determining whether a word or passage should be understood in its primary (*mukhya*) or secondary (*lakṣya*) sense and in distinguishing between the different forms of the latter. *Manana* is a process provoked by the teacher, as various kinds of arguments are used to create certainty in the student. Doubts are often resolved in dialogue with the teacher during *śravaṇa*. *Manana* is also useful for refuting the views of systems opposed to *Advaita*. Śaṅkara explains that although the entire *Brahma-sūtra* is meant only for showing that the *Upaniṣads* have *brahman* as their purport, and not for proving or disproving any conclusion by pure logic, it is necessary to repudiate the views which run counter to right knowledge. This need arises because of the reputation which some of these alternative views enjoy and the difficulty of properly evaluating their worth.[36] This function is approached by Śaṅkara in a twofold way. If the views of these schools are based on their interpretations of *śruti*, the validity of these interpretations are questioned by exegesis. If they are based on mainly rational grounds, their inconsistencies and contradictions are exposed.[37] In this way, an attempt is made to show that they are untenable.

Because *brahmajñāna* is born out of the *śruti* as *śabda-pramāṇa*, the role of *manana* must, therefore, be a largely negative one. It releases and relieves knowledge from doubt. If *brahmajñāna* is not produced by the investigation of the *pramāṇa*, it is difficult, in the context of Śaṅkara, to conceive how it can be produced only by *manana*. The problem is like the relationship between any means of knowledge and its respective object. If a form is not perceived by the eye, for instance, because of the intervention of some obstacles, these must be eliminated and the eye again employed. It is the only appropriate organ. Similarly, if the *śruti* does not give rise to knowledge because of doubts, it is the function of *manana* to remove such doubts in order that knowledge is unobstructed. Because of its radical challenge to our habitual conception of ourselves, it is difficult to imagine *śravaṇa* not provoking doubts of different kinds. It is consistent with Śaṅkara's views to suggest, however, that if doubtless knowledge is gained during *śravaṇa*, there is no need for *manana*. The suggestion here is that if *śravaṇa* fails to engender direct knowledge, it is not because of the absence of intention to do so or the presence of any natural limitations. The reasons are to be found in the various obstacles to the emergence of knowledge related to the preparedness of the student.

5.3 *Nididhyāsana* (Contemplation)

The view presented in the Introduction, that *nididhyāsana* is necessary for an experience in which alone *brahmajñāna* is conclusively gained, raises several problems in relation to Śaṅkara's central views. Besides the misunderstanding and underestimation of the role of *śravaṇa*, the argument seems self-contradictory. It accepts that the aim and achievement of *manana* is the creation of doubtless knowledge. It then immediately suggests that this well-ascertained and doubtless knowledge is inadequate. This contradiction is never resolved, and we are not made aware of what then is the exact status of *brahmajñāna* after *manana*. That *brahmajñāna* is the product of an act of meditation is at variance with Śaṅkara's recurrent distinction between knowledge and meditation and his view that the sentences of the *Upaniṣads* are not meant for the latter. His view, as we have seen, is that the *Vedānta-vākyas* directly give rise to knowledge, the results of which are immediate. Knowledge does not need to be followed by any physical or mental act.[38] In fact, meditation cannot follow knowledge, for it presupposes a duality which is already negated in *brahmajñāna.*[39] The entire weight of Śaṅkara's arguments is opposed to the view that an act of meditation is necessary over and above the knowledge gained from the *śruti* for *brahmajñāna.* The view that only through *anubhava* afforded by *nididhyāsana* is *brahman* really ascertained displaces *śruti* as the definitive *pramāṇa.*

Avidyā is not an absolute ignorance of the *ātman* but an erroneous knowledge of it, which leads to the superimposition (*adhyāsa*) of attributes properly belonging to the body, senses, and mind. It is a confusion arising from the inability to discriminate and distinguish between the Self and non-Self. It is obvious, therefore, that *avidyā* at the individual level is a mental modification (*antaḥkaraṇa vṛtti*) but of an erroneous nature. A *vṛtti* is a mode or modification of the internal organ (*antaḥkaraṇa*), and it is clear that Śaṅkara conceives all mental processes — cognitive, conative, and emotive — as modifications of the internal organ.[40] This incorrect mental modification can only be negated and corrected by another *antaḥkaraṇa vṛtti* which coincides with the object to be known and which is produced by an adequate and appropriate *pramāṇa.* It is exceedingly important to note that Śaṅkara all along sees *brahmajñāna* as a mental process occurring in the mind and not transcending it. *Brahmajñāna* is of the nature of an *antaḥkaraṇa vṛtti* coinciding with the nature of *brahman* and produced by its authoritative *pramāṇa,* the *śruti.* There is no basis in Śaṅkara for conceiving of its nature in another way. The references in his commentaries are explicit.

> *Objection:* In this connection some conceited pedants say: To no man can arise the conviction "I am the immutable Self, the One, the nonagent, devoid of the six changes, such as birth, to which all things in the world are subject; which conviction arising, renunciation of all works is enjoined."
>
> *Answer:* This objection does not apply here. For, in vain then would be the Scriptural teaching, such as "the Self is not born," etc. (B.G. 2:20). They (the objectors) may be asked why knowledge of the immutability, non-agency, unity, etc., of the Self cannot be produced by the Scripture in the same way as knowledge of the existence of *dharma* and *adharma* and of the doer passing through other births is produced by the teaching of the Scripture?
>
> *Opponent:* Because the Self is inaccessible to any of the senses.

> *Answer*: Not so. For the Scripture says "It can be seen by the mind alone" (BR.U. 4.4.19). The mind refined by *Sama* and *Dama* — i.e., by the subjugation of the body, the mind, and the senses — and equipped with the teaching of the Scripture and the teacher, constitutes the sense by which the Self may be seen. Thus, while the Scripture and inference teach the immutability of the Self, it is mere temerity to hold that no such knowledge can arise.[41]

Meditation or any experience that might arise from it is nowhere envisaged by Śaṅkara as independently capable of producing the appropriate *antaḥkaraṇa vṛtti* which can eliminate self-ignorance (*ātma-avidyā*).[42] Śaṅkara accepts that this *vṛtti*, produced in the mind by the *Vedānta-vākyas*, does not enjoy the status of absolute reality (*pāramārthika sattā*). Its reality would be the same as that of the world, the *Vedas*, and the *antaḥkaraṇa*. He sees no difficulty, however, in its capacity to negate ignorance and effect the knowledge of the absolutely real.[43] He willingly concedes that once *brahmajñāna* is effected, the absolute reality of the *Vedas* is also negated.[44] The *Vedānta-vākyas*, having negated from *brahman* all *upādhis*, eventually negate themselves.

Sureśvara develops a line of argument which is fully consistent with what we have so far seen in Śaṅkara about the nature of *brahmajñāna* and the function of meditation. In the *Naiṣkarmyasiddhi*, he deals with the argument that the knowledge derived from *śabda-pramāṇa* is mediate and indirect (*parokṣa*) and becomes a direct conviction only through meditation (*prasaṁkhyāna*).[45] According to Sureśvara, if the properly understood and interpreted *Vedānta-vākyas* do not produce immediate knowledge, continuous contemplation on their purport in the form of hearing and reasoning will not do so.[46] Meditation can only produce the ability to habitually concentrate the mind, but it is not through meditation that the *pramāṇas* yield knowledge.[47] They do so directly. Besides, according to Sureśvara, if someone gains knowledge through the *śruti* and then denies the same, knowledge through any other source is likely to be rejected.[48] If one does not accept that the *śruti* is capable of producing direct knowledge, then the texts cease to be authoritative. *Mokṣa* becomes noneternal if it is conceived of as the product of an act of meditation.[49] By emphasizing the need for *prasaṁkhyāna* over and above the *Vedānta-vākyas*, one elevates *prasaṁkhyāna* to the status of a *pramāṇa*. This is as absurd as trying to take food with one's eyes.[50] Sureśvara all along emphasizes that direct knowledge is the result of inquiry into the Vedic texts.[51] Sureśvara, however, accepts that *prasaṁkhyāna*, as repeated hearing and pondering of the *Vedānta-vākyas*, is acceptable. He grants that a clear comprehension of the texts may not result from a single hearing but may do so after repeated listening.[52] In this sense, *prasaṁkhyāna* becomes an integral part of *śravaṇa* or the process of ascertaining the meaning of the texts. Like Śaṅkara, he emphasizes the importance of mental purity (*citta-śuddhi*) as a precondition of *brahmajñāna*.[53]

Sadananda defines *nididhyāsana* as "a stream of ideas of the same kind as those of *Brahman*, the One without a second, to the exclusion of such foreign ideas as those of the body, etc."[54] This definition is reconcilable with a function that Śaṅkara assigns to contemplation after *brahman* has been apprehended from the *śruti*. In addition to doubts, which it is the function of *manana* to eliminate, *brahmajñāna* may be subject to a further impediment. Even after the gain of *brahmajñāna*, the deep impressions (*vāsanā*) formed as a result of habitual identification with the body, sense organs, and mind may reassert themselves, and there is a possibility of lapse from self-knowledge. This possibility is increased by the fact that the effects of actions which have given rise to this particular embodiment and life experience continue to bear fruit.

> Since the resultant of past actions that led to the formation of the present body must produce definite results, speech, mind, and body are bound to work even after the highest realization, for actions that have begun to bear fruit are stronger than knowledge; as for instance an arrow that has been let fly continues its course for some time. Hence the operation of knowledge, being weaker than they, (is liable to be interrupted by them and) becomes only a possible alternative. Therefore, there is need to regulate the train of remembrance of the knowledge by having recourse to means such as renunciation and dispassion.[55]

For *brahmajñāna* to be meaningful and fruitful to the aspirant, it should continuously and steadily abide in one's mind and not be displaced by age-old tendencies and inclinations.[56] Śaṅkara argues, therefore, that *Upaniṣad* sentences such as "The Self alone is to be meditated upon" (BR.U. 1.4.7) and "The intelligent aspirant after *Brahman*, knowing about this alone, should attain intuitive knowledge" (BR.U. 4.4.21) are meant for impressing upon us the need for sustaining a continuous trend of thought centered on the nature of the Self, so that knowledge is not overwhelmed by erroneous past tendencies.[57] Sentences such as these, he explains, are not intended for indicating any act for the production of a new result over and above the knowledge of *brahman* gained from the *śruti*. This contemplation of the *ātman* is not different from the knowledge that is gained during *śravaṇa*.[58] They do not constitute original injunctions, enjoining something entirely unknown.

> The very knowledge of the nature of the Self removes the ignorance about it, consisting in identification with

> the non-Self, and the superimposing of action, its factors, principal and subsidiary, and its results (on the Self). When that is removed, evils such as desires cannot exist, and consequently thinking of the non-Self is also gone. Hence on the principle of residuum, thinking follows as a matter of course. Therefore, meditation on it, from this point of view, has not to be enjoined, for it is already known from other sources.[59]

On the evidence of Śaṅkara's commentaries, it is quite clear that the idea of contemplation after *śravaṇa* and *manana* is understood to mean continuous fixing of attention on knowledge already gained. It is not seen as an avenue to any new knowledge.[60] In the context of this view, even as *manana* is an integral part of *śravaṇa*, *nididhyāsana* is not distinct in intention and purpose from both, except that it presupposes the gain of *brahmajñāna*. *Nididhyāsana* ensures that *brahmajñāna* becomes a natural and spontaneous part of one's thinking, even as the former limited notions of oneself. *Nididhyāsana*, therefore, must be carefully distinguished from what is understood as meditation (*upāsanā*) proper by Śaṅkara. The latter, according to Śaṅkara, is a mental action which does not necessarily depend upon or conform to the exact nature of the meditated object. The object may be thought of as something else.[61] *Nididhyāsana*, on the other hand, is the contemplation of an object, already conclusively known from a valid *pramāṇa*, as it really is. This contemplation is not meant for gaining anything beyond the knowledge already gained from the authoritative *pramāṇa*. *Nididhyāsana* is, therefore, strictly speaking, identical with valid knowledge or *pramā* rather than *upāsanā* (meditation). To contemplate a thing as it is can only be knowledge, for such a contemplation would be dependent on the nature of the object (*vastutantram*) and not on the will of the contemplator (*puruṣatantram*).[62]

That *nididhyāsana* is identical with *brahmajñāna* and distinct from the concept of meditation as a probable means of knowledge is supported by Śaṅkara's clear refutation of *Yoga* and its disciplines as a direct means to *brahmajñāna*.[63] Commenting on *Brahma-sūtra* 2.1.3, Śaṅkara justifies the need for a special rebuttal of *Sāṅkhya* and *Yoga*. This is necessary, he explains, because of the claim of *Yoga* to be a means to the knowledge of reality and the references to this method in the *Vedas*.[64] The fact that these schools share some views and practices in common with *Advaita* does not justify their claim as independent paths to the knowledge of *brahman*.

> Though there is agreement in respect of a portion of the subject matter, still since disagreement is in evidence in respect of others, as shown above, an effort is being made against the *Sāṁkhya* and *Yoga Smṛtis* alone, though many *Smṛtis* dealing with spiritual matters are extant. For the *Sāṁkhya* and *Yoga* are well

> recognized in the world as means for the achievement of the highest human goal (liberation), and they are accepted by the good people and are supported by the Vedic indicatory marks, as in "One becomes freed from all the bondages after realizing the Deity that is the source of these desires and attained through *Sāṁkhya* and *Yoga*" (SV.U. 6.13). Their refutation centers only round this false claim that liberation can be attained through *Sāṁkhya* knowledge or the path of *Yoga* independently of the *Vedas*. For the *Upaniṣads* reject the claim that there can be anything apart from the Vedic knowledge of the unity of the Self that can bring about liberation, as is denied in "By knowing Him alone, one goes beyond death. There is no other path to proceed by" (SV.U. 3.8). But the followers of *Sāmkhya* and *Yoga* are dualists, and they do not perceive the unity of the Self.[65]

The *Sāṅkhya* view of the qualityless nature of the *puruṣa* and the *Yoga* emphasis on detachment are only acceptable because they are harmonious with *śruti*'s own revelations. Although these schools might be indirectly conducive to the gain of self-knowledge, that knowledge itself, however, contends Śaṅkara, can be had only from the texts of the *Upaniṣads*.[66] Although Śaṅkara admits that extraordinary powers are attainable through *Yoga* practices, he denies that the mere discipline of mind control or concentration is a means to freedom.[67] The *Upaniṣads*, he says, do not prescribe these as leading to *mokṣa*.[68] This is a denial, therefore, of meditation as generally understood, as a means to *brahmajñāna*. In fact, Śaṅkara sees mental control as being impossible without *brahmajñāna* and the continuous abiding of the mind in that knowledge.[69]

Elsewhere, Śaṅkara argues that any perfection possible is attainable only through the practice of *dharma* and that the latter is revealed exclusively in the injunctions of the *Veda*.[70] Hence, the validity of a scriptural text cannot be overridden on the personal authority of someone who has attained perfection through the practice of it.[71] Besides, if one has to rely on the personal authority of adepts, there is a difficulty of contradictory assertions. These conflicts, according to Śaṅkara, can only be resolved by a consideration of their agreement with the *Vedas*.[72] Like all other mental and physical disciplines outside of the *Vedānta-vākyas*, *Yoga* can assist the gain of knowledge by helping to bring about concentration and mental purity (*citta-śuddhi*).[73]

5.4 Śaṅkara's Use of *Anubhava* in *Brahma-sūtra bhāṣya* 1.1.2.

In current studies, the most often-cited statement from Śaṅkara in support of *anubhava* as a *pramāṇa* of *brahman* occurs in his commentary on the *Brahma-sūtra*. Here Śaṅkara says that *anubhava*, etc., (*anubhavādayaśca*) can be used as a means of inquiry about *brahman*.[74] In view of the significance attached to this statement, it is important that we examine the context in which it occurs.

The discussion in which Śaṅkara expresses this view is prompted by an objection that the second *sūtra*, "That (is *Brahman*) from which (are derived) the birth, etc., of this universe," seeks to establish *brahman* by an inferential argument.[75] Śaṅkara emphatically denies this view. The *sūtras*, he says, are meant for "stringing together the flowers of the sentences of the *Upaniṣads*." They only cite and analyze the *Vedānta-vākyas* because

> the realization of *Brahman* results from the firm conviction arising from the deliberation on the (Vedic) texts and their meanings, but not from other means of knowledge like inference, etc.[76]

Having said this, Śaṅkara adds that after *brahman* is revealed as the world-cause by the *śruti*, inferential arguments not opposed to the Upaniṣadic texts can be employed as a means of reinforcing these texts. The *śruti* itself, Śaṅkara points out, in texts such as "(The Self is) to be heard of, to be reflected on" (BR.U. 2.4.5) and "A man well informed and intelligent can reach the country of the *Gāndhāras*; similarly in this world, a man who has a teacher attains knowledge," prescribes and accepts the aid of human intelligence and reasoning.[77]

It is in the immediate context of suggesting a supplementary role for all other *pramāṇas* that Śaṅkara mentions *anubhava* as a means of knowledge. It is also significant that he adds "etc." after *anubhava* (*anubhavādayaśca*). This would suggest that no special significance is being attached to *anubhava*. The inevitable conclusion here is that *anubhava* is grouped along with all other *pramāṇas* whose roles are conceived by Śaṅkara as only subordinate and supplementary to *śruti*. There seems no justification from this discussion for the deliberate singling out of *anubhava* and the claim that it is the ultimate *pramāṇa* of *brahman*. The context and the development of the argument here does not vindicate such an interpretation.

Śaṅkara clearly explains why it is possible to have supplementary *pramāṇas* in inquiring about *brahman*. In the case of the inquiry into *dharma*, for example, *śruti* alone can be employed, for the result is yet to be produced and is dependent on human effort. The result cannot be experienced prior to its production.[78] The inquiry into *brahman*, however, Śaṅkara says, relates to an already existing entity and admits, therefore, of the use of other *pramāṇas*.[79] The clear idea of the contrast which Śaṅkara introduces here is to suggest that because *brahman* is not outside the range of one's knowledge and experience, other *pramāṇas* are employable alongside *śruti*.[80] Besides, *anubhava* here seems to be used in a very wide sense. It can include any experience which can be analyzed to support and reinforce the revelations of *śruti*. The analysis of the three states of experience and the demonstration of a persisting and unchanging awareness are good examples of the supportive use of everyday experience.

The important point is that there are no grounds here or elsewhere for seeing any of these other sources of knowledge as independent or alternative means to *brahmajñāna* in Śaṅkara. This is reinforced in the course of the same discussion in which an objection is raised that if *brahman* is an existing reality, it should be the object of other means of inquiry and *Upaniṣad* inquiry is futile. Śaṅkara's reply leaves no room for doubt.

> Not so; for *Brahman*'s relation with anything cannot be grasped, It being outside the range of sense perception. The senses naturally comprehend objects and not *Brahman*. Had *Brahman* been an object of sense-perception, knowledge would have been of the form "This product is related to (i.e., produced by) *Brahman*." Again, even when the mere effect (i.e., universe) is cognized, one cannot ascertain whether it is related to *Brahman* (as its cause) or to something else. Therefore, the aphorism "That from which" etc., is not meant to present an inference.[81]

The issue is put even further beyond doubt when Śaṅkara says that the next *sūtra* (1.1.3), "Since the scriptures are its valid means" (*śastrayonitvat*), is meant for establishing *śruti* as the only *pramāṇa* of *brahman*.[82] We are left with no choice, therefore, but to see this reference to *anubhava* in the same light as Śaṅkara's mention of any other *pramāṇa* in relation to *śruti* and *brahmajñāna*. It is difficult to accept that if Śaṅkara wished to establish *anubhava* as the definitive *pramāṇa* of *brahman*, he would have chosen to do so through this single reference. The direct revelation of *brahman* is the concern of *śruti* alone, but other methods of inquiry and reasoning can assist us in removing doubt and in understanding this revelation.

In the discussion on *śravaṇa, manana*, and *nididhyāsana*, I sought to refute the sharp distinctions made between them and the claim that they are intended for different ends. All three processes, according to Śaṅkara, have the same end in view. I have also argued that they do not necessarily follow each other in sequence. In the properly qualified aspirant, *brahmajñāna* can be gained in the initial *śravaṇa*. If this does not occur, it is not because this is not the aim of *śravaṇa* or that it is incapable of bringing about knowledge. The aspirant may lack any one of the qualities described in *sādhana-catuṣṭaya*. If there are any doubts about the *pramāṇa* or the *prameya* (object revealed), then *manana* is required for the elimination of these. *Manana*, however, does not seek to establish the truth of *brahman* by logic independent of the *śruti*. It only releases *jñāna* from doubts.

In the discussion of *nididhyāsana*, I sought to refute the view that it is conceived by Śaṅkara as a special act of meditation which truly produces *brahmajñāna*. The habitual tendency of identifying the *ātman* with the mind, senses or body may reassert itself even after the gain of *brahmajñāna*. *Nididhyāsana*, as conceived by Śaṅkara, is that process of continuous contemplation by which one seeks to uninterruptedly focus one's mind on the true nature of the Self, gleaned from the *śruti*. At this stage, valid knowledge is already gained, and the purpose of *nididhyāsana* is not to produce new knowledge. It is contemplation of the *ātman* as it is, having already ascertained its nature from its valid source. Its aim is to bring about firmness or steadiness (*niṣtha*) in *jñāna*. Contrary to current views, it appears to me that *śravaṇa*, the process during which we correctly comprehend the nature of *brahman*, should be accorded primacy in Śaṅkara.

Conclusion

The great challenge to the *Pūrva-Mīmāṁsā* system was to provide a rationale for the authority of the *Vedas* which was not connected to the nature or character of a personal author. *Pūrva-Mīmāṁsā* is atheistic in outlook and posits the view that the *Vedas* are authorless (*apauruṣeya*). It is as a response to this dilemma that one best understands the arguments of this school for the validity of the *Vedas*. The fact that these texts are authorless, *Pūrva-Mīmāṁsā* claims, is precisely why they are authoritative. They are free from any possible defects and limitations of authorship. *Pūrva-Mīmāṁsā* asserts that the *Vedas*, as a source of valid knowledge, are eternal and uncreated. This view is supported by the doctrine that the words of the *Vedas*, since they primarily signify eternal universals and not the transitory particulars of the creation, are also eternal. The connection between Vedic words and their referents is eternal and free from error.

The *Pūrva-Mīmāṁsā* justification of the *Vedas* by reference to their eternity is adopted and defended by Śaṅkara and forms part of his own rationale for the authoritativeness of this *pramāṇa*. Unlike *Pūrva-Mīmāṁsā*, however, *Advaita* accepts the existence of *īśvara* and posits Him as the revealer of the *Vedas*. *Īśvara* only reveals the *Vedas* as they were revealed in previous creations. Despite the ascribing of this function to *īśvara*, Śaṅkara does not argue for the authority of the *Vedas* on the basis of *īśvara's* omniscience. Because the latter fact is known only from the *Vedas*, to use it to justify the Vedas would be to employ a circular argument. When, however, we learn from the *Vedas*, of *īśvara's* existence and nature and of God as the source of the *Vedas*, we can use rational arguments to support this knowledge, since it is not contradictory to reason. This is the kind of argument used by Śaṅkara in *Brahma-sūtra* 1.1.3 to demonstrate why *brahman* alone can be the source of the *Vedas*. It is an important dimension of Śaṅkara's rationale for the *Vedas*, which is different from that of *Pūrva-Mīmāṁsā*.

The system of *Pūrva-Mīmāṁsā*, however, does not accept that the *Vedas* are a *pramāṇa* for the knowledge of *brahman*. In their view, the purport of the *Vedas* lies only in the inculcation of *dharma*. *Dharma* is accomplished through appropriate action, physical and mental, and so this system asserts that a direct and independent authority can only be ascribed to injunctions (*vidhi*) inculcating the performance of acceptable acts and to prohibitions (*niṣedha*) instituting restraint from acts opposed to *dharma*. Sentences which do not exhort us to perform a desirable action or restrain us from an undesirable one are, by themselves, meaningless, and are meant only to subserve injunctive sentences. This view of *Pūrva-Mīmāṁsā* about the authority of the *Vedas* is entirely opposed to Śaṅkara's claim that the *Vedānta-vākyas* have an independent authority in revealing an already existent *brahman* and do not seek to impel us into any activity. While Śaṅkara, therefore, used *Pūrva-Mīmāṁsā* arguments about the eternity of the *Vedas* as part of his proof for their authority, he was obliged to develop an entirely independent rationale and justification for *śruti* as a *pramāṇa* of *brahmajñāna*. It is here that the originality of Śaṅkara is very evident and the forcefulness, consistency, and appeal of his arguments are best demonstrated. It is the significance of this rationale which modern commentators seem largely to have missed and which falsifies the argument that Śaṅkara appealed to the *śruti* merely to gain the support of an established authority for his views.

Śruti, according to Śaṅkara, affords a knowledge which is necessary for the happiness naturally pursued by all human beings and which cannot be obtained through any other source. It is not the concern of the *śruti* to inform us of ends and means which we can learn about through other *pramāṇas*. For Śaṅkara, the sphere of the *śruti*'s authority is confined to the revelation of *dharma* and *brahman*. *Dharma* is the authoritative concern of the *karmakāṇḍa* sections of the *Vedas*, while the *Upaniṣads* (i.e., *Vedānta-vākyas*) have an entirely independent purpose in the revelation of the knowledge of *brahman*.

The cornerstone of Śaṅkara's case for *śruti* as the only valid means of knowing *brahman* is that because of the very nature of *brahman*, *śruti* as a *pramāṇa* in the form of words is the only logical means. While his contention for *śruti* as the only *pramāṇa* of *brahmajñāna* is not divorced from his wider views about its authoritativeness, in this case the argument is as much centered on the logic of words (*śabda*) as the only conceivable means through which this knowledge could be imparted and attained. It is really a justification of *śabda* as opposed to any other *pramāṇa*, and this fact lends to his rationale a certain undogmatic character. What gives Śaṅkara's argument its force and makes it difficult to dismiss is the logical interdependence which he demonstrates between the appropriateness of the *pramāṇa* and the nature of the entity to be known. The relationship here is between *brahman*, as the entity to be known, and *śabda*, as the means of knowledge. Modern commentators, upholding *anubhava* as the ultimate *pramāṇa* of *brahmajñāna* in Śaṅkara, seem, on the whole, to have missed the significance of this logical interdependence between *śabda* and *brahman*.

The case for *śabda* (the word) as the only appropriate vehicle of *brahmajñāna* consists also of showing why this knowledge cannot be attained through other ways of knowing, and this Śaṅkara convincingly does at every available opportunity in his commentaries. *Brahman* cannot be known through sense perception because it is *nirguṇa* (qualityless). It is free from all the qualities (form, taste, smell, touch, and sound) through which the various sense organs apprehend their respective objects. In addition, the sense organs can only know the nature of things by objectifying them. *Brahman*, being the knower, the awareness in the sense organs, can never become the object of their knowledge. It can never be the object of any organ or kind of perception. To claim any kind of experience as the means through which the knowledge of *brahman* can be gained requires proof that this is possible without presupposing *brahman* as an object.

The impossibility of knowing *brahman* through any of the senses means that the other four *pramāṇas* (inference, comparison, postulation, and noncognition), dependent as they are on sense perception for their data, cannot afford any conclusive knowledge of *brahman*. It is Śaṅkara's often-stated view that independent reasoning cannot establish anything final about the nature of *brahman*. The summation, therefore, is that if *brahman* is to be known, it can only be through an authoritative source of knowledge consisting of words (*śabda*). This, affirms Śaṅkara, is what the *Upaniṣads* are and what they declare themselves to be. This dimension of Śaṅkara's rationale for the *śruti* as the *pramāṇa* of *brahman*, although it goes beyond the simple dogmatic assertions about the eternity of the *Vedas*, will still have little appeal for the skeptic who doubts even the existence of *brahman*. This fact, however, does not invalidate the reasoning behind it, and one imagines that it is intended for someone who accepts the existence of *brahman* but has doubts about the appropriate means of knowledge.

The aspect of Śaṅkara's rationale which I am emphasizing at this point is that given the nature of *brahman*, *śruti* as a means of knowledge consisting of words is the only logical and credible *pramāṇa*. The other important and complementary dimension of this rationale is that given the nature of *brahman* and the fact that the fundamental human problem is one of *avidyā* (ignorance), the knowledge derived from the words of the *śruti* is a fully adequate solution. For Śaṅkara, therefore, *śruti* as a *pramāṇa* is both logical and adequate. Modern commentators argue that Śaṅkara himself posits *anubhava* as the ultimate *pramāṇa* which certifies the provisional statements of the *śruti*. This view not only falsifies Śaṅkara's epistemology but also misses the substance of his assertion that the knowledge afforded through words is adequate. It is unfortunate that this significance has not been apprehended even by scholars such as R.V. de Smet and K.S. Murty, who have treated Śaṅkara's exegesis in some detail.[1]

Śaṅkara's arguments for the logic of words (*śabda*) as the *pramāṇa* of *brahmajñāna* center on the nature of *brahman*. His arguments for the adequacy of *śabda* also derive from the fact. The gist of these arguments is that *śruti* is not required to reveal *brahman* in the sense of demonstrating its existence. As awareness, the content and basis of the "I" notion, *brahman* is self-revealing and always manifest. Because *brahman*, as the Self, is self-illumining, no one doubts his or her own existence. While no human being is unaware of the existence of the Self, its true nature remains unknown. The consequence of this ignorance (*avidyā*) is that the limited attributes of the body and mind are wrongfully superimposed on the Self. The task of the *śruti*, therefore, is not the revelation or production of an unknown entity, but the imparting of correct knowledge about a Self which is misunderstood. This is all that is required. In Śaṅkara, the *śruti*, rather than being subservient to the authority of an experience, interprets and corrects the meaning of experience. This suggests that our experiences do not necessarily give rise to right knowledge and that, in relation to the knowledge of *brahman*, they do not provide a valid self-interpretation.

It is clear that as far as Śaṅkara is concerned, valid knowledge (*pramā*) is attained only by the application of a valid means of knowledge (*pramāṇa*), and he nowhere posits an experience as a spontaneous source of *brahmajñāna*. We cannot, therefore, emphasize strongly enough the misleading nature of the common contemporary tendency to classify Śaṅkara's *Advaita* as a form of mysticism on the basis that he posits a special experience as the source of ultimate knowledge. Human experiences, in the widest sense, may be employed in a secondary manner to support and clarify the propositions of the *śruti*, and this is what Śaṅkara does in his commentaries. The experiences of dream and deep sleep, for example, are analyzed by him to elucidate and reinforce *śruti* revelations about the nature of the Self. This is possible, however, only after the Self is known from the *śruti*, and these experiences are not affirmed by Śaṅkara to be independent, authoritative sources of knowledge.

Knowledge derived from inquiry (*jijñāsā*) into the meaning of words can be an adequate solution if the problem involved is merely one of ignorance (*avidyā*). In *Advaita*, *brahman* does not have to be attained. As the very Self of every human being, it is already fully accomplished. Actions (*karman*), which are necessary if one wants to create, modify, purify, or reach an object, are redundant in the case of *brahman*. No actions are required for the attainment of one's own Self, and the problem is only an incorrect apprehension of its nature. Knowledge is the sufficient solution to a problem of ignorance, and in this case the words of the *śruti* afford valid knowledge of the Self. *Brahmajñāna* is fully identified by Śaṅkara with knowledge gained from the *śruti*. Like the connection between *brahman* and the means through which it can be known, there is also a logical interrelationship in Śaṅkara between *avidyā*, as the problem, and knowledge (*jñāna*), derived from the words of the *śruti*, as the solution.

Śaṅkara's argument about the adequacy of knowledge derived from the sentences of the *śruti* as a solution to a problem of ignorance is underlined by his emphasis on the fruitfulness of these sentences. This is another element of Śaṅkara's understanding of the *śruti* overlooked by modern commentators. Śaṅkara reiterates the immediate fruitfulness of the knowledge derived from the sentences of the *śruti*. Even as the comprehension of the sentence "This is a rope, not a snake" can at once eliminate the fear of someone who mistakenly takes a rope for a snake, the knowledge gained from the sentences of the *śruti* directly removes the ignorance, grief, and fear associated with erroneously taking oneself to be the finite body. The fruitfulness of this knowledge, contends Śaṅkara, is apparent in the transformed life of one who appreciates the true nature of the Self.

It is significant and interesting that the argument about the efficacy of the *Vedānta-vākyas* in eliminating fear and sorrow is a principal one employed by Śaṅkara in responding to the *Pūrva-Mīmāṁsā* challenge of the independent authority of these sentences. *Pūrva-Mīmāṁsā*, it must be remembered, contend, that the *Vedānta-vākyas* do not have a purport of their own but are subservient to sentences enjoining ritual (*karman*). This is a challenge which Śaṅkara could not answer by a dogmatic assertion about the authority of the *Vedas* as derived from their eternity, since this is the very basis on which the *Vedas* are accepted by *Pūrva-Mīmāṁsā*. He seeks, therefore, to demonstrate the authority of these sentences by reference to their independent fruitfulness as a viable solution to the human problem of existential fear and sorrow. In the light of this fact, we wonder whether Śaṅkara, if he were alive today, might not have employed this as a leading argument in his appeal to those, Hindu or non-Hindu, lacking a traditional faith (*śraddha*) in the authority of the *śruti*. Perhaps the argument about the obvious and immediate fruitfulness of *brahmajñāna* in the lives of those who have understood and accepted it might have been combined with the less-dogmatic aspects of his rationale. It might have been connected with arguments that the knowledge afforded by the *śruti* is otherwise unobtainable, that it is reasonable, and that it is neither refuted nor contradicted by what is known through other *pramāṇas*. In other words, for Śaṅkara, novelty, fruitfulness, and noncontradiction might have been sufficient as the leading elements of a contemporary rationale for the *śruti*.

Modern commentators have failed to grasp the epistemological significance of Śaṅkara's affirmation that *mokṣa* is coincident with the gain of knowledge from the *śruti*. Modern commentators treat the attainment of *brahmajñāna* in Śaṅkara as proceeding in three stages. *Śravaṇa* (listening), the first of these, is described as acquainting us with the teachings of the *śruti*. In the second stage of *manana* (reflection), one seeks through reason to remove any doubts about these teachings. At the end of these two stages, however, knowledge still only has a tentative and provisional validity. It is really the final stage of *nididhyāsana* (contemplation) which affords an experience through which the claims of the *śruti* are directly apprehended and verified beyond all doubt. This experience, therefore, is presented as the true *pramāṇa* of *brahmajñāna*.

We have emphasized strongly in this study that Śaṅkara does not distinguish the nature and aims of these three processes in the manner of modern commentators. They are all intended for the understanding and assimilation of knowledge derived from the *śruti* sentences, not from any alternative source. Consistent with his view that *brahman*, as the Self, is immediately available and "unattained" only because of ignorance, he sees this clear understanding as all that is required. The relationship obtained between *brahman* and *śruti* is one between an existent but incorrectly known entity and the appropriate means of its knowledge. It is not the creation or attainment of anything new but the right knowledge of something already there.

Śaṅkara repudiates the need for any action, mental or physical, beyond the understanding of the *śruti*-sentences. In this he is very specific about the redundancy of meditation (*upāsanā*). In view of the indispensable function ascribed by modern interpretations to meditation in the attainment of *brahmajñāna*, Śaṅkara's lucid distinction between *jñāna* (knowledge) and meditation (*upāsanā*) is most revealing. He categorically distinguishes the nature and functions of these two processes. The substance of this distinction is focused on his understanding of meditation (*upāsanā*) as a mental activity in which the true nature of the object meditated upon is irrelevant. The object is conceived to be different from its actual nature, and each form of *upāsanā* has as its aim a hitherto nonexistent result. This is one important reason why meditation is classified as a variety of action by Śaṅkara, and not identified with *jñāna*. Meditation is not envisaged by Śaṅkara as concerned with or as having as its aim the attainment of knowledge corresponding with the exact nature of an object. It is extremely important to note that Śaṅkara condemns the view that after the knowledge of *brahman* is gained from the *śruti*, this knowledge must then be meditated upon to produce a further knowledge which is truly valid and capable of eliminating *avidyā*. This is the function which modern commentators ascribe to *nididhyāsana* in Śaṅkara. A theory/practice dichotomy is posited in which *śruti*-derived knowledge is affirmed as theory and meditation as the practice which leads to a verification of this theory. Śaṅkara's unmistakable position, however, is that the clear understanding of the nature of *brahman* from the sentences of the *śruti* is all that is required. This is the aim of inquiry into the *śruti*, the significance of which modern commentators who have worked on Śaṅkara's exegesis have overlooked. Even though, in considering Śaṅkara's epistemology, this study has had to cover certain common exegetical grounds with some of these commentators, it differs radically in its understanding of the aim of exegesis in Śaṅkara and of the status of knowledge gained at the end of it.

Meditation, then, in the view of Śaṅkara, has for its aim the creation of a previously nonexistent result, and its nature is not to concern itself with the true character of objects. *Jñāna* (knowledge), on the other hand, has for its aim the proper understanding of the true nature of existing objects. It cannot create or alter these objects but seeks simply to know them as they are. The indispensable requirement for any kind of *jñāna* is an appropriate and valid means of knowledge (*pramāṇa*) capable of revealing the entity as it is. For taste, it is the tongue; for sound, it is the ear; and for forms, it is the eye. *Brahman* is the ever-manifest Self of every human being and, indeed, of everything that exists. As the Self, *brahman* is already attained but incorrectly known. The words of the *śruti* constitute, for Śaṅkara, the valid means of knowing *brahman*. What is required, therefore, is the knowledge of *brahman*, derived from inquiry into the meanings of these words. This is the attainment of *brahmajñāna* and the joyful freedom of *mokṣa*.

Today, in *Advaita*, and more widely in Hinduism, the status of the *śruti* is ambiguous and contradictory. There is a disposition, noted in many of the studies reviewed in the Introduction, to assert its authority while simultaneously positing a view which undermines that authority. Hinduism seems, in general, to be embarrassed by the authority of the *śruti*, without proper critical evaluation of the alternative sources of spiritual knowledge set before it. There is a rational justification for *śruti* as a *pramāṇa* of *brahmajñāna* in Śaṅkara, centered on its logicality, its adequacy, and its fruitfulness. There is an urgent need in *Advaita* and in Hinduism to take a fresh look at the traditional understanding of the *śruti* as a *pramāṇa* and to unfold, clarify, and evaluate this understanding. This process needs to be undertaken, even as Śaṅkara did in his time, with reference to contemporary views and concerns. It is a task which calls for a unity between the commitments of both faith and scholarship. The elements of this traditional understanding derived from *Pūrva-Mīmāṁsā* need, in particular, to be studied and reinterpreted. Must the concept of the *śruti* as *śabda-pramāṇa* be necessarily linked to the eternity of a language (viz., Sanskrit)? Is the argument for the eternity of a language necessary to show that the *śruti* is of a nonhuman origin? In a secular and skeptical age, many difficult questions will have to be asked, but as Hinduism will unhesitatingly admit, meaningful answers will never be given or discovered until meaningful questions are asked.

Notes

Introduction

1. Swami Prabhavananda, *The Spiritual Heritage of India* (London: Allen and Unwin, 1962) p. 15.
2. S. Radhakrishnan, *The Hindu View of Life* (London: Allen and Unwin, 1927; Unwin Paperbacks, 1980), p. 13.
3. C. Sharma, *A Critical Survey of Indian Philosophy* (Delhi: Motilal Banarsidass, 1976), p. 13. Not all writers, however, accept this use of the word *darśana*. Hiriyanna, for instance, uses the word to mean "philosophic opinion," and sees it as specifying a school of thought. See M. Hiriyanna, *Outlines of Indian Philosophy* (London: Allen and Unwin, 1932; first Indian reprint ed., Bombay: Allen and Unwin, 1973), p. 182.
4. Radhakrishnan's main discussion of Śaṅkara occurs in his work, *Indian Philosophy*, 2 vols. (London: Allen and Unwin, 1971), 2, 445–658. Of all the thinkers treated by Radhakrishnan in the two volumes, Śaṅkara has been accorded the most detailed analysis. Radhakrishnan is himself regarded as an Advaitin, and his exposition of Śaṅkara is in a large measure an attempt to defend *Advaita* against many common criticisms.
5. Radhakrishnan, *Indian Philosophy*, 2, 494–496.
6. Radhakrishnan, *The Hindu View of Life*, pp. 14–15. See also, Prabhavananda, *The Spiritual Heritage of India*, p. 17.
7. T.M.P. Mahadevan, "The Place of Reason and Revelation in the Philosophy of an Early Advaitin," in *Proceedings of the Tenth Philosophical Congress of Philosophy, Amsterdam, August 11–18, 1948* (Amsterdam: North-Holland, 1949), p. 248.
8. See M.A. Buch, *The Philosophy of Śaṁkara* (Baroda: A.G. Widgery, 1921), p. 271.
9. See M.K. Iyer, *Advaita Vedānta* (New York: Asia Publishing House, 1964), pp. 152–153.
10. Radhakrishnan, *Indian Philosophy*, 2, 518.
11. Mahadevan, "The Place of Reason," p. 248.
12. Y.K. Menon and R.F. Allen, *The Pure Principle: An Introduction to the Philosophy of Śaṅkara* (Michigan State University Press, 1960), pp. 17–18.
13. See R.P. Singh, *The Vedānta of Śaṅkara — a Metaphysics of Value*, vol. 1 (Jaipur: Bharat Publishing House, 1949), pp. 202–203.
14. Radhakrishnan, *Indian Philosophy*, 2, 514.
15. Ibid.

16. Mahadevan, "The Place of Reason...," p. 249. See also S.K. Belvalkar, *Vedānta Philosophy* (Poona: Belrakunja Publishing House, 1929), p. 14.
17. Menon and Allen, *The Pure Principle*, p. 18.
18. Iyer, *Advaita Vedānta*, p. 153.
19. Radhakrishnan, *Indian Philosophy*, 2, 518.
20. Ibid., p. 514.
21. Belvalkar, *Vedānta Philosophy*, pp. 15–16.
22. Buch, *The Philosophy of Śaṅkara*, p. 274.
23. Radhakrishnan, *Indian Philosophy*, 2, 510.
24. Ibid., p. 617.
25. Ibid., p. 534. Radhakrishnan's concern to emphasize the mystical origin and foundation of Śaṅkara's conclusion seems to conflict with his equal concern to characterize *Advaita* as a "purely philosophical scheme." This description, whenever employed, is intended to distinguish it from a theological scheme. The distinction is obviously based on his own view of the respective roles of the theologian and the philosopher, the nature of the two disciplines, and his own interpretation of Śaṅkara's position. In Radhakrishnan's view, the theologian is one who takes a stand on a particular denominational basis. He/she is identified with a particular religious tradition and the purpose is to systematize, expand and defend the doctrines of that tradition. The philosopher, on the other hand, is not bound by any particular religious tradition considered to be true. Religion in general is the province of the investigation. It is interesting to note that this is a quite common description of *Advaita* employed by many writers, most of whom do not provide any clear definitions of philosophy or theology. See, for example, Prabhavananda, *The Spiritual Heritage of India*, p. 293.
26. Prabhavananda, *The Spiritual Heritage of India*, pp. 293–294. Very revealing of the authority attributed by Prabhavananda to direct experience is the manner in which he treats *anubhava* as nondifferent from *śruti*, or as an additional *pramāṇa*. He subjects *anubhava* to the criteria normally used for certifying a *pramāṇa*. He argues that for the experience to be genuine, it must reveal an entity unknowable through any other means and that the content of its revelation must not be contradicted by any other means of knowledge. See p. 16.
27. C. Sharma, *A Critical Survey of Indian Philosophy*, p. 289.
28. R.P. Singh, *The Vedānta of Śaṅkara*, p. 186. The determination of epistemology by experience is, according to Singh, what Śaṅkara means by the concept of *vastutantram*. I submit, however, that this is a misunderstanding of this concept. In Śaṅkara, the idea of *vastutantram* as opposed to *puruṣatantram* is used to distinguish the entire

process of knowledge from the process of activity. The distinction and its significance will be considered subsequently.

29. Ibid., p. 168.
30. S.K. Belvalkar, *Vedānta Philosophy*, pp. 17–18. One wonders about the validity of Belvalkar's argument for the superiority of experience over reason in ordinary life. It is very common for experience to be corrected and interpreted by reason. Even while seeing a mirage of water, for example, one knows it to be false.
31. N.K. Devaraja, *An Introduction to Śaṅkara's Theory of Knowledge*, 2nd ed., rev. (Delhi: Motilal Banarsidass, 1972).
32. Ibid., p. 66.
33. One wonders here whether Devaraja has apprehended the special sense in which the word object is used by Śaṅkara in this context. This significant point will be discussed later.
34. Ibid., p. 67.
35. Śaṅkara, quoted in ibid., p. 57.
36. Śaṅkara, quoted in ibid., p. 62. Devaraja, however, refrains from discussing Śaṅkara's reply to this contention. For full discussion, see B.S.B. 2.1.4–6, pp. 307–15.
37. M. Hiriyanna, *Outlines of Indian Philosophy*, pp. 336–82.
38. Ibid., p. 358.
39. Ibid., pp. 380–381.
40. See M. Hiriyanna, *Indian Philosophical Studies* (Mysore: Kavyalaya Publishers, 1957), pp. 48–49.
41. N. Smart, *Doctrine and Argument in Indian Philosophy* (London: Allen and Unwin, 1964), p. 98.
42. Ibid., p. 104. The view that *Advaita* is essentially nondifferent from *Mahāyāna* has been seriously questioned. Devaraja, *Śaṅkara's Theory of Knowledge*, pp. 12–22, discusses very central differences of method and content between the two schools. It is a theme to which he returns throughout his study.
43. Smart, *Doctrine and Argument in Indian Philosophy*, p. 150.
44. Smart, *The Yogi and the Devotee* (London: Allen and Unwin, 1968). In this work, Smart traces the development of *Advaita* from a synthesis between the non-Vedic religions (Buddhism, Jainism, *Sāṅkhya-Yoga*) and Vedic religions. The latter contributed the concept of *brahman*, and the former the idea of Self, etc. He traces a similar process in *Mahāyāna* Buddhism. In both cases, the distinctive element is the higher role assigned to *dhyāna* as the ultimate means of freedom. This distinguishes it from the theism of Mādhava and Rāmānuja. Smart's thesis rests upon his presupposition about the place of *dhyāna* in Śaṅkara. One wonders also whether the differences between Śaṅkara

and Rāmānuja could be explained as the results of the application of the different techniques of *dhyāna* and *bhakti*. Smart reduces his thesis to a mathematical-like formula:

2 *dhyāna*	+	1 *bhakti*	=	Absolutism
2 *bhakti*	+	1 *dhyāna*	=	Theism
2 *dhyāna*	+	0 *bhakti*	=	Non-theistic Pluralism

See p. 50.

45. R.V. de Smet, "Śaṅkara's Non-Dualism," in R.V. de Smet and J. Neuner, eds., *Religious Hinduism* (Allahabad: St. Paul's Publications, 1964), pp. 52–61.
46. Ibid., p. 55.
47. Ibid., p. 56. This conflict is also very evident in a most recent work of Eric Lott. There is a clear statement of Śaṅkara's assertion that knowledge of *brahman* results from grasping the meaning of the Vedic statements indicating identity, followed by an affirmation of the finality of intuition. See Lott, *Vedāntic Approaches to God* (London: Macmillian Press, 1980), p. 169.
48. BR.U. 2.4.5.
49. Jacob Kattackal, *Religion and Ethics in Advaita* (Freiburg: Herder, 1980), pp. 122–123.
50. Mahadevan, "The Place of Reason," p. 251.
51. Iyer, *Advaita Vedānta*, p. 174. Also, Menon and Allen, *The Pure Principle*, pp. 21–22.
52. R.V. de Smet, "The Theological Method of Śaṁkara" (Ph.D. thesis, Gregorian University, 1953), p. 333.
53. Singh, *The Vedānta of Śaṅkara*, p. 186. The only difference, according to this writer, between sensuous perception and internal perception is that the latter is also a consciousness of value. Singh's claim that Śaṅkara describes *śruti* as intuitional perception is based on a misreading of B.S.B. 1.3.28. Śaṅkara's description of *śruti* as *pratyakṣa* is in relation to his reference to *smṛti* as inference. *Smṛti* is related to *śruti* even as inference is to direct perception. The former is dependent on the latter for its data and authority. See B.S.B. 1.3.28, p.210.
54. Singh, *The Vedānta of Śaṅkara*, p. 197.
55. Iyer, *Advaita Vedānta*, p. 188.
56. Buch, *The Philosophy of Śaṅkara*, p. 260.
57. S.N. Dasgupta, *Hindu Mysticism* (Chicago: Open Court Publishing Co., 1927).
58. Ibid., pp. 46–47.
59. Ibid., Preface, viii.
60. Ibid., p. 81.

61. R.C. Zaehner, *Mysticism Sacred and Profane* (Clarendon Press, 1957; rpt. ed., London: Oxford University Press, 1978). Also *Hindu and Muslim Mysticism* (London School of Oriental and African Studies, 1960; New York: Schocken Books, 1972).
62. Geoffrey Parrinder, *Mysticism in the World's Religions* (London: Sheldon Press, 1976).
63. Ibid., pp. 11–12.
64. Ibid., p. 32.
65. Ibid., p. 37.
66. For a most recent and typical consideration of *Advaita* as mysticism, see Kattackal, *Religion and Ethics in Advaita*, Chs. 1–2. According to Kattackal, the transcendental experience is regarded by *Advaita* as the true state of *jñāna*, and the major conclusions of *Advaita* are deduced from the nature of this experience.
67. In a recent article, Kim Skoog has identified a number of writers (K. Potter, E. Deutsch, S. Mayeda and S. Murty) whom, he claims, emphasize the significance of *śruti* in Śaṅkara. While there is a greater recognition among these writers for the role of *śruti* in Śaṅkara, it is not clear, however, that they affirm the views adopted in this study. See Skoog, "Śaṁkara on the Role of *Śruti* and *Anubhava* in Attaining *Brahmajñāna*," *Philosophy East and West*, 39, No. 1 (January 1989), 67–74.

Chapter 1

1. *Advaita Vedānta* epistemology borrows a great deal from the orthodox *Pūrva-Mīmāṁsā* school. The word *Mīmāṁsā* means inquiry, and this system undertakes a systematic analysis of the first (*pūrva*) parts of the *Vedas*, the *mantras* (hymns in praise of various deities), the *brāhmaṇas* (guide books for the performance of sacrifices), and the *āraṇyakas* (philosophical interpretations of the sacrifices). *Vedānta* is referred to as *Uttara-Mīmāṁsā* because its concern is with the analysis of the last (*uttara*) sections of the *Vedas*, the *Upaniṣads*.

   The *sūtras* of Jaimini (ca. 200 B.C.) are the earliest work of this system and form its basis. There are over twenty-fixe hundred *sūtras* discussing one thousand topics. Jaimini's work was commented upon by Śabara Swāmi (ca. A.D. 400) and his work was further commented upon by Prabhākara and Kumārila Bhaṭṭa, who differ from each other in certain important respects and form the two principal schools of *Mīmāṁsā*, named after them. Śaṅkara generally follows the *Bhāṭṭa* school but with considerable differences, as will become evident later.
2. For Śaṅkara and his immediate disciples, epistemology and metaphysical issues were treated together. The *Vedānta-Paribhāṣā* of

Dharmarājā, a seventeenth-century *Advaitin*, is the first systematic exposition of *Advaita* epistemology. It is a classic work in the history of *Advaita*, and its study is a must for all serious students of this system. It discusses the *pramāṇas* in detail and offers an *Advaita* interpretation of the nature and validity of knowledge. The *Vedānta-Paribhāṣā* is divided into eight chapters. In the first six chapters, he defines and discusses the six means of knowledge accepted in common by *Pūrva-Mīmāṁsā* and *Advaita*. The seventh chapter is devoted in the main to an analysis of the terms *tat* and *tvam* and the final chapter discusses the nature of *mokṣa* and the means of its attainment. Frequent references will be made to this important work in the course of my discussions. See Ch. 1, p. 5.

3. D.M. Datta, *Six Ways of Knowing* (London: Allen and Unwin, 1932), p. 27.
4. Ibid.
5. BR.U.B. 2.1.20, p. 214.
6. B.S.B. 1.1.4, p. 34.
7. B.S.B. 1.1.2, pp. 16–17.
8. V.P., Ch. 1, p. 5.
9. Ibid., p. 7.
10. *Advaita* posits three orders of existence: (1) Absolute (*pāramārthika*) existence belongs to nondual *brahman* alone. (2) Empirical (*vyāvahārika*) is the objective universe, the independent reality which endures until *brahman*, its substratum, is known. (3) Illusory (*prātibhāsika*) existence is the false appearance of something where it does not exist, such as the perception of mirage water in the desert. It comes to an end as soon as the obstacles to proper perception are removed and its locus is correctly apprehended. See V.P., Ch.2, p. 81.
11. B.S.B., Intro., p. 4.
12. The word generally is used because of the exceptional case of the *jīvan-mukta*, who, having gained self-knowledge, continues in the embodied state. It should not be thought that access to information through the *pramāṇas* is impossible for this person. The difference is that the employment of the instruments of knowledge proceeds from the clear understanding of the distinction between Self and non-Self and is, therefore, not founded in *avidyā*. It would be absurd to contend that having gained self-knowledge, the *jīvan-mukta* is incapable of any further kind of knowledge because the *pramāṇas*, founded in *avidyā*, cease to be operative. This is why it was important to point out the nature of the relationship between *avidyā* and the *pramāṇas*. The *pramāṇas* are operative both in the presence and absence of the

notion of superimposition. The *Bhagavadgītā* beautifully describes the attitude of the *jīvan-mukta* to the *pramāṇas.*

> "I do nothing at all"; thus would the truth-knower think, steadfast, — though seeing, hearing, touching, smelling, eating, going, sleeping, breathing, speaking, letting go, seizing, opening and closing the eyes, — remembering that the senses move among sense-objects (B.G. 5:8–9).

13. BR.U.B. 4.3.6, p. 425.
14. B.S.B. 2.2.28, pp. 419–420.
15. For an outline of the *Advaita* views, see V.P., Ch. 6., pp. 143–149.
16. Some general textbooks carry brief summaries of this theory. See C. Sharma, *A Critical Survey of Indian Philosophy*, Ch. 13.
17. Ibid., pp. 146–148.
18. V.P., Ch. 6, pp. 144–145. It must be noted that the *Advaita* theory of *svataḥ-prāmāṇya-vādā* advocates that the same causes which produce a particular cognition also give rise to its validity (*svataḥ-prāmāṇyam-utpadyate*) as well as a belief in that validity (*prāmāṇyam-svataḥ-jñāyate*). The theory is proposed in these two aspects. It may be argued that there is a contradiction in proposing that the same causes which produce a particular cognition also produce its validity. What happens when there is a false cognition? Is this also produced by the same causes that produce the valid cognition? The *Advaita* position, however, is that the same causes do not produce valid and invalid cognitions. When a cognition is found to be invalid, this invalidity is explained as arising not from the causes themselves but from a defect which has entered into those causes. *Advaita* considers this defect to be an extraneous factor. Valid cognitions arise when the causes are free from defects, while invalid ones are traced to some defect in those causes. See P. K. Sundaram, *Advaita Epistemology* (Madras: University of Madras, 1968), pp. 178–81. Also Swami Satprakashananda, *Methods of Knowledge* (Calcutta: Advaita Ashrama, 1974), pp. 111–114 and S. Chatterjee and D. Datta, *An Introduction to Indian Philosophy* (Calcutta: University of Calcutta, 1968), pp. 329–332.
19. For a brief summary of the *Nyāya* position, see Devaraja, *An Introduction to Śaṅkara's Theory of Knowledge*, pp. 122–126.
20. See Datta, *Six Ways of Knowing*, p. 21.
21. B.S.B. 1.1.4, p. 23. This argument will become even clearer when the nature of scripture as a *pramāṇa* is subsequently discussed.
22. Ibid., 2.2.31, p. 426.
23. B.G. 13:1–2.

24. Ibid., 9:18.
25. See N.K. Devaraja, *An Introduction to Śaṅkara's Theory of Knowledge*, pp. 112–113. Also G.P. Bhatt, *Epistemology of the Bhāṭṭa School of Pūrva Mīmāṁsā* (Varanasi: The Chowkhamba Sanskrit Series Office, 1962), pp. 51–56.
26. B.G.B. 18:50, pp. 488–490.
27. PR.U.B. 6.2, p. 487.
28. The schools of Indian philosophy have defined the nature and number of the *pramāṇas* differently, and a discussion of considerable sophistication and detail has developed concerning each one. It is neither possible nor relevant for me to attempt a detailed and comparative treatment of each *pramāṇa*. My concern here is primarily with *śabda-pramāṇa*, and my purposes will be served by a general outline of the nature and function of each one. A few references will be made to other schools where they highlight the *Advaita* definition. For a detailed comparative treatment and attempt to vindicate the six *pramāṇas*, see Datta, *Six Ways of Knowing*.
29. V.P., Ch. 1, p. 66.
30. Ibid., p. 12.
31. T.B., pp. 17–22. The authenticity of *Tattvabodha* as a work of Śaṅkara is under question. See K.H. Potter, ed., *The Encyclopedia of Indian Philosophies*, vol. 3 (Delhi: Motilal Banarsidass, 1981), pp. 331–333.
32. The five organs of action (*karmendriyas*) evolve from the *rajas* aspect of the five elements. The organ of speech is born from the *rajas* aspect of space; the hands from the *rajas* aspect of air; the legs from the *rajas* aspect of fire; the genitals from the *rajas* aspect of water; and the anus from the *rajas* aspect of earth. From the total *rajas* aspect of these five elements is evolved the five *prāṇas*. The *tamas* aspect of the five elements, by undergoing the process of grossification, evolve into the five gross elements. The first stage in this process is the division of each element into two equal halves. One half of each element remains intact, while the other half divides into four equal parts. In the final stage, the intact half combines with one part of each of the other four elements, and the process is completed. From these grossified elements, the visible physical body is formed.
33. BR.U.B. 2.4.11, p. 254.
34. Ibid., 1.5.3, p. 148. It should be noted that terms such as *manas* and *buddhi*, which strictly speaking denote functions of the *antaḥkaraṇa*, are sometimes used by Śaṅkara to denote the entire organ. *Manas* is that mode (*vṛtti*) of the *antaḥkaraṇa* characterized by doubt and indecision, while *buddhi* indicates the function of decision and determination.

35. Ibid.
36. The *ātman* and the *antaḥkaraṇa* are entirely distinct. Like the sense objects, the states of the mind are knowable, and the *antaḥkaraṇa* stands in relation to the *ātman* as known and knower. Being composed of the subtlest substance, the *antaḥkaraṇa* easily reflects the light that is the Self. Through the contact with the *antaḥkaraṇa*, the sense organs receive consciousness, and through these it is transmitted to the physical body. The Self thus successively illumines the aggregate of body and organs. See BR.U.B. 4.3.7, p. 428.
37. Two of the organs, the senses of seeing and hearing, reach out to their objects, while the organs of touch, taste, and smell generate cognition while abiding in their locations. See V.P., Ch. 1, p. 66. For an argument in favor of this view, see D.M. Datta, *Six Ways of Knowing*, pp. 39–71. Datta tries to show it as a more favorable explanation of perception than other available theories.
38. BR.U.B. 1.4.10, p. 103; 5.14.4, p. 592.
39. "Invariable concomitance is co-existence with the thing to be inferred that must abide in all substrata of the reason" (V.P., Ch. 2, p. 73).
40. There is a broad consensus among Indian schools of philosophy about the general principles of inference, but important differences as regards to its particulars. While *vyāpti*, for instance, is accepted as the essential element of *anumāna*, there is disagreement about its ascertainment. *Nyāya*, as one would expect, has taken the lead in the methodic study of this source of knowledge.
41. V.P., Ch. 2, p. 73.
42. Ibid., p. 74. *Advaita* sees negative invariable concomitance as a case of postulation.
43. BR.U.B. 4.3.7, pp. 436, 433; B.S.B. 2.3.26, p. 485.
44. V.P., Ch. 2, p. 76. Śaṅkara himself is usually satisfied with stating the first two stages and occasionally adding the example.
45. V.P., Ch. 3, p. 83.
46. Ibid., p. 85.
47. "It is the assumption of an explanatory fact (*upapādaka*) from a knowledge of the thing to be explained (*upapādya*)" (V.P., Ch. 5, p. 117).
48. See D.M. Datta, *Six Ways of Knowing*, pp. 236–237.
49. V.P., Ch. 5, p. 124.
50. V.P., Ch. 6.
51. This view of *Advaita* contrasts strongly with the *Nyāya* argument that nonexistence is available for sense perception. According to *Nyāya*, each sense organ can perceive the existence as well as the nonexistence of its respective object. It argues that the nonexistence

of an object in a particular locus is related to the locus as an attribute. The room, for example, has as its attribute the nonexistence of the table. Because of this relation, the perception of the floor leads to the perception of the nonexistence of the table through a special contact between the organ of vision and the nonexistence of the table. *Advaita* argues, however, that in no case can the sense organ come in contact with any kind of nonexistence. See V.P., Ch. 6, p. 133.

52. "Only a nonapprehension that is possessed of capacity is (to be regarded as) the instrument of an apprehension of nonexistence" (V.P., Ch. 6, p. 126). See also pp. 127–128.

53. *Śabda-pramāṇa* can be viewed in two ways. It can be seen as inclusive of all knowledge, secular and sacred, transmitted through language. It can also be seen as referring specifically to the *Vedas* as a unique form of *śabda-pramāṇa.* It is with the analysis and understanding of *śabda-pramāṇa* in the latter sense that *Advaita* is primarily concerned. There are important differences between the understanding of the concept in the general and specific senses. In the former sense, for example, *śabda* is of human origin (*pauruṣeya*), while in the latter sense it is of nonhuman origin (*apauruṣeya*). These terms will be considered in more detail later. In the discussion which immediately follows, *śabda* is treated in the general sense. I have only provided some brief remarks here since the discussion in the following chapters is intended to give a detailed analysis of the conception of the *Vedas* as *śabda-pramāṇa.*

54. *Śabda-pramāṇa* is commonly translated as "testimony" or "authority." I find, however, as I hope to demonstrate, that neither of these two terms reflects the complexity of the concept. It is difficult to find a simple expression which accurately communicates the notion. I have chosen, therefore, to leave the expression untranslated.

55. This argument is central to the claim that *brahman* can be known from *śruti* as *śabda-pramāṇa.*

56. See D.M. Datta, *Six Ways of Knowing*, pp. 330–332. Datta's work provides many useful insights, but its main limitation is that it discusses *śabda-pramāṇa* and its associated theories with little or no reference to the justification of *śruti* as a *pramāṇa.* It is apparent that most of the *Advaita* arguments evolved with this concern in mind, and their rationale can only be understood in this context.

Chapter 2

1. This does not contradict my previous argument that the nature and method of *śabda-pramāṇa* distinguishes it as an independent source of knowledge.

2. Some *Advaitins*, however, argue that even in the empirical world, *śabda-pramāṇa* alone can inform us of another person's thoughts and emotions.
3. The *Vedas* are collectively referred to as *śruti* (literally, "that which is heard"). This term suggests the oral transmission of knowledge in a succession of teachers and students. It is suggested that the reason for the oral transmission of Vedic knowledge was the absence of a written script at the time when the *Vedas* were composed. It appears that even long after writing was introduced, there was a clear preference for the oral transmission of scripture, and religious learning through the written word was looked down upon. Perhaps it was felt that the oral transmission of a tradition was a far better way of ensuring its living continuity. Vedic words had to be handed down exactly as they had been heard, and correct sounds and pronunciations became all-important. Continuous repetition became the mode of learning, and *śravaṇa* (listening) became the first procedure in assimilating knowledge. See William Cenker, "The Pandit: The Embodiment of Oral Tradition," *Journal of Dharma*, 5 (1980), pp. 237–251.
4. B.G.B., Intro., pp. 2–3.
5. B.G. 4:7–8.
6. Ibid., 4:6.
7. Ibid., 4:5.
8. Ibid., 7:26.
9. Ibid., 3:22.
10. Ibid., 3:23–24.
11. B.G.B., Intro., p. 4.
12. Ibid. "Know this by long prostration, by inquiry, by service, those men of wisdom who have realized the truth will teach thee wisdom" (ibid., 4:34).
13. B.G. 4:1–3.
14. B.S.B. 1.1.1, p. 12.
15. Ibid., Intro., p. 3.
16. B.G.B. 2:16, pp. 34–37.
17. B.S.B. 1.1.1, p. 12.
18. Ibid., 1.3.28, p. 209.
19. This contrasts with the *Nyāya* view of universals as real, eternal, and independent of their respective particulars, to which they are related by inherence.
20. For a summary of these views, see Datta, *Six Ways of Knowing*, pp. 259–273.
21. B.S.B. 1.3.28, p. 209.

22. V.P., Ch. 4, p. 94.
23. B.S.B. 1.3.28, p. 209. *Pūrva-Mīmāṁsā* deals with this objection by arguing that such words as *Vasu* refer to unique individuals who are eternal, and thus the connection between them and the words signifying them is eternal. They also contend that gods are birthless, deathless, and unembodied. This theory, however, is not acceptable to Śaṅkara. On the evidence of various texts, he argues that gods are also embodied. It is only through extraordinary merit that this status is achieved, and it is, in fact, lost when this merit is exhausted. See ibid., 1.3.26–27, pp. 204-207.
24. Ibid., 1.3.28, p. 213. The *sphoṭa* doctrine was postulated by Indian grammarians to explain how the individual and separate syllables which comprise any word can reveal its meaning. The syllables are presented separately to the hearer. Corresponding to each word and sentence, there is a latent and indivisible *sphoṭa* which conveys its meaning. As the sounds of a word are sequentially uttered, the corresponding *sphoṭa* is progresively revealed. Since the *sphoṭa* is conceived by its advocates to be eternal and indivisible, there is no question of a time sequence, and it can be grasped as a whole. The theory of *sphoṭa* is rejected by Śaṅkara.
25. Ibid.
26. Ibid.
27. Ibid., p. 214.
28. The doctrine of the eternity of the word and its connection with its referent is taken over by Śaṅkara from the *Pūrva-Mīmāmśā* school. See M.S.J. 1.1.5–23, pp. 8–16. *Sūtras* 6–11 detail several arguments against the eternity of the word. In *sūtras* 12–17, Jaimini attempts to refute each argument individually and follows this, in *sūtras* 18–23, with independent arguments for the eternal word. According to Jaimini, the momentary nature of the word is not due to its noneternity but is the result of the function of its manifesting agency. Utterance only manifests what is already existing. When we speak of the production of a word, we only indicate its utterance and not its creation anew. Changes in pronunciation are only indicative of changes in tone and not in the word itself. If the uttered word was transient, it would vanish immediately, and there would be no possibility of comprehension. We should be reminded that the intention behind the *Mīmāṁsā* view is the justification of the *Vedas* as a defect-free source of knowledge. The view here seems to be that if the relationship between words and their meanings is fixed by human convention, like everything human it will be liable to error. The argument, therefore, is that this relationship is natural, eternal, and free from error.
29. B.S.B. 1.3.29, p. 216.

30. See Ganganatha Jha, *The Pūrva-Mīmāṁsā in Its Sources* (Benares: Benares Hindu University, 1942), p. 153.
31. M.S.J. 1.1.27, p. 19.
32. Ibid., 1.1.30, p. 20.
33. B.S.B. 1.3.28, p. 211.
34. Ibid., pp. 209–10.
35. Ibid., pp. 210–11.
36. Ibid., 1.3.30, p. 217.
37. Ibid., pp. 217–21.
38. Ibid., pp. 218–19.
39. Ibid., 4.1.4, p. 821. Śaṅkara cites BR.U. 4.3.22: "The *Vedas* are no *Vedas*." See also V.P., Ch. 4, p. 113.
40. The attitude of early *Mīmāṁsā* writers about God is a matter of some controversy. It is sometimes argued that they did not discuss God because they were primarily concerned with establishing the *Vedas* as a self-evident, eternal source of knowledge and inquiring into ritual. Jaimini says nothing about God. Kumārila Bhaṭṭa, on the other hand, severely criticized theistic arguments for God and an omniscient person and seems to find the concept absurd. It is of interest to note a few of his arguments. It is not proper, he argues, to attribute the creation of a world that is full of pain and suffering to God. Suffering cannot be traced back to merit and demerit, which are nonexistent at the beginning of creation. Compassion cannot be the motive for creation, since there are no beings to whom compassion can be shown. Besides, on this view, the world would be made entirely happy, for there is nothing that could deter the compassionate activity. If it is deterred, God could not be omnipotent. Why should God create? If God's activity is purposeless, God is not an intelligent person. If God creates because of God's desire for sport (*līlā*), God cannot be regarded as one who is complete. If the theist is concerned about finding a cause to explain the world process, *karman* can be regarded as a sufficient cause. Against the notion of an omniscient person, Kumārila argues that whether a person knows all can only be verified by someone who is omniscient. Logically, therefore, there should be many omniscient persons. See Jha, *The Pūrva-Mīmāṁsā* in Its Sources, pp. 47–52.
41. B.S.B. 1.2.2, p. 111.
42. Ibid., 1.1.3, pp. 18–19.
43. "Those that are called the *Ṛg-Veda* (*Yajur-Veda*, etc.) are but the exhalation of this great Being" (BR.U. 2.4.10).
44. BR.U.B. 2.4.10, p. 251.

45. B.S.B. 1.3.28, p. 210. See also B.G.B. 15:15, p. 409. Here also he interprets authorship in the sense of initiating the regular succession of teaching.
46. "The sacrificers, having acquired fitness to receive the *Veda* as a result of the earlier performance of good deeds, received it as it had already existed among the *ṛṣis*" (*Ṛg-Veda mantra*, quoted in B.S.B. 1.3.29, p. 217). Or, "In the days of yore, the great *ṛṣis* received through austerities, with the permission of the self-born One, the *Veda*, together with the anecdotes, that had remained withdrawn during dissolution" (ibid). See also 1.3.30, p. 219.
47. V.P., Ch. 4, pp. 115–116.
48. Vācaspati Miśra flourished in the first half of the 9th century A.D. He occupies a very important place in the history of *Advaita* thought. His two most important works are *Bhāmatī* and *Tattvasmīkṣā*. *Bhamātī* is a commentary on a portion of Śaṅkara's commentary on the *Brahma-sūtra*, while *Tattvasmīkṣā* is a commentary on the *Brahma-siddhi* of Maṇḍanamiśra. The first work is supposed to have been named in honor of his wife.
49. *Bhāmatī*, 1.1.2, pp. 141–42.
50. BR.U.B., Intro., 1.1, pp. 1–5.
51. B.S.B. 2.1.6, p. 314.
52. Ibid., 3.1.25, pp. 585–586.
53. *Mīmāṁsā* is in full agreement with Śaṅkara on this point, even though they do not agree, as we shall see, that the *Vedas* are also a *pramāṇa* for *brahman*. The *Mīmāṁsā* argument is that although *dharma* is an object of knowledge, it is not amenable to senseperception. Perception can only apprehend objects which are in existence at the time and are in contact with the organs. *Dharma*, however, is not in existence at the time of perception and has to be brought into being by certain acts. In addition, it has no external or tangible form and cannot be in contact with any of the sense organs. The other *pramāṇas* such as inference, presumption, etc., are more or less dependent on perception and are not, therefore, applicable. See M.S.J. 1.1.4, pp. 6–7. Also, Jha, *The Pūrva-Mīmāṁsā in Its Sources*, pp. 175–176.
54. BR.U.B., Intro., 1.1, pp. 1–2.
55. Ibid., pp. 2–3.
56. It is very important to note the specific sense in which Śaṅkara is using the concepts of *dharma* and *adharma* in this discussion. Here it implies *puṇya* (merit) and *pāpa* (demerit) accruing particularly from the performance and nonperformance of recommended ritual activities. Actions are understood as having a twofold result: seen (*dṛṣṭa*) and unseen (*adṛṣṭa*). Śaṅkara's contention is that the unique relation between any action and its unseen result can be known only from

the *Vedas*. The *adṛṣṭa* result is conceived of as a subtle, persisting impression that has the potency of bearing good or evil in the course of time.

57. BR.U.B., Intro., 1.1, pp. 3–5. Śaṅkara's attribution of an independent authoritative aim to the *jñānakāṇḍa* of the *Vedas* is perhaps the most important exegetical divergence from *Pūrva-Mīmāṁsā*, whose views he adopts on so many other matters. *Pūrva-Mīmāṁsā* considers only the injunctive statements of the *Vedas* to be authoritative. All other passages serve as auxiliaries to injunctions. We shall consider the details of this interesting controversy later. For further statements of Śaṅkara on the limitations of the ritual portions of the *Vedas*, see B.G.B. 2:42–44, p. 61; MU.U.B. 1.2.12, pp. 109-111.
58. BR.U.B. 2.3.6, p. 236.
59. Ibid., 4.4.6, p. 504. "The ultimate aim of the *Upaniṣads* is to teach Self-knowledge" (BR.U.B. 3.5.1, p. 336).
60. The terms *brahman* and *ātman* are interchangeable here because of their identity.
61. B.S.B. 1.1.2, p. 17; 1.1.4, p. 22.
62. BR.U.B. 3.9.26, pp. 388–389.
63. See above, Ch. 1.4.
64. The other elements, the particular qualities which they manifest, and the organs evolved out of them are as follows:

Space	Sound	Ear
Air	Touch	Skin
Water	Taste	Tongue
Earth	Smell	Nose

65. "One becomes freed from the jaws of death by knowing that which is soundless, touchless, colourless, undiminishing and also tasteless, eternal, odourless, without beginning and without end, distinct from *Mahat*, and ever constant" (KA.U. 1.3.15).
66. B.G.B. 13:12, pp. 345–346. Also 2:25, p. 51.
67. "This body, O son of Kunti, is called the Field (*Kshetra*); that which knoweth it is called the Knower of the Field (*Kshetrajña*)" (B.G. 13:1).
68. Ibid., 13:17.
69. BR.U.B. 2.4.14, p. 261. Also, KE.U.B. 2.1, pp. 59–60.
70. "It being an established fact that the object and the subject, that are fit to be the contents on the concepts "I" and "it" (respectively) and are by nature contradictory as light and darkness, cannot logically have any identity, it follows that their attributes can have it still less. Accordingly, the superimposition of the object, referable through the concept "it" and its attributes on the subject that is conscious by

nature and is referable through the concept "I" (should be impossible), and contrariwise the superimposition of the subject and its attributes on the object should be impossible" (B.S.B., Intro., p. 1).

71. AI.U.B. 2.1, pp. 48–49.
72. See above, Ch. 1.4.
73. B.S.B. 2.1.6, p. 314.
74. Ibid., 2.1.27, p. 355.
75. Ibid., 2.1.11, p. 322.
76. It should be pointed out that there is no twisting of the text here, for the compound does indeed offer both possibilities of meaning.
77. B.S.B. 1.1.3, pp. 18–20.
78. The possibilities and limitations of reason in relation to the acquisition of *brahmajñāna* will be considered later. It must be mentioned that although Śaṅkara dismisses perception, etc., as valid primary sources of the knowledge of *brahman*, this does not imply that they have absolutely no role in the process of gaining this knowledge. The subsidiary functions which they are assigned will become apparent as we proceed.
79. See, for example, S.K. Mukherjee, "Śaṅkara on the Limits of Empirical Knowledge," in *Annals of the Bhandarkar Oriental Research Institute*, 12 (1930–31), 68.
80. KE.U. 2.1–3. For one of Śaṅkara's finest discussions on this paradox, see his full commentary on Part 2 of this *Upaniṣad*.
81. BR.U.B. 3.6.1, p. 343.
82. Ibid., p. 344.
83. KE.U.B. 1.3, p. 49. The word *āgama* literally means "traditional knowledge." See also B.G.B. 18:50, p. 487.
84. Radhakrishnan, *Indian Philosophy*, 2, 617.
85. N.K. Devaraja, *An Introduction to Śaṅkara's Theory of Knowledge*, p. 66.
86. B.S.B. 1.1.1, p. 9. These views of Śaṅkara are to be understood with reference to the theory of *svataḥ-prāmāṇya-vāda*. See above, Ch. 1.2.
87. B.S.B. 2.1.1, p. 304.
88. Ibid., 1.1.4, p. 23. The argument here is that the dependence of one *pramāṇa* on another leads to infinite regression.
89. Ibid., 2.1.4, p. 307. In support, he cites a well-known text, "I ask you of that Being who is to be known only from the *Upaniṣads*" (BR.U. 3.9.26).
90. BR.U.B. 1.4.14, p. 123.
91. B.S.B. 2.3.6, p. 453.

92. B.G.B. 13:4, pp. 336–337.
93. BR.U.B. 1.3.1, p. 32. See also, B.S.B. 2.1.1, p. 302: "One cannot surmise the possibility of perceiving supersensuous things without the *Vedas*." "Vedic texts are the valid means to us in the matter of generating knowledge about supersensuous things" (B.S.B. 2.3.32, p. 945).
94. BR.U.B. 1.4.7, p. 92.
95. CH.U.B. 8.12.1, p. 475. This should be seen in the context of our discussion on the criterion of valid knowledge. See above, Ch. 1.1.
96. Sureśvara (ca. A.D. 800) is a direct disciple of Śaṅkara and was installed by him in charge of the *Math* at Sringeri. Until very recently, though, that he was identical with Maṇḍanamiśra, the disciple of Kumārila Bhaṭṭa. It is now held, however, that Sureśvara is closer in view to Śaṅkara than Maṇḍana. See E. Deutsch and J.A.B. van Buitenen, *A Source Book of Advaita Vedānta* (Honolulu: University Press of Hawaii, 1971), pp. 223–224. Sureśvara's chief works are, *Naiṣkarmya siddhi* and *Bṛhadāraṇyakopaniṣad-bhāṣya-vārttika.*
97. See N.S. 3:34–38, pp. 168-170.
98. *Bhāmatī*, 1.1.4, pp. 157–160.
99. B.S.B. 2.2.38, p. 436.
100. For a summary of some of the *Nyāya* arguments about God, see Radhakrishnan, *Indian Philosophy*, 2, 165–173. Also, G. Chemparathy, *An Indian Rational Theology* (Vienna: De Nobili Research Library, 1972).
101. B.S.B. 1.1.2, p. 17. The *Nyāya* argument might have difficulty in proving that there is a single creator. On the analogy of common experience, one could argue that complex effects are generally produced by several agents acting in coordination.
102. See ibid., 2.2.37–41, pp. 434–438. We may notice here the parallels in argument with Kumārila Bhaṭṭa.
103. Ibid., 2.2.38, pp. 435–436.
104. Ibid., 2.1.31, pp. 359–360.
105. Perhaps the best examples of this are to be found in those parts of his *Brahma-sūtra* commentary where he sets out to refute the *Sāṅkhya* doctrine of the evolution of the world from insentient matter. For example,

> It is not seen in this world that any independent insentient thing that is not guided by some sentient being can produce modifications to serve some special purpose of man; for what is noticed in the world is that houses, palaces, beds, seats, recreation grounds, etc., are made by the intelligent engineers and others at

the proper time and in a way suitable for ensuring or avoiding comfort or discomfort. So how can insentient *Pradhāna* create this universe, which cannot even be mentally conceived of by the intelligent and most far-famed architects, which is seen in the external context to consist of the earth, etc., that are fit places for experiencing the results of various works, and in the context of the individual person, of the body and other things having different castes, etc., in which the limbs are arranged according to a regular design, and which are the seats for experiencing various fruits of actions? (B.S.B. 2.2.1, p. 369).

106. See above, Introduction.

107. Radhakrishnan, *Indian Philosophy*, 2, 518. Radhakrishnan's views are contrary to the main argument of Śaṅkara for justifying the *Vedas*. According to Śaṅkara, the *Vedas* as *śabda-pramāṇa* are necessary because the knowledge which they afford is not available through any other means. If this knowledge was available through human faculties, Śaṅkara's argument would not stand.

108. The term includes texts like the *Manu Smṛti*, the *Bhagavadgītā*, the *Purāṇas*, and the *Mahābhārata*. It is also used with reference to the works of other schools such as *Nyāya*, *Vaiśeṣika*, and *Yoga*.

109. B.S.B. 1.3.28, p. 210.

110. Ibid., 2.1.1, p. 304.

111. Ibid., pp. 303–304.

112. Ibid., 2.1.3, pp. 306–307.

113. B.G.B. 18:19, p. 461.

114. B.S.B. 1.2.25, p. 149. Śaṅkara's conclusions on the respective authority of *śruti* and *smṛti* are derived from *Pūrva-Mīmāṁsā* writers who have discussed this matter in interesting detail. See M.S.J. 1.3.1–6, pp. 55-68. With regard to the *smṛtis* composed by Manu and others, Kumārila has proposed five alternatives: (1) That the authors of these texts were entirely mistaken about what they wrote. (2) That their assertions were derived from personal observation. (3) That they learnt about what they wrote from others. (4) That they intentionally made wrong statements to mislead others. (5) That their assertions are based on Vedic injunctions. He advances various arguments for the rejection of all alternatives, except the last. For most of the *smṛti* injunctions, Kumārila says, corroborative Vedic texts are easily found. In the case of texts for which no such corroboration can be found, we must presume that such Vedic texts were known to the *smṛti* compilers but are now lost along with many others. The basis of this presumption is the fact that the compilers of the *smṛtis* had

also learned and studied the *Vedas*. Kumārila, however, does not accept all *smṛti* literature to be equally authoritative. Only those parts of the *smṛtis* which are concerned with *dharma* have their origin directly in the *Vedas*. Those that relate to pleasure and pain as experienced in the world are derived from direct perception. Stories, which are encountered from time to time, are meant for praising *dharma* and condemning *adharma*. See Jha, *Pūrva-Mīmāṁsā in Its Sources*, pp. 214–218.

115. B.G.B. 18:66, p. 513.

116. Ibid. Also, B.S.B. 2.1.12, p. 324.

117. PR.U.B. 6.2, p. 490.

118. BR.U.B. 2.1.20, p. 209. *Pūrva-Mīmāṁsā* writers have also considered the question of whether Vedic words and their denotations are the same as those in common use. They have concluded that the words must be the same if Vedic injunctions are to be understood and meaningful. See M.S.J. 1.3.30, p. 91. In fact, *Pūrva-Mīmāṁsā* accepts that there are cases in which the meaning of the Vedic word may have to be sought among non-Aryan people. Such a situation arises if the word used by a non-Aryan is exactly the same as used in the *Vedas* but unknown to the Aryan vocabulary. See M.S.J. 1.3.10, p. 74.

119. BR.U.B. 2.1.20, p. 209, 217.

120. See N.S. 3:84–86, pp. 207–208.

121. Ibid., p. 208.

122. BR.U.B. 1.4.7, pp. 81–82. Also N.S. 3:44–45, pp. 173-174.

123. BR.U.B. 2.1.20, pp. 218–219. The general view of *Advaita* on this point is that the fields of perception and *śruti* are different. Perception is concerned with the empirical world while *śruti* discloses absolute reality. *Śruti* does not deny the empirical validity of perception.

124. "As for the argument that creation after deliberation is seen in the world only in cases of such efficient causes as the potter and others, but not in the case of materials, that is being answered. Any argument from common sense is not applicable here; for this is not truth to be arrived at from the *Vedas* (alone); its meaning should conform to Vedic statements" (B.S.B. 1.4.27, p. 296).

125. BR.U.B. 3.3.1, pp. 318–319.

126. B.S.B. 1.4.14, pp. 272–273.

127. Ibid., 1.3.7, p. 166.

128. B.G. 3:17–18.

129. AI.U.B., Intro., p. 8. Also, B.G.B. 2:46, 69. The fact that the *brahmajñāni* transcends the necessity for the *śruti* does not in any

way detract from its indispensability as a *pramāṇa* of *brahman*. The point is that a *pramāṇa*, having successfully given birth to knowledge, is no longer needed for that purpose. Its value is not thereby reduced, nor does it suggest that knowledge is otherwise attainable.

Chapter 3

1. "Nor can the scriptures speak about an unknown thing without having recourse to conventional words and their meanings" (BR.U.B. 2.1.20, p. 209).
2. The view that the words of the *Vedas* are the same as those of conventional usage is accepted even by the orthodox *Pūrva-Mīmāṁsā* system. See M.S.J. 1.3.30, p. 91.
3. B.G.B. 13:12, pp. 346–347. Also KE.U.B. 1.3, p. 49.
4. KA.U. 2.2.15. Also B.G. 13:17.
5. B.S.B., Intro., pp. 3–4.
6. Ibid., p. 3.
7. Ibid., 1.1.1, p. 11.
8. Ibid., p. 12. Also 2.3.7, p. 455. In the *Bhagavadgītā bhāṣya*, a similar argument is made:

   > For, the Self is not a thing unknown to anybody at any time, is not a thing to be reached or got rid of or acquired. If the Self be quite unknown, all undertakings intended for the benefit of oneself would have no meaning. It is not, indeed, possible to imagine that they are for the benefit of the physical body or the like which has no consciousness; nor is it possible to imagine that pleasure is for pleasure's sake and pain is for pain's sake. It is, moreover, the Self-knowledge which is the aim of all endeavour. Wherefore, just as there is no need for an external evidence by which to know one's body, so there is no need for an external evidence to know the Self who is even nearer than the body (B.G.B. 18:50, p. 488).

9. B.S.B. 1.1.2, pp. 12–13.
10. Ibid., Intro., pp. 1–2.
11. Ibid., p. 6.
12. "Therefore we have only to eliminate what is falsely ascribed to *Brahman* by *avidyā*; we have to make no more effort to acquire a knowledge of *Brahman* as He is quite self-evident. Though thus quite self-evident, easily knowable, quite near, and forming the very Self, *Brahman* appears — to the unenlightened, to those whose reason is

carried away by the differentiated phenomena of names and forms created by *avidyā* — as unknown, difficult to know, very remote, as though He were a separate thing. But to those whose reason has turned away from external phenomena, who have secured the grace of the *Guru* and attained the serenity of the Self (*manas*), there is nothing else so blissful, so well-known, so easily knowable, and quite so near as *Brahman*" (B.G.B. 18:50, p. 487). Also 2:18, p. 39.

13. Śaṅkara does not absolutely dismiss the value of *karman* in the pursuit of freedom. The role which he assigns to it will be considered later.
14. B.S.B. 1.1.4, pp. 32–34. Also TA.U.B. 1.11.4, p. 286.
15. B.S.B. 1.1.4, p. 32.
16. Ibid. The idea here is that *brahman* is free from all qualities and unconnected with anything.
17. Ibid., pp. 32–33.
18. See BR.U.B. 1.4.7, p.83. Also TA.U.B. 2.1.1, p. 300.
19. Other examples are used by Śaṅkara to illustrate the idea of a notional loss. A prince, discarded by his parents soon after his birth, grew up in a fowler's home. Not aware of his princely identity, he took himself to be a fowler and identified with that role. When told by a compassionate man of his royal descent, he immediately gave up his mistaken identity and assumed his rightful royal status. (BR.U.B. 2.1.20, pp. 210–211). Another common example used by *Advaita* teachers is the story of a necklace wearer, who somehow thinks that he has lost the necklace which is all the time around his neck.
20. BR.U.B. 1.4.7, p. 96.
21. The word *dharma* in this context indicates any action, ritualistic or otherwise, which results in the production of merit (*puṇya*) and leads to enjoyment in this or in other worlds.
22. M.S.J. 1.1.2, p. 3.
23. Ibid., 1.2.1, p. 22.
24. Ibid., 1.2.7, p. 26. A sentence which subserves an injunction by praising the act or its result is termed an *arthavāda*.
25. For example, it is argued that a sentence such as, "*Vāyu* is a swift deity," is purposeless by itself. When, however, it is seen in relation to the injunction, "One who wants prosperity should touch a goat relating to *Vāyu*," it serves as a praise of the deity and a recommendation of the ritual.
26. See M.S.J. 1.1.4–6, pp. 6–7. The argument here is that *dharma* is not amenable to any other *pramāṇa* because it has no external or tangible form. It also has to be brought into existence by prescribed acts. Vedic injunctions are the only source of its knowledge. We should

remind ourselves that Śaṅkara accepts the *Vedas* as the authoritative *pramāṇa* for *dharma*.

27. There is a linguistic dimension to the *Mīmāṁsā* argument that the central concern of the *Vedas* is the initiation of activity through injunctive statements. They hold the view that in all sentences, words derive their meaningfulness only from their relationship with the verb. The pivot of any sentence is the verb, and all usage is thus meant for instituting action. A factual statement, therefore, is never an end in itself but has its reference in some activity. See M.S.J. 1.1.25, p. 18.
28. B.S.B. 1.3.33, p. 225.
29. BR.U.B. 1.3.1, p. 33.
30. B.S.B. 1.1.4, p. 22.
31. BR.U.B. 1.4.7, p. 92.
32. B.S.B. 1.1.4, p. 25.
33. Ibid., pp. 39–40. Also BR.U.B. 1.4.7, pp. 92–93 and 1.4.10, p. 103.
34. "For it is the very nature of the negative to convey the idea of the nonexistence of the action with which it gets connected. The idea of nonexistence causes inactivity, and that idea ceases to exist automatically, like fire that has exhausted its fuel" (B.S.B. 1.1.4, pp. 38–39). Also BR.U.B. 1.3.1, pp. 34–35.
35. TA.U.B. 1.11.4, p. 290. Also B.S.B. 1.1.4, pp. 22–23. Śaṅkara does not deny that there are some Vedic texts which subserve injunctions. He maintains, however, that this is not the case with *Vedānta-vākyas*, which have their own result.
36. B.S.B. 1.1.4, p. 22.
37. For good definitions of the sixfold criteria, see Sadānanda's *Vedāntasāra*, Ch. 5. There is little information on Sadānanda's (ca. A.D. 1450) life. It is not known whether he wrote any work other than the *Vedāntasāra*. The text itself systematically presents the main doctrines of *Advaita*. It is held in high esteem and widely studied by students of *Advaita*.
38. The nature of the reasoning process acceptable to *Advaita* is discussed in detail later.
39. The desirable ends attainable by adopting the means prescribed in the *karmakāṇḍa* are sometimes classified as *dharma*, *artha* (wealth), and *kāma* (pleasure). These three human goals (*puruṣārthas*) are also referred to as *pravṛtti-dharma* (the way of works).
40. The *jñānakāṇḍa* is also, of course, collectively referred to as *Vedānta*. The word *Vedānta* (*Veda* + *anta* "end") literally means the end of the *Vedas* (i.e., the *Upaniṣads*). The *puruṣartha* of this section is *mokṣa* also referred to as *nivṛtti dharma* (the way of renunciation).

41. B.S.B. 1.1.1, pp. 6–13.
42. MU.U. 1.2.12.
43. See B.G.B., Intro., pp. 2–3.
44. BR.U.B. 5.1.1, pp. 560–61.
45. Ibid., 2.1.20, p. 216.
46. Ibid., pp. 216–17.
47. It is clear that Śaṅkara denies the reality of actions and results, etc., only from the absolute standpoint (*paramārtha*). This is the standpoint of *brahmajñāna*. Their empirical (*vyavahāra*) reality is not denied. The term *prātibhāsika* describes the illusory, such as the rope mistaken for a snake. Dream experiences also come under this category. The universe enjoys a *vyavahāra* status.
48. BR.U.B. 2.1.20, p. 217. Also 4.5.15, pp. 549–551.
49. See above, Ch. 2.4.
50. KE.U.B. 1.4, pp. 51–52. "Knowledge alone which is imparted by those who have realised the truth — and no other knowledge — can prove effective" (B.G.B. 4:34, p. 149).
51. KA.U.B. 1.2.7–9, pp. 137–140.
52. CH.U. 6.14.1–2. See also Śaṅkara's *bhāṣya* on same.
53. MU.U. 1.2.12. The qualification of *brahmaniṣṭham* emphasizes the necessity of *jñāna* becoming an assimilated and integrated part of his outlook. Śaṅkara's repeated demand for scriptural mastery does not find echo in modern interpretations of *Advaita*. This is directly related to the different perceptions of the role of the *Vedas* in the acquisition of *brahmajñāna*.
54. Ibid., 1.2.13. Also Śaṅkara's *bhāṣya*.
55. B.S.B. 1.1.8, p. 57. A similar illustration is also explained by Śaṅkara in CH.U.B. 8.12.1, p. 472.
56. The method is also mentioned by Sadānanda in B.S. 1:31.
57. B.G. 13:12.
58. See Śaṅkara's commentary on ibid.
59. The word *sat* is often used to describe *brahman*. It is interesting to note here the very ordinary sense in which he understands the term.
60. B.G. 13:13.
61. Ibid., 13:14.
62. See IS.U. 2.4–5; KA.U. 1.2.20; KE.U. 1.4.9, 2.2.
63. In *Advaita*, definitions through nonessential characteristics (*upādhis*) are referred to as *taṭasthalakṣaṇa*. The nonessential attributes are referred to as *upalakṣaṇa*. Definitions which focus on the essential

nature of the object are referred to as *svarūpalakṣaṇa*. These will be discussed shortly.

64. TA.U. 3.1.1.
65. KE.U. 1.6.
66. "As a spider spreads out and withdraws (its thread), as on the earth grow the herbs (and trees), and as from the living man issues out hair on the head and body, so out of the Immutable does the universe emerge" (MU.U. 1.1.7).
67. MU.U. 1.1.6.
68. KA.U. 1.3.15; 2.1.2; Also PR.U. 4.9; IS.U. 6.8.
69. KA.U. 1.2.14.
70. BR.U. 3.8.8.
71. BR.U.B. 1.4.7, p. 95.
72. Ibid., 2.3.6, p. 239.
73. According to a classification in the *Vedānta Paribhāṣā* (Ch. 4, pp. 96–98), *laksaṇā* is of three kinds:
    1. Exclusive implication (*jahallakṣaṇā*). One resorts to exclusive implication when the primary meaning of a word or sentence is excluded or abandoned in favor of its implied meaning. The standard example of *jahallakṣaṇā* is "The village is on the Ganges." It is obvious that the direct meaning of "Ganges" is incompatible with the purport of the other words. The village could not be located on the surface of the water. Therefore, by exclusive implication, the term should be understood to refer to the banks of the river.
    2. Nonexclusive implication (*ajahallakṣaṇā*). This occurs when the primary meaning is not excluded but included with its implied meaning. An example of it is "The red is winning the race." Here "red" implies red horse. Thus the word *red*, without relinquishing its primary meaning of red color, indicates, by nonexclusive implication, the red horse.
    3. Exclusive–nonexclusive implication (*jahadajahallakṣaṇā*). In this type, only a part of the original meaning is retained, while the rest is rejected. In the example, "This is that Devadatta," the primary meaning of "this" is present time and place, and "that" points to an alternative time and place. These two being incompatible, they are negated in favor of the individual free from spatial and temporal qualifications. The point of this example is not that Devadatta under two different sets of conditions is absolutely identical. The aim is to point out an identity.

    Implication is necessitated primarily by the intention of a sentence rather than the logical connection of its words. There is a need for recourse to implication only when the direct meaning is clearly impossible. (See B.S.B. 1.4.11, p. 264.) The implied meaning is discovered through the application of an *arthāpatti* (postulation) type of reasoning. The data for this are the recollected primary meanings and the intention of the speaker. The latter can be inferred from the general context.

74. TA.U. 2.1.1.
75. The following discussion is based largely on Śaṅkara's commentary on this definition. See TA.U.B. 2.1.1, pp. 299–319.
76. Śaṅkara goes on to deny the idea that this text suggests that the *ātman* can know itself. The Self, he argues, is without parts and cannot simultaneously be both knower and known. If the Self became a knowable, there will be no knower. Moreover, if the *ātman* is in any way cognizable, scriptural instruction about it will become useless, even as instruction about a pot. See ibid., pp. 305–306.
77. TA.U.B. 2.1.1, pp. 309–310.
78. The reason is that *brahman* is free from all attributes through which words directly signify objects.
79. TA.U.B. 2.1.1, p. 310.
80. CH.U.B. 7.1.3, p. 370.
81. BR.U.B. 4.3.32, pp. 475–476. Also CH.U.B. 7.23.1, p. 402.
82. BR.U.B. 3.9.28.7, pp. 395–396.
83. Also referred to as *bhāgalakṣaṇā*.
84. B.S.B. 3.2.22, pp. 625–626. See full commentary on this *sūtra*.
85. These *mahāvākyas* are generally considered to be four in number, one from each of the four *Vedas*:
    (1) "That Thou Art" (*tat tvam asi*) (CH.U. 6.8.7) of the *Sāma-Veda*.
    (2) "Consciousness is *brahman*" (*prajñānam brahma*) (AI.U. 3.1.3) of the *Ṛg-Veda*.
    (3) "I am *brahman*" (*aham brahmāsmi*) (BR.U. 1.4.10) of the *Yajur-Veda*.
    (4) "This *ātman* is *brahman*" (*ayam ātmā brahma*) (MA.U. 2) of the *Atharva-Veda*.
86. The *māhavākya* is then repeated nine times during the course of the instruction. Śaṅkara, however, only comments elaborately on CH.U. 6.16.3 and 6.8.7.
87. CH.U.B. 6.8.7, p. 339. See entire *bhāṣya* on this verse.
88. Ibid., 6.16.3, p. 361.
89. Ibid., p. 362.
90. "We hold that the scriptures aim at establishing the identity of the transmigrating soul with God Himself by removing from the soul all

vestiges of transmigration. From this point of view, it becomes affirmed that God is possessed of the characteristics of being untouched by sins, etc., and that the opposite characteristics of the soul are unreal" (B.S.B. 4.1.3, p. 820).

91. See V.S. 4: 144–147.
92. CH.U.B. 6.16.3, pp. 363–364.

Chapter 4

1. For the basis of the discussion below on this distinction, see B.S.B. 1.1.2, pp. 16–18.
2. BR.U.B. 5.1.1, pp. 558–559. One of the very important reasons for emphasizing the distinction between *jñāna* and *karman* is that if *jñāna* is classified as an activity, *mokṣa* will become the result of an action, and, therefore, noneternal.
3. B.S.B. 1.1.4, p. 34.
4. Ibid.
5. Ibid.
6. Ibid., p. 35.
7. Ibid., p. 31.
8. The root meaning of *upāsanā* is "to sit by the side of."
9. BR.U.B. 1.3.9, p. 45.

> Meditation consists in a current of uniform concepts, not interspersed with dissimilar ones, which proceeds according to the scriptures and relates to an object enjoined in the scriptures (TA.U.B. 1.3.4, p. 247).
>
> *Upāsanā* consists in setting up a current of similar thoughts (B.S.B. 4.1.7, p. 831).

10. See B.S.B. 1.1.4, pp. 29–30.
11. See BR.U. 3.1.9.
12. BR.U.B. 1.5.2, pp. 144–145.
13. For another example of *adhyāsā upāsanā*, see BR.U.B. 1.1.1, p. 6.
14. B.S.B. 1.1.4, pp. 30–31. Also BR.U.B. 1.4.10, pp. 105–106.
15. For example, "When that Self, which is both high and low, is realized, the knot of the heart gets untied, all doubts become solved, and all one's actions become dissipated" (MU.U. 2.2.8).
16. Each meditation has its own distinctive result. See BR.U.B. 2.1.14, p. 186.
17. B.S.B. 1.1.1, pp. 8–9.

18. See CH.U.B., Intro., 1.1, p. 4, and TA.U.B. 1.11.4, pp. 291–292. The prerequisites of *jñāna* will be considered in detail later.

19. See B.S.B. 1.1.4, pp. 28–29. Śaṅkara himself cites the following texts in support of the simultaneity of *jñāna* and *mokṣa*: "Anyone who knows *Brahman* becomes *Brahman*" (MU.U. 3.2.19). "When that *Brahman*, the basis of all causes and effects, becomes known, all the results of his (i.e., aspirant's) actions become exhausted" (MU.U. 2.2.8).

> One who knows the Bliss (that is the very nature) of *Brahman* ceases to have 'fear from anything (TA.U. 2.9).
>
> O Janaka, you have certainly attained (*Brahman* that is) fearlessness (BR.U. 4.2.4).
>
> Then what delusion and what sorrow can there be for that seer of unity? (IS.U. 7).

20. B.S.B. 1.1.4, p. 28.

21. MU.U.B. 1.15, p. 88.
Also, "This identity of the embodied soul, that is taught, is a self-established truth, and it has not to be accomplished through some extraneous effort. From this it follows that like the idea of the rope removing the ideas of snake, etc., (superimposed on it), the acceptance of the unity of the (individual) Self with *Brahman*, as declared in the scripture, results in the removal of the idea of an individual soul bound up with the body, that is a creation of beginningless ignorance" (B.S.B. 2.1.14, p. 328).

22. B.S.B. 1.1.4, p. 36. Also BR.U.B. 1.4.7, p. 93.

23. BR.U.B. 1.4.10, p. 114.

24. BR.U.B. 1.4.7, pp. 87–90.

25. In B.G.B. 13:2, pp. 329–30, a similar objection is formulated as follows:

> The Lord Himself is the *Kṣetrajña* and *Kṣetra* is quite distinct from *Kṣetrajña* who perceives it; but I am a *samsārin* subject to pleasure and pain. To bring about the cessation of *samsāra*, I should first acquire a discriminative knowledge of *Kṣetra* and *Kṣetrajña*, then attain a direct perception of *Kṣetrajña*, the Lord, by means of *dhyāna* or meditation of the Lord and dwell in the true nature of the Lord.

Śaṅkara says that this is the view of someone who lacks the traditional method of understanding the *śāstra*. Such a person, according to Śaṅkara, is "the slayer of the Self. Ignorant in himself, he confounds others, devoid as he is of the traditional key (*saṁpradāya*) to the teaching of the *śāstras*. Ignoring what is directly taught, he suggests what is not taught. Therefore, not being acquainted with the traditional interpretation, he is to be neglected as an ignorant man, though learned in all śāstras."

26. BR.U.B. 1.4.7, p. 89.
27. Ibid., pp. 90–92. See also B.S.B. 2.1.4, pp. 331–332.
28. BR.U.B. 4.5.15, pp. 548–549.
29. MU.U. 1.1.4–5 distinguishes between *aparā vidyā* (lower knowledge) and *parā vidyā* (higher knowledge). *Parā vidyā* is described as that by which the immutable is known.
30. CH.U. 7.1.3. See Śaṅkara's commentary, p. 371.
31. Other terms used for the *antaḥkaraṇa* are *buddhi*, *citta*, and *manas*.
32. "Among thousands of people, one perchance strives for perfection; even among those who strive and are perfect, only one perchance knows me in truth" (B.G. 7:3). Also BR.U.B. 4.4.12, p. 512.
33. See BR.U.B. 2.4.1, p. 242 and B.S.B. 3.4.26, p. 783.
34. B.G.B. 15:11, p. 405. Also KA.U.B. 1.2.24, pp. 155–156.
35. MU.U.B. 3.1.8, pp. 155–156. Also KE.U.B. 4.8, pp. 93-94.
36. B.S.B. 1.1.1, pp. 6–9.
37. See above, Ch. 3.2.
38. B.S.B. 1.1.1, p. 9.
39. The nature of the arguments employed in these discussions is addressed subsequently.
40. See for example, KA.U. 1.3.4–9; 1.3.12–14.
41. See ibid., 1.1.1–29.
42. Ibid., 1.1.26–27.
43. MU.U.B. 1.2.12, p. 110.
44. B.G. 9:21. Also 2:42–44 and KA.U. 1.2.10.
45. See KA.U. 1.2.1–2 and Śaṅkara's commentary.
46. For brief definitions of all prerequisites, see V.S. 1:15–26.
47. B.G.B. 6:26. Also 6:34–35; 2:62–64.
48. Ibid., 2:54.
49. KA.U. 2.1.1–2.
50. Ibid., 1.3.3–9.
51. V.S. 1:21.

52. B.G. 2:14–15.
53. CH.U.B. 6.12.2, pp. 347–348. Also 4.1.1, p. 176; 4.10.2, p. 199; B.G.B. 4:39, pp. 151–152, 9:3, pp. 240–241.
54. For another detailed enumeration of qualities conducive to *brahmajñāna*, see B.G. 13:7–11.
55. See MU.U.B. 1.2.13, pp. 111–112 and B.G.B. 18:67, pp. 516–517.
56. B.G. 3:34.
57. Ibid., 5:3.
58. Ibid., 2:57.
59. Ibid., 2:64. See also 12:17; 14:22; 18:10.
60. B.G.B. 8:27, pp. 219–220.
61. "Thy concern is with action alone, never with results. Let not the fruit of action be thy motive, nor let thy attachment be for inaction" (B.G. 2:47).
62. B.G.B. 5:8, p. 165. Also 5:11–12.
63. Ibid., 18:9, p. 450.
64. Ibid., Intro., pp. 5–6. See also 2:46–50; 2:59; 3:4–5; 3:8–9; 3:30; 18:3–11; BR.U.B. 3.3.1, p. 318; 4.4.22, p. 523; B.S.B. 4.1.18, p. 845; TA.U.B. 1.11.4, pp. 291–292.
65. B.G.B. 3:18–19, p. 104.
66. Ibid., 5: Intro., pp. 154–159.
67. Ibid., 3:20–29, pp. 104–109.
68. See above, Introduction.
69. See R.V. de Smet, "Śaṅkara's Non-Dualism," in *Religious Hinduism*, pp. 52–61.
70. B.G.B. 13:11, pp. 342–343.

Chapter 5

1. See BR.U. 2.4.5 and 4.5.6.
2. See B.S.B. 1.1.4, pp. 34–36.
3. See above, Ch. 4.1.
4. B.S.B. 1.1.4, p. 35.
5. Ibid., 3.2.21, p. 622. See also 1.1.4, pp. 35–36.
6. Śaṅkara proposes for refutation the view that *manana* and *nididhyāsana* are enjoined as actions after *śravaṇa*. See B.S.B. 1.1.4, p. 25.
7. B.S.B. 1.1.4, pp. 43–44.
8. V.S. 5:182.

> Hearing is a mental activity leading to the conviction that the Vedāntic texts inculcate only *Brahman*, the One without a second (V.P., Ch. 8, p. 213).

9. KE.U. 1.5–7.
10. See BR.U.B. 1.4.10, p. 107.

> The man who knows not the Self is ruined, as also the man who has no faith in the teachings and the words of his *Guru*, and the man who is full of doubts. No doubt the ignorant and the faithless are ruined, but not to the same extent as a man of doubting mind. He is the most sinful of all. — How? — Even this world which is common to all men is not won by a skeptic, nor the other world, nor happiness: for even these things come within the sweep of his doubt (B.G.B. 4:40, p. 152).

11. V.S. 5:191

> Reflection is a mental operation producing ratiocinative knowledge that leads to the refutation of any possible contradiction from other sources of knowledge regarding the meaning established by scriptural testimony (V.P., Ch. 8, p. 213).

12. For the basis of the discussion below, see B.S.B. 2.1.11, pp. 320–323.
13. Kapila is the reputed founder of the *Sāṅkhya* system of thought, while Kaṇada is supposed to have initiated the *Vaiśeṣika* school. There is no reliable historical evidence on either thinker.
14. B.S.B. 2.1.11, pp. 322–323. For related arguments, see BR.U.B. 1.4.6, p. 75, and KA.U.B. 1.2.8, pp. 140–141.
15. For a discussion of these types, see M. Hiriyanna, *Indian Philosophical Studies*, pp. 45–46.
16. B.S.B. 2.1.6, p. 314.
17. Ibid., 1.1.1, pp. 12–13.
18. Ibid., 1.1.2, p. 15. The two texts cited by Śaṅkara here are "The Self is to be heard of, to be reflected on" (BR.U. 2.4.5) and "A man, well-informed and intelligent, can reach the country of the *Gandhāras*; similarly in this world, a man who has a teacher attains knowledge" (CH.U. 4.14.2).
19. BR.U.B. 3.1.1, Intro., p. 285.
20. Ibid., 3.8.9, p. 362.
21. See above, Ch. 2.5.
22. MA.U.K.B. 3.1, Intro., p. 268.

23. Ibid., 4.99, p. 402. It is important to note that the genuineness of Śaṅkara's commentary on the *Kārikā* of Gaudapada is under question. For a view on this matter, see Devaraja, *An Introduction to Śaṅkara's Theory of Knowledge*, pp. 222–224.
24. TA.U. 2.5.1.
25. B.S.B. 2.1.6, pp. 314–315.
26. For Śaṅkara's detailed analysis of the three states, see MA.U.B. 1–6, pp. 179–190.
27. B.G. 2:13.
28. B.S.B. 1.3.19, p. 193. Also BR.U.B. 2.1.20, p. 212.
29. MU.U 1.1.7, p. 91.
30. B.S.B. 2.1.14, p. 327; CH.U.B. 6.1.4–6, pp. 293–295.
31. B.G. 13:32; 9:6.
32. B.S.B. 1.3.7, p. 166.
33. Ibid., 3.2.18, p. 615.
34. See ibid., 3.2.19, pp. 615–616.
35. Ibid., 3.2.20, pp. 616–617.
36. Ibid., 2.2.1, pp. 367–368.
37. Ibid.
38. BR.U.B. 1.4.7, p. 89.
39. See B.S.B. 1.1.4, p. 23.
40. See BR.U.B. 1.5.3, pp. 147–150; B.S.B. 2.3.31, pp. 492–493; AI.U.B. 3.1.2, pp. 67–70.
41. B.G.B. 2:21, p. 46. There are innumerable references in Śaṅkara to the mental nature of *brahmajñāna* and the functions of the mind in its production. See B.G.B. 18:50, p. 487; 18:55, p. 493; 18:66, p. 500; BR.U.B. 4.4.19, p. 517; 2.2.1, p. 177; B:S.B. 1.1.4, p. 34; KA.U.B. 1.3.12, p. 169; MU.U.B. 3.1.9, pp. 156–157.
42. The mental modification which destroys *avidyā* is sometimes conceived as a final thought or *vṛtti*, the crystallization of *brahmajñāna*. As such, it is termed as *brahmākāravṛtti* (a thought coinciding with the nature of *brahman*) or *akhandākāra cittavṛtti* (a mental modification centered on nonduality).
43. B.S.B. 2.1.14, pp. 330–331.
44. Ibid., 4.1.4, pp. 820–821; B.G.B. 2:69, pp. 78–79.
45. In the history of *Advaita* thought, the *prasaṁkhyāna* argument is associated with the name of Maṇḍanamiśra, an elder contemporary of Śaṅkara. His most famous work is the *Brahma-siddhi*. According to Maṇḍana, the *mahāvākyas* are incapable, by themselves, of bringing about *brahmajñāna*. The *Vedānta-vākyas* convey an in-

direct knowledge which is made direct only by deep meditation (*prasaṁkhyāna*). The latter is a continuous contemplation of the purport of the *mahāvākyas*. *Śravaṇa* alone, according to Maṇḍana, is incapable of eliminating the deeply ingrained false impressions of *avidyā*. Vācaspati, following Maṇḍana, emphasizes the role of deep meditation in producing *brahmajñāna*. According to Vācaspati, it is the mind, perfected and refined through deep meditation, which is the immediate cause of *brahmajñāna*. This argument is associated with the *Bhāmatī* school of *Advaita*, named after Vācaspati's famous work. For a summary of the *Brahma-siddhi*, see K.H. Potter ed., *The Encyclopedia of Indian Philosophies*, 3, 346–420. Also, E. Deutsch and J.A.B. van Buitenen, *A Source Book of Advaita Vedānta*, Ch. 10.

46. N.S. 3:124–125.
47. Ibid., 3:90.
48. Ibid., 3:118.
49. Ibid., 3:91.
50. Ibid., 3:117.
51. Ibid., 2:1–9.
52. Ibid., 3:125–126.
53. Ibid., 1:47–51.
54. V.S. 5:192.
55. BR.U.B. 1.4.7, p. 93. In *Advaita*, the results of actions are classified in a threefold manner. First, there is the sum total of the results of actions done in all previous existences, yet to bear fruit (*saṁcita-karman*). Second, there are the results of actions presently performed and those likely to be done in the future (*āgāmi-karman*). These would eventually form part of the (*saṁcita-karman*). Third, there are the results of actions which have given rise to and are currently being experienced in this particular birth (*prārabdha-karman*). *Brahmajñāna* is seen as immediately destroying *saṁcita-karman*. Actions done by the *jīvan-mukta* after the gain of knowledge are incapable of producing results to be experienced, because they are unaccompanied by any sense of doership. Even while acting, one is identified with the actionless Self. The results of actions which have given rise to this particular body, however, are compared by Śaṅkara to an arrow which is already released from the bow. In spite of *brahmajñāna*, its momentum will continue until naturally exhausted. This is evidenced, according to Śaṅkara, by the fact that there are knowers of *brahman* who still retain the body after knowledge. The *jñāni*, however, experiences the results of *prārabdha-karman*, knowing that the *ātman* is always free and unaffected. When *prārabdha-karman* exhausts itself and the body falls, the *jīvan-mukta* is not reborn.

See B.G.B. 4:37, p. 150; 13:23, pp. 362–365; B.S.B. 4.1.13–15, pp. 835–841.

56. The prerequisites of *sādhana-catuṣṭaya* are, in fact, intended to create the state of mind in which *jñāna* can occur and abide uninterruptedly.

57. BR.U.B. 1.4.7, pp. 93–94.

58. Ibid., pp. 90–91.

59. Ibid., p. 87.

60. See also, B.S.B. 1.1.4, p. 43. It is perhaps very significant that Śaṅkara himself does not pursue the detailed distinction between *śravaṇa*, *manana*, and *nididhyāsana* which has characterized later and modern *Vedānta*.

61. B.S.B. 1.1.4, pp. 34–35. Although *nididhyāsana* is most commonly translated as "meditation," I think that in order to preserve the clear distinction which Śaṅkara makes between the nature of *upāsanā* or *dhyāna* and *nididhyāsana*, it is more appropriate to render *nididyāsana* as "contemplation." "Meditation" can be reserved for translating *upāsanā* or *dhyāna*.

62. It is significant that in the *Upaniṣad* (BR.U. 2.4.5 and 2.5.7), the teacher Yajñavalkya, while prescribing *śravaṇa*, *manana*, and *nididhyāsana*, substitutes in the next sentence the word *vijñāna* (right knowledge or apprehension) for *nididhyāsana*.

63. Śaṅkara's refutation is of the classical system of Patañjali (ca. fifth century A.D.), formulated in the *Yoga-sūtra*. (See S.N. Dasgupta, *Yoga Philosophy in Relation to Other Systems of Indian Thought*.)

64. It is very interesting to note the references in the *Upaniṣads* which Śaṅkara cites as alluding to *Yoga*:

> The Self is to be realized — to be heard of, reflected on, and profoundly meditated upon (BR.U. 2.4.5).
>
> Holding the body in balance with three limbs (chest, neck, and head) erect (SV.U. 2.8).
>
> The holding of the senses and organs unperturbed and under control is called *Yoga* by adepts (KA.U. 2.3.18).
>
> Getting fully this knowledge (of *Brahman*) and the process of *Yoga* (KA.U. 2.3.18).

See B.S.B. 2.1.3, p. 305.

65. B.S.B. 2.1.3, p. 306.

66. Ibid., p. 307. This should be seen in the context of his view that supersensuous things can be known only through the *Vedas*. See ibid., 2.1.1, p. 302, and 2.3.1, p. 445.
67. Ibid., 1.3.33, pp. 228–229.
68. BR.U.B. 1.4.7, p. 91.
69. Ibid. Also MA.U.K.B. 3:39–40, pp. 316–317.
70. B.S.B. 2.1.1, pp. 302–304.
71. Ibid., p. 302.
72. Ibid. In addition to the other evidence presented, this is also a refutation of personal authority as a basis for the validity of the *śruti*.
73. B.G.B. 5:26–29, pp. 177–178.
74. B.S.B. 1.1.2, p. 16. For citings of this text, see, for example, Buch, *The Philosophy of Śaṅkara*, pp. 261–262; Singh, *The Vedānta of Śaṅkara*, p. 193; Iyer, *Advaita Vedānta*, p. 155; Hiriyanna, *Indian Philosophical Studies*, p. 49; Radhakrishnan, *Indian Philosophy*, 2, 510.
75. The inference suggested here is the *Nyāya* argument that any purposeful effect must have an intelligent cause. The aim of this *purvapakṣa* is to challenge the claim of *śruti* as the only *pramāṇa* of *brahman*.
76. B.S.B. 1.1.2, p. 15.
77. Ibid.
78. Ibid., p. 16. Where *śruti*, for instance, mentions a certain result as the effect of a particular ritual, there is no scope for reinforcing such a connection by resorting to any supplementary *pramāṇa*. One is dependent entirely on the authority of the *śruti*. Even reasoning has little scope in helping to establish that such and such a ritual will produce such and such a result. One is called upon merely to implement the mandate.
79. B.S.B. 1.1.2, p. 16.
80. See above, Ch. 4.1.
81. B.S.B. 1.1.2, p. 17.
82. Ibid., 1.1.3, pp. 19–20.

Conclusion

1. I have referred to de Smet's study in my Introduction. For Murty's analysis, see K. Satchidananda Murty, *Revelation and Reason in Advaita*.

Bibliography

Primary Sources (The Commentaries of Śaṅkara)

Ten Principal Upaniṣads with Śaṅkarabhāṣya (Īśa, Kena, Kaṭha, Praśna, Muṇḍaka, Māṇḍūkya, Taittirīya, Aitareya, Chāndogya, and Bṛhadāraṇyaka). Works of Śaṅkarācārya in Original Sanskrit, Vol. I. Delhi: Motilal Banarsidass, 1964; reprint ed., 1978.

Bhagavadgītā with Śaṅkarabhāṣya. Works of Śaṅkarācārya in Original Sanskrit, Vol. II. Poona: Motilal Banarsidass, 1929; reprint ed., Delhi, 1981.

Brahma-sūtra with Śaṅkarabhāṣya. Works of Śaṅkarācārya in Original Sanskrit, Vol. III. Delhi: Motilal Banarsidass, n.d.

Primary Sources in English Translation

* Indicates those translations which
have been cited in this study.

* Alston, A.J., trans. *The Realization of the Absolute: The Naiṣkarmya Siddhi of Sureśvara.* 2nd ed. London: Shanti Sadan, 1971.

Date, Vinayak Hari, trans. *Vedānta Explained, Śaṁkara's Commentary on the Brahma-sūtra.* 2 vols. Bombay: Bookseller's Publishing Co., 1954.

* Gambhīrānanda, Swāmi, trans. *Eight Upaniṣads: with the Commentary of Śaṅkarācārya* [*Īśa*, *Kena*, *Kaṭha*, and *Taittirīya* in vol. I; *Aitareya*, *Muṇḍaka*, *Māṇḍūkya* and *Kārikā*, and *Praśna* in vol. II]. 2nd ed. Calcutta: Advaita Ashrama, 1965–1966.

* ____, trans. *The Brahma-sūtra Bhāṣya of Śaṅkarācārya.* 3rd ed. Calcutta: Advaita Ashrama, 1977.

Jagadananda, Swami, trans. *Upadeśasāhasrī of Śrī Śaṅkarācārya (A Thousand Teachings).* 5th ed. Madras: Sri Ramakrishna Math, 1973.

* Jha, Ganganatha, trans. *The Chāndogyopanishad (A Treatise on Vedānta Philosophy Translated into English with the Commentary of Śaṅkara).* Poona: Oriental Book Agency, 1942.

* ____, trans. *The Pūrva-Mīmāṅsā-Sūtras of Jaimini: with an Original Commentary in English.* Varanasi: Bharatiya Publishing House, 1979.

* Mādhavānanda, Swāmī, trans. *The Bṛhadāraṇyaka Upaniṣad: with the Commentary of Śaṅkarācārya.* 5th ed. Calcutta: Advaita Ashrama, 1975.

* ____, trans. *The Vedānta-Paribhāṣā of Dharmarāja Adhvarīndra.* Belur Math, Howrah: The Ramakrishna Mission Saradapitha, 1972.

Mayeda Sengaku, trans., *A Thousand Teachings.* Tokyo: University of Tokyo Press, 1979.

* Nathan, R.S., trans. *Tatwa Bodh of Samkaracharya*. Calcutta: Chinmaya Mission, n.d.

* Nikhilananda, Swāmī, trans. *Vedāntasāra or The Essence of Vedānta of Sadānanda Yogīndra*. 6th ed. Calcutta: Advaita Ashrama, 1974.

* Sastri, S.S. Suryanarayana, and Raja, C. Kunhan, eds. and trans. *The Bhāmatīof Vācaspati: on Śaṅkara's Brahmasūtrabhāṣya (Catūssūtri)*. Adyar, Madras: The Theosophical Publishing House, 1933.

* Sastry, A. Mahadeva, trans. *The Bhagavad Gita: with the Commentary of Sri Śaṅkaracharya*. Madras: Samata Books, 1977; reprint ed., 1979.

____, trans. *The Taittiriya Upanishad: with the Commentaries of Sri Śaṅkaracharya, Sri Suresvaracharya* and *Sri Vidyaranya (Including Introduction to the Study of Upanishads by Sri Vidyaranya and the Atharvana Upanishads: Amritabindu, Kaivalya)*. Madras: Samata Books, 1980.

Sharma, Pandit Har Dutt, trans. *Brahmasūtra—Catuḥsūtrī: The First Four Aphorisms of Brahmasūtras along with Śaṅkarācārya's Commentary*. Poona: Oriental Book Agency, 1967.

Swāhānanda, Swāmī, trans. *The Chāndogya Upanishad*. Madras: Sri Ramakrishna Math, 1975.

Tyāgīśānanda, Swāmī, trans. *Śvetāśvataropanishad*. 7th ed. Madras: Sri Ramkrishna Math, 1979.

Venkararamiah, D., trans. *The Pañcapādikā of Padmapāda*. Gaekwad's Oriental Series, Vol. 107. Baroda: Oriental Institute, 1948.

* Vidyābhūṣaṇa, M.M. Satisa Chandra, trans. *The Nyāya Sūtras of Gotama*. Edited by Nandalal Sinha. Allahabad, 1930; reprint ed. Delhi: Motilal Banarsidass, 1981.

Secondary Sources

Alston, A.J. *A Śaṁkara Source-Book*.
Vol. 1: *Śaṁkara on the Absolute*.
Vol. 2: *Śaṁkara on the Creation*.
Vol. 3: *Śaṁkara on the Soul*.
London: Shanti Sadan, 1980–1981.

Banerjee, N.V. *The Spirit of Indian Philosophy*. Delhi: Arnold Heinemann Publishers (India), 1974.

Belvalkar, S.K. *Vedānta Philosophy*. Poona: Bilrakunja Publishing House, 1929.

Bhatt, G.P. *Epistemology of the Bhāṭṭa School of Pūrva Mīmāṁsā*. Varanasi: Chowkhamba Sanskrit Series Office, 1962.

Bhattacharya, A.S. *Studies in Post-Śaṅkara Dialectics*. Calcutta: University of Calcutta, 1936.

Bhattacharya, K.C. *Studies in Vedāntism*. Calcutta: University of Caluctta, 1909.

Bowes, Pratima. *Hindu Intellectual Tradition*. Delhi: Allied Publishers, 1977.

Buch, M.A. *The Philosophy of Śaṁkara*. Baroda: A.G. Widgery, 1921.

Cenker, William. "The Paṇḍit: The Embodiment of Oral Tradition," *Journal of Dharma* 5 (1980), 237–51.

Chatterjee, S., and Datta, D. *An Introduction to Indian Philosophy*. Calcutta: University of Calcutta, 1968.

Chemparathy, G. *An Indian Rational Theology*. Vienna: De Nobili Research Library, 1972.

____. "The *Nyāya-Vaisesikas* as Interpreters of *Śruti*," *Journal of Dharma* 3 (1978), 274–294.

Das, Ras-Vihari. *The Essentials of Advaitism*. Lahore: Motilal Banarsidass, 1933.

Das, Saroj Kumar. *A Study of the Vedānta*. Calcutta: University of Calcutta, 1937.

Dasgupta, S.N. *Hindu Mysticism*. Chicago: Open Court Publishing Co., 1927.

____. *Yoga Philosophy in Relation to Other Systems of Indian Thought*. Delhi: Motilal Banarsidass, 1930; reprint ed., 1974.

____. *Yoga as Philosophy and Religion*. London: 1924; reprint ed., Delhi: Motilal Banarsidass, 1978.

____. *A History of Indian Philosophy*. First Indian ed. 5 vols. Delhi: Motilal Banarsidass, 1975.

Datta, D.M. *Six Ways of Knowing*. London: Allen and Unwin, 1932.

____. "Testimony as a Method of Knowledge," *Mind* 36 (1927), 354–58.

____. "Epistemological Methods in Indian Philosophy." In *The Indian Mind*, pp. 118–136. Edited by C.A. Moore. Honolulu: East-West Center Press, 1967.

De Smet, R.V. "The Theological Method of Śaṁkara." Ph.D. thesis, Gregorian University, 1953.

____, "Śaṅkara and Aquinas on Creation," *Indian Philosophical Annual* 6 (1971), 112–118.

____, "Śaṅkara and Aquinas on Liberation (Mukti)," *Indian Philosophical Annual* 5 (1970), 239–247.

____, and Neuner, J., eds. *Religious Hinduism*. Allahabad: St. Paul's Publications, 1964.

Deutsch, Eliot. *Advaita Vedānta: A Philosophical Reconstruction.* Honolulu: East-West Center Press, 1969.

____, and van Buitenen, J.A.B. *A Source Book of Advaita Vedānta.* Honolulu: University of Hawaii Press, 1971.

Devaraja, N.K. *An Introduction to Śaṅkara's Theory of Knowledge.* 2nd ed. rev. Delhi: Motilal Banarsidass, 1972.

Doherty, Barbara Ann. "The Path to Liberation: Śaṅkara, Metaphysician, Mystic, and Teacher." Ph.D. thesis, Fordham University, 1979.

Feuerstein, G. *The Philosophy of Classical Yoga.* Manchester University Press, 1980.

____, and Miller, J. *A Reappraisal of Yoga.* London: Rider & Co., 1971.

Guénon, René. *Man and His Becoming According to the Vedānta.* Translated by Richard C. Nicholson. New York: Noonday Press, 1958.

Gupta, Sanjukta. *Studies in the Philosophy of Madhusūdana Saraswatī.* Calcutta: Sanskrit Pustak Bhandar, 1966.

Gupta, Sisir Kumar. *Madhusūdana Saraswatī on the Bhagavadgita.* Delhi: Motilal Banarsidass, 1977.

Hasurkar, S.S. *Vācaspati Miśra on Advaita Vedānta.* Darbhanga: Mithila Institute, 1958.

Hino, Shoun. *Sureśvara's Vārtika on Yājñavalkya-Maitreyī Dialogue.* Delhi: Motilal Banarsidass, 1982.

Hiriyanna, M. *Indian Philosophical Studies.* Mysore: Kavyalaya Publishers, 1957.

____. *Outlines of Indian Philosophy.* London: Allen and Unwin, 1932; first Indian reprint ed., Bombay: Allen and Unwin, 1973.

Iyer, M.K. *Advaita Vedānta.* New York: Asia Publishing House, 1964.

Jha, Ganganatha. *Pūrva Mīmāṁsā in Its Sources.* Benares: Benares Hindu University, 1942.

____. *The Prābhākara School of Pūrva Mīmāṅsā.* Allahabad, 1911; reprint ed., Delhi: Motilal Banarsidass, 1978.

Kattackal, Jacob. *Religion and Ethics in Advaita.* Freiburg: Herder, 1980.

Lott, Eric *Vedantic Approaches to God.* London: Macmillan Press, 1980.

Macdonell, A.A. *A Practical Sanskrit Dictionary.* London: Oxford University Press, 1924.

Mahadevan, T.M.P. *Outlines of Hinduism.* Bombay: Chetana, 1956.

____. *The Philosophy of Advaita.* 3rd ed. Madras: Ganesh & Co., 1969.

____, ed. *Preceptors of Advaita.* Secunderabad: Kanchi Kamakoti Śaṅkara Mandir, 1968.

____. "The Place of Reason and Revelation in the Philosophy of an Early Advaitin." In *Proceedings of the Tenth Philosophical Congress of Phi-*

losophy, Amsterdam, August 11–18, 1948, pp. 247–55. Amsterdam: North-Holland, 1949.

Malkani, G.R. *Vedantic Epistemology.* Amalner: Indian Institute of Philosophy, 1953.

Menon, Y.K., and Allen, R.F. *The Pure Principle: An Introduction to the Philosophy of Śaṅkara.* Michigan State University Press, 1960.

Monier-Williams, M. *A Sanskrit-English Dictionary.* Oxford: Oxford University Press, 1899; reprint ed., 1974.

____. *A Dictionary of English and Sanskrit.* 4th Indian ed. Delhi: Motilal Banarsidass, 1976. reprint ed., 1982.

Mukherjee, S.K. "Śaṁkara on the Limits of Empirical Knowledge," *Annals of the Bhandarkar Oriental Research Institute* 12 (1930–31), 64–70.

____. "Śaṅkara on the Relation Between the *Vedas* and Reason," *Indian Historical Quarterly* 6 (1930), 108–113.

____. "Śaṁkara on Empirical and Transcendental Knowledge," *Journal of the Department of Letters, University of Calcutta* 21 (1931), 1–30.

Murty, K. Satchidananda. *Revelation and Reason in Advaita.* Andhra University and Columbia University Press, 1959; reprint ed., Delhi: Motilal Banarsidass, 1974.

O'Neil, Thomas L. *Māyā in Śaṅkara: Measuring the Immeasurable.* Delhi: Motilal Banarsidass, 1980.

Organ, T.W. *The Hindu Quest for the Perfection of Man.* First Paperbound ed. Ohio: Ohio University Press, 1980.

____. *Hinduism.* New York: Barron's Educational Series, 1974.

____. *The Self in Indian Philosophy.* London: Mouton & Co., 1964.

Parrinder, Geoffrey *Mysticism in the World's Religions.* London: Sheldon Press, 1976.

Potter, K.H., ed. *The Encyclopedia of Indian Philosophies.*

Vol. 1: *Bibliography.*

Vol. 3: *Advaita Vedānta.*

Delhi: Motilal Banarsidass, 1981.

Prabhavananda, Swami. *The Spiritual Heritage of India.* London: Allen and Unwin, 1962.

Prithipal, D. *Advaita Vedānta.* Bombay: Bharatiya Vidya Bhavan, 1969.

Radhakrishnan, S. *The Hindu View of Life.* London: Allen and Unwin, 1927. Unwin Paperbacks, 1980.

____. *Indian Philosophy.* 2 vols. London: Allen and Unwin, 1971.

Ramachandran, T.P. *The Concept of the Vyāvahārika in Advaita Vedānta.* Madras: University of Madras, 1969.

Rao, R. *Śaṅkara.* Mysore: Kaivalya Publications, 1960.

Rao, K.S. Ramakrishna. *Advaita as Philosophy and Religion.* Prasaranga: University of Mysore, 1969.

Roy, S.S. *The Heritage of Śaṁkara.* Allahabad: Udayana Publications, 1965.

Saksena, S. "Authority in Indian Philosophy," *Philosophy East and West* 1 (1951), 38–47.

Saraswati, Swami Satchidanandendra. *How to Recognize the Method of Vedānta.* Holenarsipur: Adhyatma Prakasha Karyalaya, 1964.

Sastri, Kokileswar. *An Introduction to Adwaita Philosophy.* Calcutta: University of Calcutta, 1926.

Satprakashananda, Swami. *Methods of Knowledge.* London: Allen and Unwin, 1965; first Indian ed. Calcutta: Advaita Ashrama, 1974.

Sen Gupta, A. *Samkhya and Advaita Vedānta.* Lucknow: Manoranjan Sen, Gour Ashram, 1973.

Sen Gupta, B.K. *A Critique on the Vivarna School.* Calcutta: Firma K.L. Mukhopadhyaya, 1959.

Sharma, C. *A Critical Survey of Indian Philosophy.* Delhi: Motilal Banarsidass, 1976.

Sharma, I.C. *Ethical Philosophies of India.* London: Allen and Unwin, 1965.

Sharma, P.S. *Anthology of Kumārilabhaṭṭa's Works.* Delhi: Motilal Banarsidass, 1980.

Singh, R.P. *The Vedānta of Śaṅkara—a Metaphysics of Value*, Vol. 1, Jaipur: Bharat Publishing House, 1949.

____. "Radhakrishnan's Substantial Reconstruction of the *Vedānta* of Śaṁkara," *Philosophy East and West* 16 (1966), 5–32.

Sircar, Mahendranath. *Comparative Studies in Vedantism.* Bombay: Humphrey Milford, 1927.

Skoog, Kim. "Śaṁkara on the Role of *Śruti* and *Anubhava* in Attaining *Brahmajñāna*," *Philosophy East and West* 39, No. 1 (January 1989), 67–74.

Smart, Ninian. *Doctrine and Argument in Indian Philosophy.* London: Allen and Unwin, 1964.

____. *The Yogi and the Devotee.* London: Allen and Unwin, 1968.

Srivastava, R.S. *Contemporary Indian Philosophy.* Delhi: Munshiram Manoharlal, 1965.

Sundaram, P.K. *Advaita Epistemology With Special Reference to Iṣṭasiddhi.* Madras: University of Madras, 1968.

Upadhyaya, V.P. *Lights on Vedānta.* Varanasi: Chowkhamba Sanskrit Series Office, 1959.

Urquhart, W.S. *The Vedānta and Modern Thought.* London: Oxford University Press, 1928.

Warrier, A.G. Krishna. *The Concept of Mukti in Advaita Vedānta.* Madras: University of Madras, 1961.

Zaehner, R.C. *Hinduism.* Oxford: Oxford University Press, 1977.

____. *Hindu and Muslim Mysticism.* London: School of Oriental and African Studies, 1960; New York: Schocken Books, 1972.

____. *Mysticism Sacred and Profane.* Clarendon Press, 1957; reprint ed. London: Oxford University Press, 1978.

Zimmer, H. *Philosophies of India.* New York: Pantheon Books, 1951.

Glossary

The following list does not include all of the Sanskrit terms used in this study. It is a selection only of the more technical terms used in *Advaita Vedānta*. All of the Sanskrit terms, however, are fully explained in the text itself. It is very difficult to give literal translations of important *Advaita* concepts, and the following explanations should not be regarded as substitutes for the detailed discussion of each term in the text.

abhyāsa	repetition; one of the sixfold criteria used in *Advaita* for determining the purport of *śruti* passages; the frequent repetition of a text is seen as an indication of its importance
adhikārī	a qualified student or spiritual aspirant
adhyāropa	wrong attribution of the qualities of one entity upon another, e.g., the qualities of the body upon the Self
adhyāsa	superimposition; in *Advaita* the term is used to describe the erroneous identification of *brahman* with the qualities of the body and mind
Advaita	literally, "nonduality"; the school of thought systematized and expounded by Śaṅkara
āgama	traditional text or doctrine; sometimes used as a synonym for the *śruti*
āgāmi karman	results of actions done in the present and those likely to be done in the future
ahaṁkāra	ego or "I" notion
ajahallakṣaṇā	a nonexclusive form of implication, in which both the primary and implied meanings of a word or sentence are taken into considation in order to arrive at its meaning
ajñāna	ignorance, error, or invalid cognition
akhaṇḍārthaka vākyam	a sentence or statement positing identity between subject and predicate
anādi	that which is without beginning; eternal
ānanda	bliss; the very nature of *brahman* in *Advaita*
anantam	limitless, boundless, eternal
anitya	impermanent, changing, transient
antaḥkaraṇa	literally, "the internal organ"; used as a general designation for the mind and all of its functions

anubhava — experience, firm opinion; the term is also used to designate knowledge gained from any valid source other than memory

anumāna — inference; one of six sources of valid knowledge accepted by *Advaita*

anupalabhi — noncognition; one of six sources of valid knowledge accepted by *Advaita*

aparā vidyā — literally, "lower knowledge"; in *Advaita*, it includes all kinds of knowledge other than that of *brahman*; the latter alone is posited as leading directly to *mokṣa*

aparokṣa — literally, "not invisible"; used as an adjective of *jñāna*, it signifies knowledge which is directly and immediately gained

apauruṣeya — that which is not of human origin or nature; used as a description of the *śruti* to distinguish it from texts having a human origin

apavāda — negation or refutation; in *Advaita*, it refers to the negation, through knowledge, of qualities wrongly superimposed on *brahman*

apramā — invalid or incorrect knowledge

āpta — a credible, trustworthy, or authoritative person

āptavākya — the statement of an authoritative person

apūrva — novelty; one of the sixfold criteria used in *Advaita* for determining the purport of *śruti* passages; the idea here is that if the subject is knowable through other *pramāṇas*, it cannot be the central purport of the *śruti*; *śruti* aims only to inform us of things which we cannot know otherwise

arthāpatti — postulation; one of the six sources of knowledge accepted in *Advaita*

arthavāda — praise or commendation; one of the sixfold criteria used in *Advaita* for determining the purport of the *śruti*; the term is also used in *Pūrva-Mīmāṁsā* to describe Vedic sentences which subserve injunctions by praising the act or its result

asat — unreal, impermanent, false; the opposite of *sat*

ātman	the Self; in *Advaita*, the *ātman* is posited as being identical with *brahman*
ātmajñāna	knowledge of the *ātman*; synonymous with *ātmavidyā*
avidyā	ignorance, misapprehension, erroneous knowledge; in *Advaita*, it especially denotes erroneous knowledge about the nature of the *ātman*
avidyānivṛtti	the removal or negation of ignorance by knowledge
bhāṣya	a commentary or explanatory work
brahmajijñāsā	inquiry (especially into the *śruti* texts) about the nature of *brahman*
brahmajñāna	the knowledge of *brahman*; synonymous with *brahmavidyā*
brahman	the limitless reality; identical, in *Advaita*, with the *ātman*
brahmaniṣṭham	the state of being established in the knowledge of *brahman*; a qualification of the spiritual teacher in *Advaita*
caitanya/cit	awareness or consciousness; the nature of the Self in *Advaita*
citta-śuddhi	purity of the mind; a precondition, in *Advaita*, for the knowledge of *brahman*
dṛk	the knower, subject, or seer; the nature of the *ātman* in *Advaita*, emphasizing that it cannot be objectified
guṇa	quality or attribute; merit or excellence
īndriya	organ, especially sense organ
īśvara	God; the impersonal *brahman* conceived of as creator and ruler of the universe and possessing the qualities of omnipotence and omniscience
jada	insentient or inert; opposite of *caitanya*
jāgarita-avasthā	the waking state
jahadajahallakṣaṇā	an exclusive – nonexclusive type of implication in which only part of the original meaning of a word or sentence is retained, while the rest is rejected; used in *Advaita* for the exegesis of *tat tvam asi*; also referred to as *bhagalakṣaṇā*

jahallakṣaṇā	an exclusive type of implication, in which the primary meaning of a word or sentence is abandoned in favor of its implied meaning
jijñāsa	inquiry, especially into the meaning of the *śruti*
jijñāsu	one who inquires
jīvanmukta	literally, "living free"; in *Advaita*, used to describe one who retains the body after attaining *mokṣa*; such a person enjoys a sense of freedom and fullness in spite of the limitations of the body
jñāna	any kind of cognition, without regard to the question of truth or error
jñāni	the one who possesses valid (esp. spiritual) knowledge
jñānakāṇḍa	final selections of the *Vedas* (viz., the *Upaniṣads*), seen in *Advaita* as having an independent purport in revealing the knowledge of *brahman*
karaṇa	cause or instrument
karmajijñāsā	inquiry or investigation into the first sections of the *Vedas* dealing with the performance of rituals
karmakāṇḍa	first sections of the *Vedas* dealing with the performance of ritual actions; seen, in *Advaita*, as having a different aim and result from the *jñanakāṇḍa*
kṣetra	literally, "the field"; used in the *Bhagavadgītā* (13:1) to refer to the body and, by extension, to any object other than the *ātman*
kṣetrajña	literally, "the knower of the field"; used in the *Bhagavadgītā* (13:1) to define the *ātman*, pointing out its nature as the subject or knower
lakṣaṇā	definition; indirect or implied meaning; in the latter sense, it constitutes an important principle of exegesis in *Advaita*
lakṣyārtha	secondary or implied meaning of a word or sentence

mahāvākya	literally, "great sentence"; *Advaita* holds four such great sentences, taken from the four *Vedas*, to be especially meaningful in positing the identity of *ātman* and *brahman*; one of the best known is *tat tvam asi*
manana	thinking or reflection; in *Advaita*, it describes the process of pondering over the meaning or the *śruti* with the aid of reason
mokṣa	literally, "freedom," generally from the cycle of birth and death; in *Advaita*, this freedom is conceived as being coincident with the knowledge of *brahman* and is attainable while living in the body
mukhyārtha	literal or direct meaning of a word or sentence; opposite of *lakṣyārtha*
mumukṣutvam	desire for the attainment of *mokṣa*; a precondition for the gain of knowledge in *Advaita*
mumukṣu	spiritual aspirant who earnestly desires *mokṣa*
naiyāyika	follower of the *Nyāya* system of Indian philosophy
neti, neti	literally, "not this, not this"; this Upaniṣadic statement is seen in *Advaita* as a negative method of defining *brahman* by denying all false attributes or specifications
nididhyāsana	contemplation or attentive thinking
nimitta kāraṇa	the intelligent or efficient cause, as distinguished from the material cause (*upādāna kāraṇa*)
nirguṇa	devoid of all qualities; the nature of *brahman* in *Advaita*
nirvikalpa	free from change or differences; without modifications
niṣedha	prohibitions; applied by *Pūrva-Mīmāṁsā* to statements in the *Vedas* instituting restraint from acts opposed to *dharma* and seen by this school as having an independent authority
nitya	changeless or eternal
pāramārthika sattā	absolute existence or reality characteristic, in *Advaita*, of *brahman* alone
parataḥ-prāmāṇya-vāda	*Nyāya* doctrine of the extrinsic validity of knowledge

parataḥ-prakāśa-vāda	*Pūrva-Mīmāṁsā* doctrine of the extrinsic luminosity of knowledge; one of the important epistemological differences of this school with *Advaita*
parā vidyā	literally, "higher or supreme knowledge"; used in *Advaita* to refer to the knowledge of *brahman*, which alone leads to *mokṣa*
parokṣa	literally, "invisible"; used as an adjective of *jñāna*, it signifies mediate or indirect knowledge
pauruṣeya	that which is of human nature or origin; used as a definition of the *smṛti* texts to distinguish their origin from the *śruti*
phala	fruit or result; one of the sixfold criteria used in *Advaita* for determining the purport of *śruti* passages; the proposal in a passage of a distinct result is seen as evidence of its independent authoritativeness
pramā	valid knowledge
pramāṇa	a source of valid knowledge; six such sources are accepted in *Advaita*
prameya	an object of knowledge
pramiti	a correct notion or cognition; knowledge gained by the application of a valid *pramāṇa*
prārabdha karman	results of actions which have given rise to, and are currently being experienced in, this particular birth
prasaṁkhyāna	reflection, contemplation, meditation
prātibhāsika	illusory existence, such as that belonging to a mirage or any optical illusion
pratyakṣa	perception; one of the six sources of valid knowledge in *Advaita*
Pūrva-Mīmāṁsā	school of Vedic exegesis founded by Jaimini and concerned with the analysis of the first (*pūrva*) or ritualistic section (*karmakāṇḍa*) of the *Vedas*
purvapakṣa	the first objection to an assertion in any discussion; a series of such objections are generally proposed by Śaṅkara in his commentaries
ṛṣi	inspired poet or sage; thought of in Hinduism as the ones to whom the *Vedas* were originally revealed

śabda	sound or word
śabda-pramāṇa	a means of valid knowledge consisting of words; identified, in *Advaita*, with the *śruti* and posited as one of the six sources of knowledge
śabda-pramā	knowledge derived from *śabda-pramāṇa*
sādhana-catuṣṭaya	the fourfold disciplines proposed in *Advaita* as preparatory for the successful gain of knowledge from the *śruti*
saḍliṅga	the sixfold exegetical criteria employed in *Advaita* for determining the purport of the *śruti*
saguṇa (brahman)	with qualities; *brahman* conceived of as creator of all the universe and as possessing all good qualities
sākṣi	witness; the nature of *brahman* in *Advaita*
samādhi	literally, "putting together"; concentration or meditation; eighth and last stage in the *Yoga* system of Patañjali
sāmānya jñāna	knowledge of a very general kind, lacking in specificity
saṁcita karman	the sum total of the results of actions done in all previous existences, and yet to bear fruit
saṁsāra	cycle of successive births and deaths, freedom from which constitutes *mokṣa*
śāstra	any manual of teaching or sacred text; often used as a synonym for the *śruti*
sat	that which really is; absolute existence; the nature of *brahman* in *Advaita*
savikalpa	with modifications or differences; determinate; opposite of *nirvikalpa*
siddhānta	established or demonstrated conclusion of an argument
śiṣya	student or disciple
smṛti	literally, "memory"; name given to the whole body of religious texts other than the *śruti*; *smṛti* texts are subservient to the authority of the *śruti* because of their human origin
śraddha	faith; faith in the authority of the *śruti* as a source of valid knowledge and in the teacher who unfolds its meaning is an important prerequisite for the gain of knowledge in *Advaita*

śravaṇa	act of listening or hearing; in *Advaita*, it signifies the acquisition of knowledge by listening to the words of the *śruti* as unfolded by the spiritual teacher
śrotriya	one who is well versed in the meaning of the *śruti*; a qualification of the teacher in *Advaita*
śruti	literally, "that which is heard"; synonym for the *Vedas*, emphasizing that they were transmitted orally from teacher to student; unlike the *smṛti* texts, *śruti* is posited as having a nonhuman origin
sthita-prajña	one who is firm or well-established in self-knowledge
suṣupti avasthā	the state of deep sleep
svapna avasthā	the dream state
svarūpa lakṣaṇā	a definition which points out the essential or intrinsic nature of its object
svataḥ-prāmāṇya-vāda	*Advaita* and *Pūrva-Mīmāṁsā* doctrine of the self-validity of knowledge
svataḥ-prakaśa-vāda	*Advaita* doctrine of the self-luminosity of knowledge
tarka	reason or logic
tatastha lakṣaṇā	a definition which points out the non-essential or accidental characteristics of its object
tātparya	purport, intention, or meaning of a scriptural text; in *Advaita*, this is determined by the application of the sixfold exegetical criteria, on the basis of which they contend that the *tātparya* of the *Upaniṣads* is the revelation of the nondual *brahman*
upādāna kāraṇa	the material cause, as distinguished from the efficient cause (*nimitta kāraṇa*)
upādhi	a substitute or anything which may be taken for or has the appearance of another thing; in *Advaita*, the term is applied to all qualities and characteristics wrongly attributed to *brahman* but which neither belong to nor limit *brahman*

upakramopasaṁhārau — the beginning and the end; one of the sixfold criteria used in *Advaita* for determining the purport of *śruti* texts; the initial and concluding statements of any passage are considered to be especially important in determining its meaning

upalakṣanā — a nonessential attribute or quality

upamāna — comparison; one of the six sources of valid knowledge accepted by *Advaita*

upapatti — reasonableness; one of the sixfold criteria employed in *Advaita* for determining the meaning of *śruti* passages; the interpretation more satisfactory to reason is given priority when determining the purport of any text

upāsanā — the act of sitting or being near at hand; service, homage, adoration, worship, meditation

uttara-mīmāṁsā — literally, "later or higher inquiry"; term applied to the study of the last section of the *Vedas* (viz., the *Upaniṣads* or *jñānakāṇḍa*) as distinguished from inquiry into the first section of the *Vedas* (viz., *karmakāṇḍa*) dealing with ritual; often used as a synonym for the system of *Vedānta*

vākya — a sentence or statement

Vedānta — literally, "the end of the Vedas"; general term applied to the last sections of the *Vedas* (viz., the *Upaniṣads*), and to all systems of thought based on their interpretation

Vedānta-vākya — sentences of the *Upanisads*; seen in *Advaita* as having an independent purport in revealing the nature of *brahman*

vidhi — injunctions; applied by *Pūrva-Mīmāṁsā* to Vedic statements inculcating the performance of acts for the attainment of *dharma*; the *Vedas*, according to this school, are only concerned with prescribing acts for the attainment of *dharma*

viśeṣa jñāna — knowledge of a specific or detailed nature; opposite of *sāmānya jñāna*

vṛtti — any modification or change occurring in the mind

vyāvahārika satta	empirical reality or existence, such as that attributed, in *Advaita*, to the world; distinguished from the absolute reality of *brahman* and the entirely illusory existence of a mirage
yukti	reason or argument

Index

svapna avasthā 105
svataḥ-prakāśa 21

T

tarka 104
titikṣā 90–91

U

upādāna kāraṇa 106
upādhis 51, 106, 109
upakramopasaṁhara 64
upamāna 27
upaptti 64
uparati 90
upāsanā 81, 83–84, 95, 111–112

V

Vācaspati 38
vairāgya 88–90
vāsanā 111
vastutantram 80
vedānta-vākyas 62–65, 67, 78–79, 82–85, 87, 91, 96, 98, 100, 104, 107–110, 114, 117–118, 121
vidhi 61, 99, 117
viṣaya 65
viśeṣa-jñāna 57
viveka 88–89
vṛtti 109

Y

Yoga 48, 50, 112–113
yukti 101

Z

Zaehner, R.C. 12

ABOUT THE AUTHOR

Anantanand Rambachan holds a Ph.D. from the University of Leeds and is currently assistant professor of religion at St. Olaf College. Dr. Rambachan's publications have focused on the topics of Hindu epistemology and the contemporary encounter among world religions. He is active in the programs of the World Council of Churches and other international interfaith organizations, and his series of twenty-one lectures on Hinduism has been transmitted by the British Broadcasting Company.

SOCIETY FOR ASIAN AND COMPARATIVE PHILOSOPHY
MONOGRAPH SERIES
Henry Rosemont, Jr., Editor

No. 1 *The Sage and Society: The Life and Thought of Ho Hsin-Yin,* by Ronald Dimberg, 1974

No. 2 *Studies in Comparative Aesthetics,* by Eliot Deutsch, 1975

No. 3 *Centrality and Commonality: An Essay on* Chung-Yung, by Tu Wei-Ming, 1976 (out of print)

No. 4 *Discourse on the Natural Theology of the Chinese,* by Gottfried W. Leibniz, translated with an introduction, notes, and commentary by Henry Rosemont, Jr., and Daniel J. Cook, 1977 (out of print)

No. 5 *The Logic of Gotama,* by Kisor Kumar Chakrabarti, 1978 (out of print)

No. 6 *Commentary on the* Lao Tzu *by Wang Pi,* translated by Ariane Rump, introduction by Wing-tsit Chan, 1979

No. 7 *Han Fei Tzu's Political Theory,* by Wang Hsiao-po and Leo S. Chang, 1986

No. 8 *The Māṇḍūkya Upaniṣad and the Agama Śāstra: An Investigation into the Meaning of the Vedānta,* by Thomas E. Wood, 1990

No. 9 *Mind Only: A Philosophical and Doctrinal Analysis of the Vijñānavāda,* by Thomas E. Wood, 1991

No. 10 *Accomplishing the Accomplished: The* Vedas *as a Source of Valid Knowledge in Śaṅkara,* by Anantanand Rambachan, 1991

Title orders should be directed to the University of Hawaii Press, 2849 Kolowalu Street, Honolulu, Hawaii, 96822. Manuscripts should be directed to Professor Henry Rosemont, Jr., Department of Philosophy, St. Mary's College, St. Mary's City, Maryland 20686.